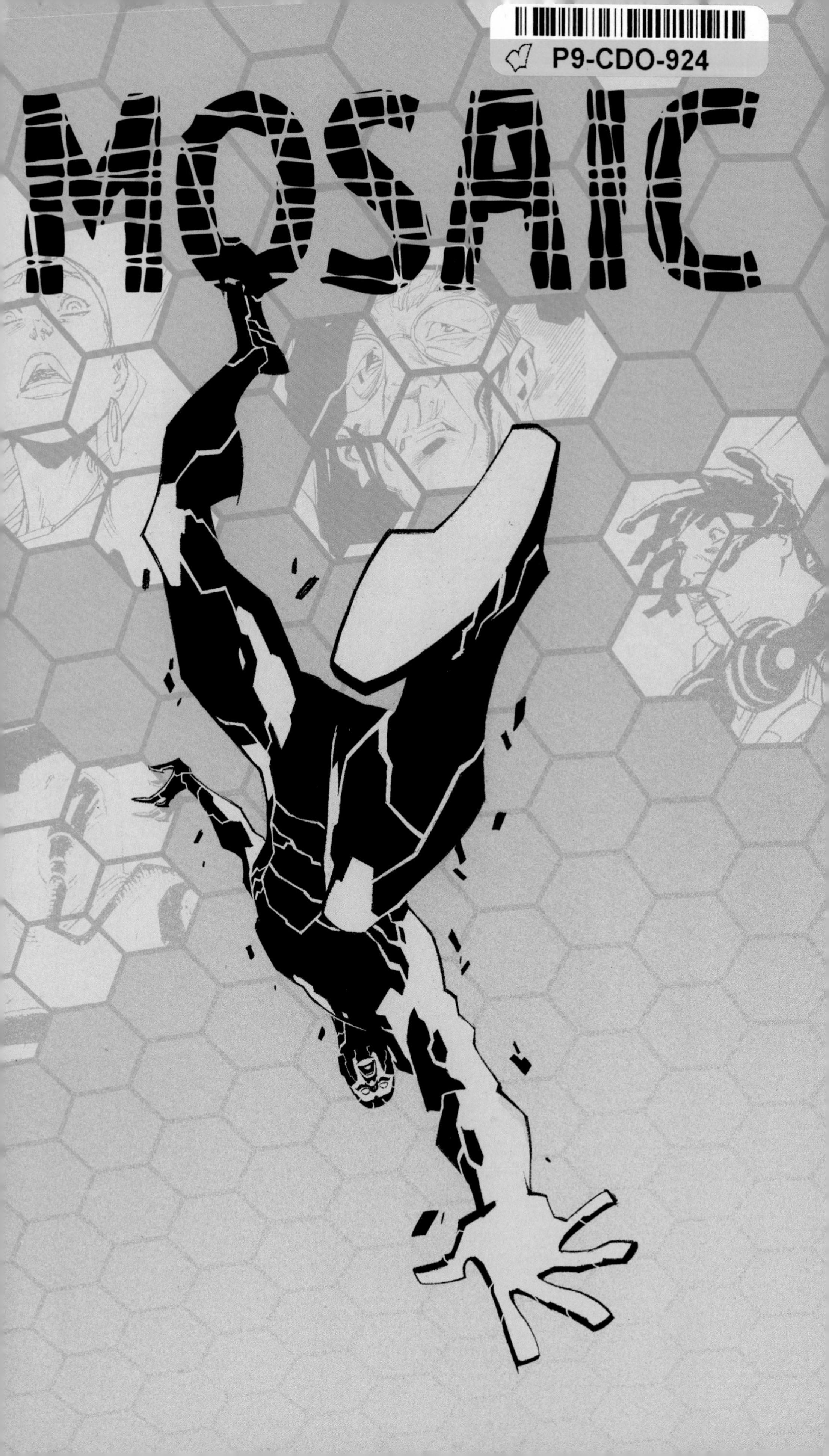
MOSAIC

COLLECTION EDITOR **JENNIFER GRÜNWALD** ▪ ASSISTANT EDITOR **CAITLIN O'CONNELL**
ASSOCIATE MANAGING EDITOR **KATERI WOODY** ▪ EDITOR, SPECIAL PROJECTS **MARK D. BEAZLEY**
VP PRODUCTION & SPECIAL PROJECTS **JEFF YOUNGQUIST** ▪ SVP PRINT, SALES & MARKETING **DAVID GABRIEL**
BOOK DESIGNER **JAY BOWEN**

EDITOR IN CHIEF **AXEL ALONSO** ▪ CHIEF CREATIVE OFFICER **JOE QUESADA**
PRESIDENT **DAN BUCKLEY** ▪ EXECUTIVE PRODUCER **ALAN FINE**

MOSAIC VOL. 1: KING OF THE WORLD. Contains material originally published in magazine form as MOSAIC #1-5. First printing 2017. ISBN# 978-1-302-90039-7. Published by MARVEL WORLDWIDE, I
subsidiary of MARVEL ENTERTAINMENT, LLC. OFFICE OF PUBLICATION: 135 West 50th Street, New York, NY 10020. Copyright © 2017 MARVEL No similarity between any of the names, characters, persons, a
institutions in this magazine with those of any living or dead person or institution is intended, and any such similarity which may exist is purely coincidental. **Printed in Canada.** DAN BUCKLEY, President, M
Entertainment; JOE QUESADA, Chief Creative Officer; TOM BREVOORT, SVP of Publishing; DAVID BOGART, SVP of Business Affairs & Operations, Publishing & Partnership; C.B. CEBULSKI, VP of Brand Manage
& Development, Asia; DAVID GABRIEL, SVP of Sales & Marketing, Publishing; JEFF YOUNGQUIST, VP of Production & Special Projects; DAN CARR, Executive Director of Publishing Technology; ALEX MOR
Director of Publishing Operations; SUSAN CRESPI, Production Manager; STAN LEE, Chairman Emeritus. For information regarding advertising in Marvel Comics or on Marvel.com, please contact Vit DeBellis
grated Sales Manager, at vdebellis@marvel.com. For Marvel subscription inquiries, please call 888-511-5480. **Manufactured between 3/3/2017 and 4/4/2017 by SOLISCO PRINTERS, SCOTT, QC, CAN**

10 9 8 7 6 5 4 3 2 1

MOSAIC

KING OF THE WORLD

WRITER **GEOFFREY THORNE**

ARTISTS **KHARY RANDOLPH**
WITH **THONY SILAS** (#3-5)

COLORISTS **EMILIO LOPEZ**
WITH **ANDRES MOSSA** (#2, #4-5)

LETTERER **VC's JOE SABINO**

COVER ART **STUART IMMONEN** (#1),
KERON GRANT (#2-4) &
MIKE DEL MUNDO (#5)

ASSISTANT EDITOR **ALLISON STOCK**
ASSOCIATE EDITOR **DARREN SHAN**
EDITOR **NICK LOWE**

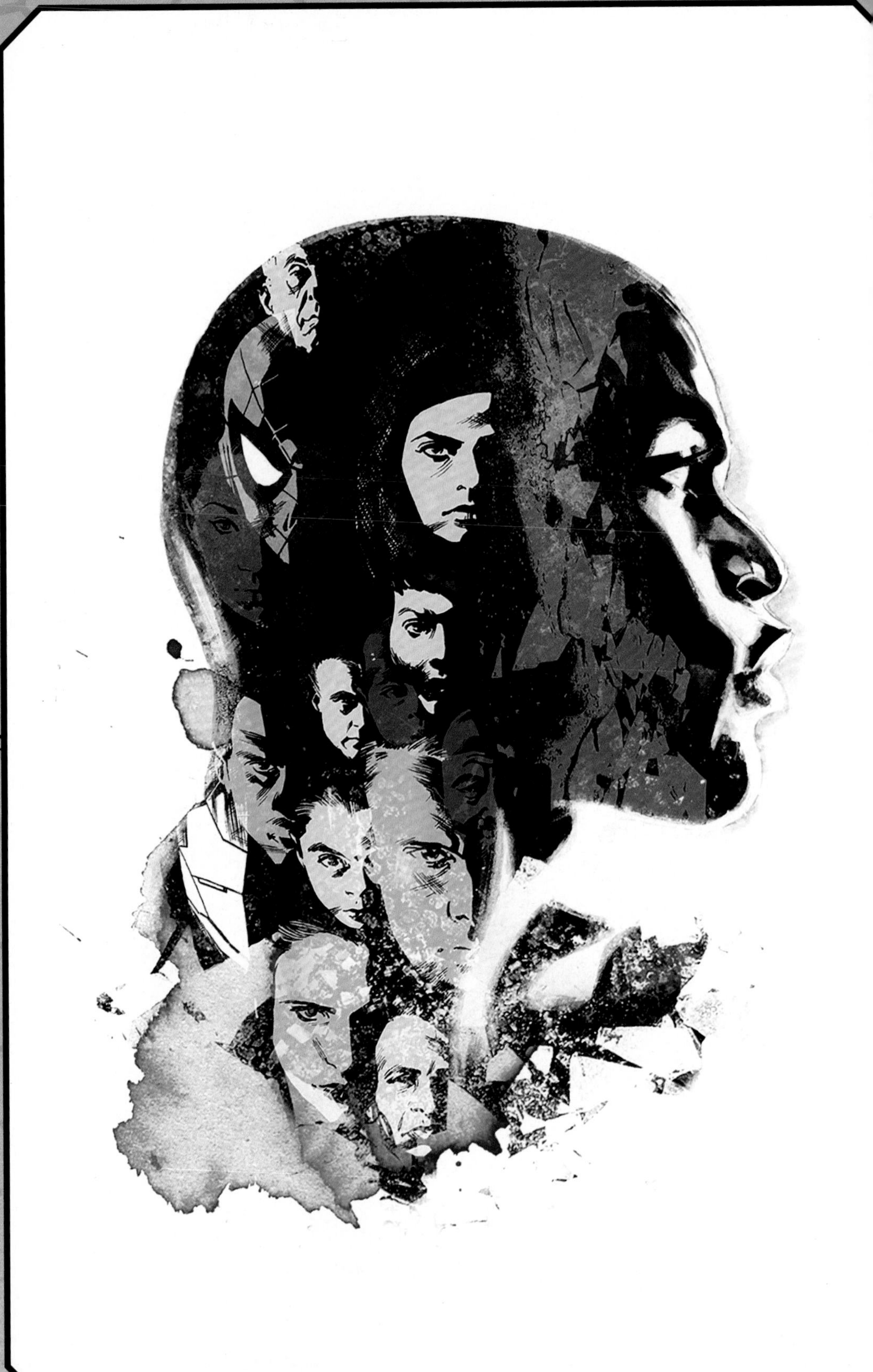

MOOD INDIGO

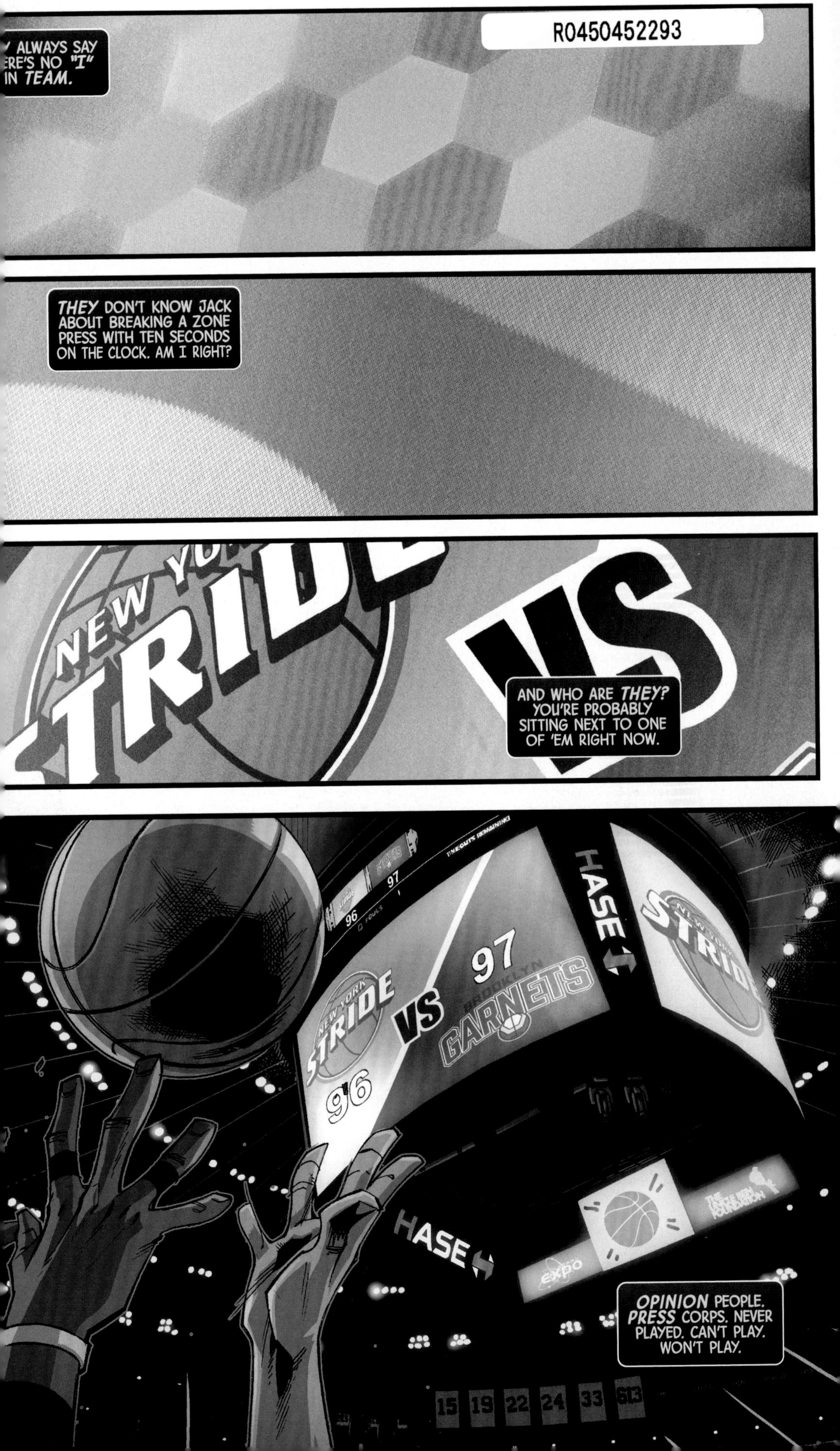

ALWAYS SAY
ERE'S NO "I"
IN TEAM.
THEY DON'T KNOW JACK ABOUT BREAKING A ZONE PRESS WITH TEN SECONDS ON THE CLOCK. AM I RIGHT?
NEW YORK STRIDE
VS
AND WHO ARE THEY? YOU'RE PROBABLY SITTING NEXT TO ONE OF 'EM RIGHT NOW.
HASE
NEW YORK STRIDE
96
VS
97
BROOKLYN GARNETS
EXPO
OPINION PEOPLE. PRESS CORPS. NEVER PLAYED. CAN'T PLAY. WON'T PLAY.
15 19 22 24 33

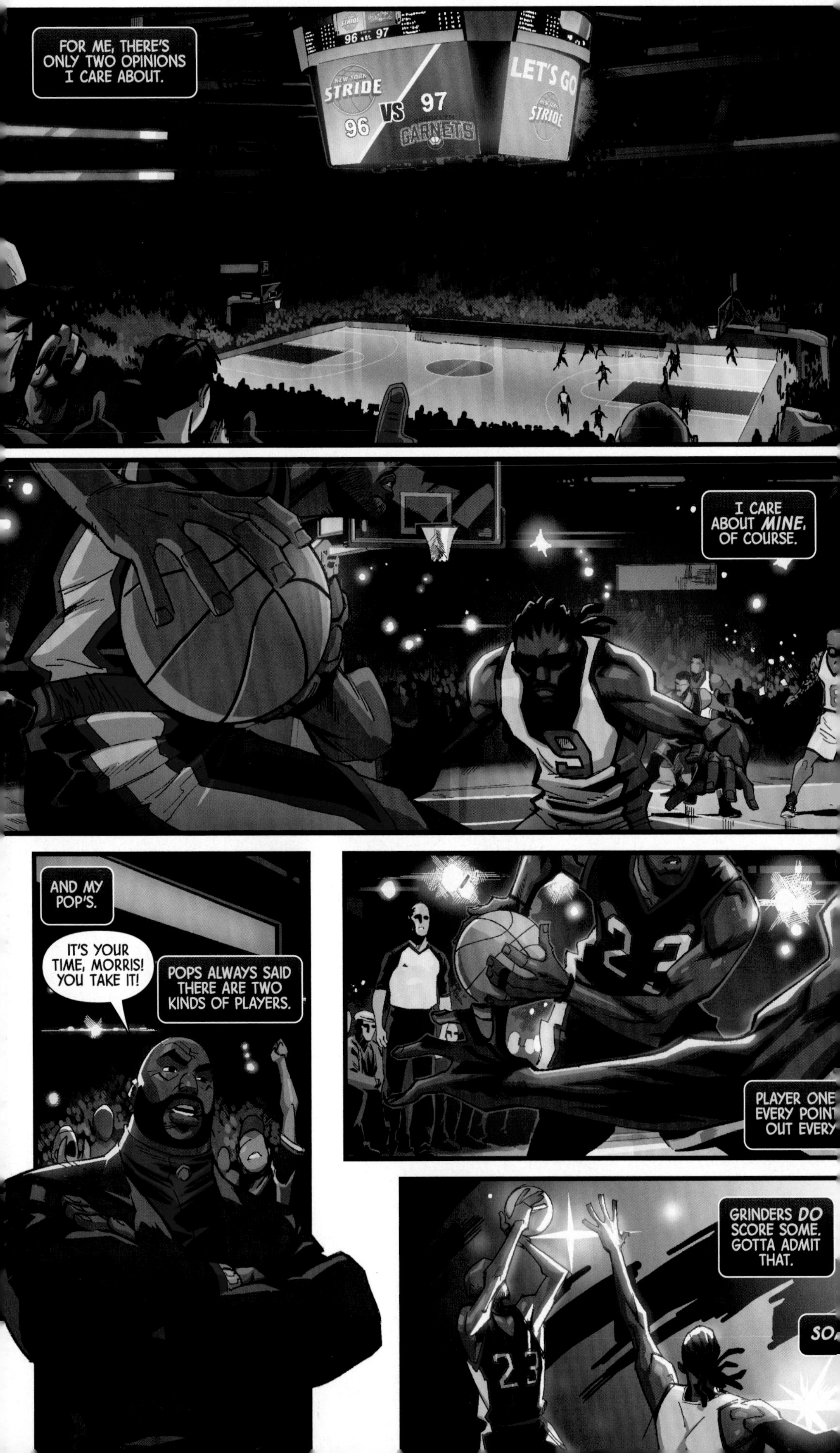

FOR ME, THERE'S ONLY TWO OPINIONS I CARE ABOUT.
96 97
NEW YORK STRIDE
96 VS 97
GARNETS
LET'S GO
NEW YORK STRIDE
I CARE ABOUT MINE, OF COURSE.
AND MY POP'S.
IT'S YOUR TIME, MORRIS! YOU TAKE IT!
POPS ALWAYS SAID THERE ARE TWO KINDS OF PLAYERS.
PLAYER ONE EVERY POIN OUT EVERY
GRINDERS DO SCORE SOME. GOTTA ADMIT THAT.
SO,

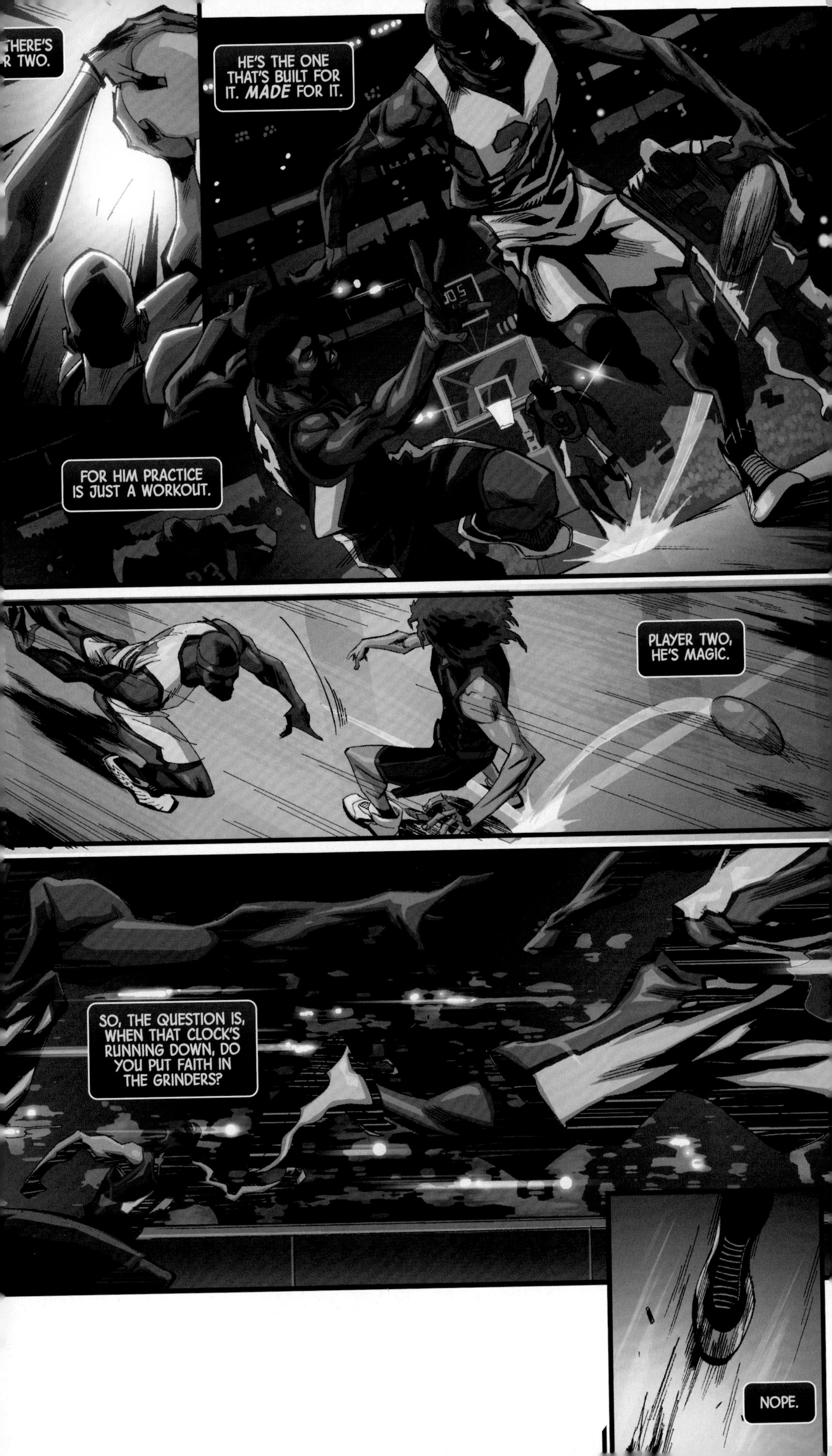

THERE'S
R TWO.
HE'S THE ONE THAT'S BUILT FOR IT. MADE FOR IT.
FOR HIM PRACTICE IS JUST A WORKOUT.
PLAYER TWO, HE'S MAGIC.
SO, THE QUESTION IS, WHEN THAT CLOCK'S RUNNING DOWN, DO YOU PUT FAITH IN THE GRINDERS?
NOPE.

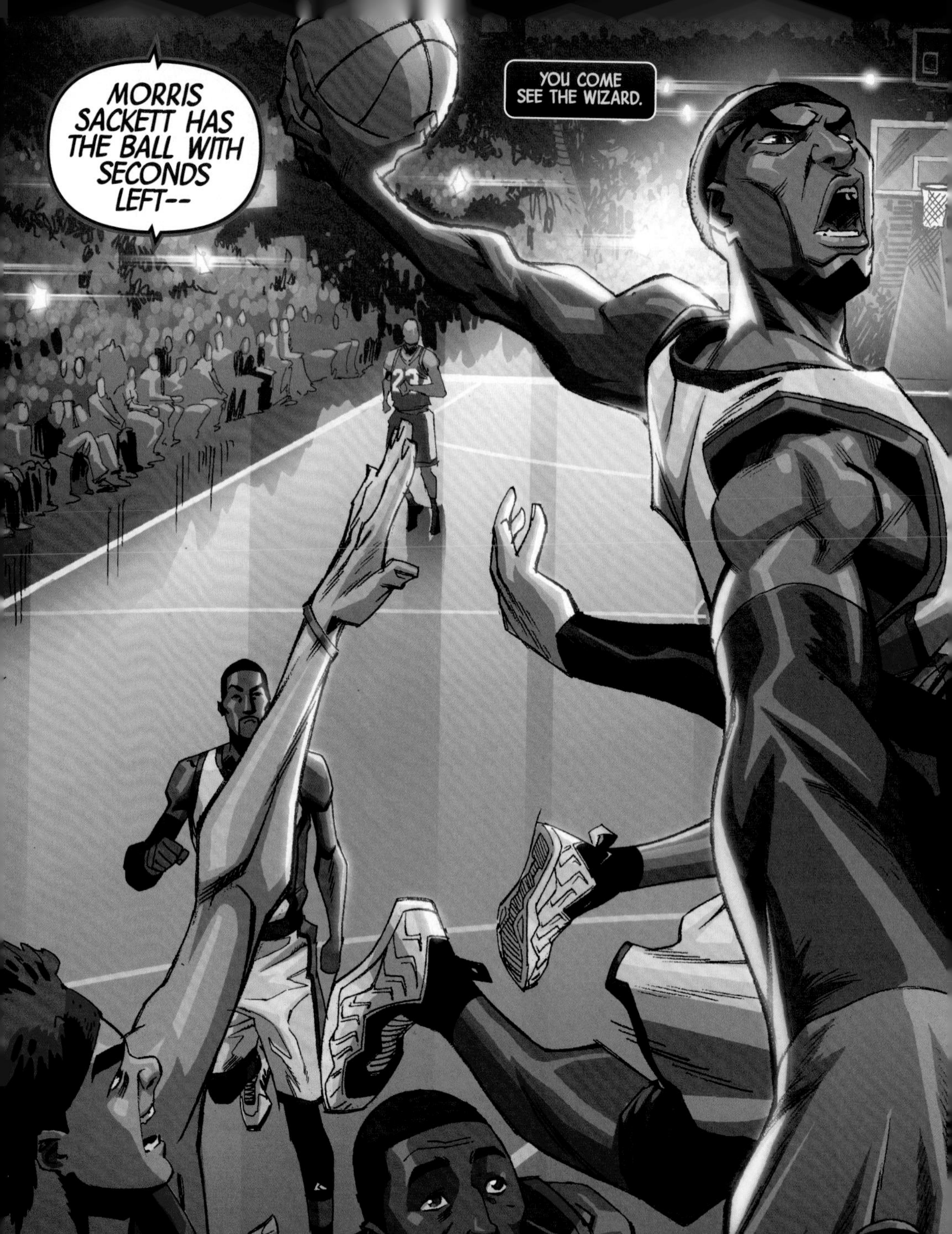
MORRIS SACKETT HAS THE BALL WITH SECONDS LEFT--
YOU COME SEE THE WIZARD.

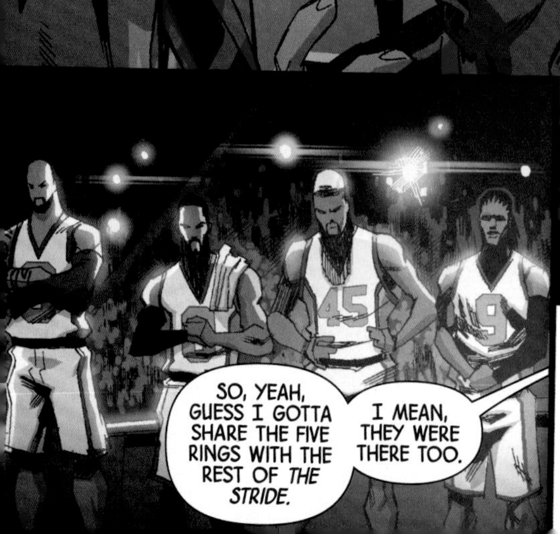
SO, YEAH, GUESS I GOTTA SHARE THE FIVE RINGS WITH THE REST OF *THE STRIDE*.
I MEAN, THEY WERE THERE TOO.

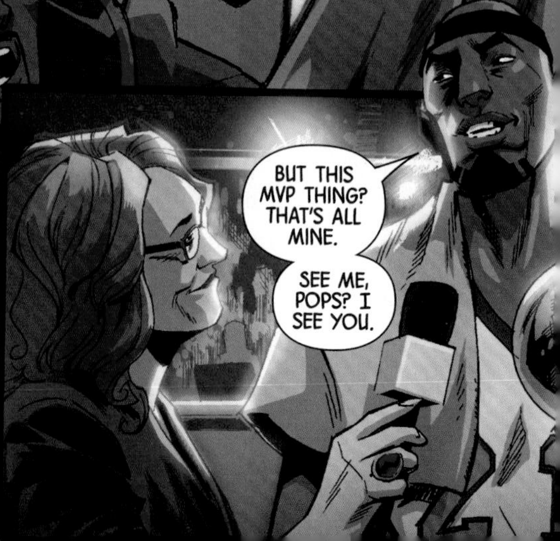
BUT THIS MVP THING? THAT'S ALL MINE.
SEE ME, POPS? I SEE YOU.

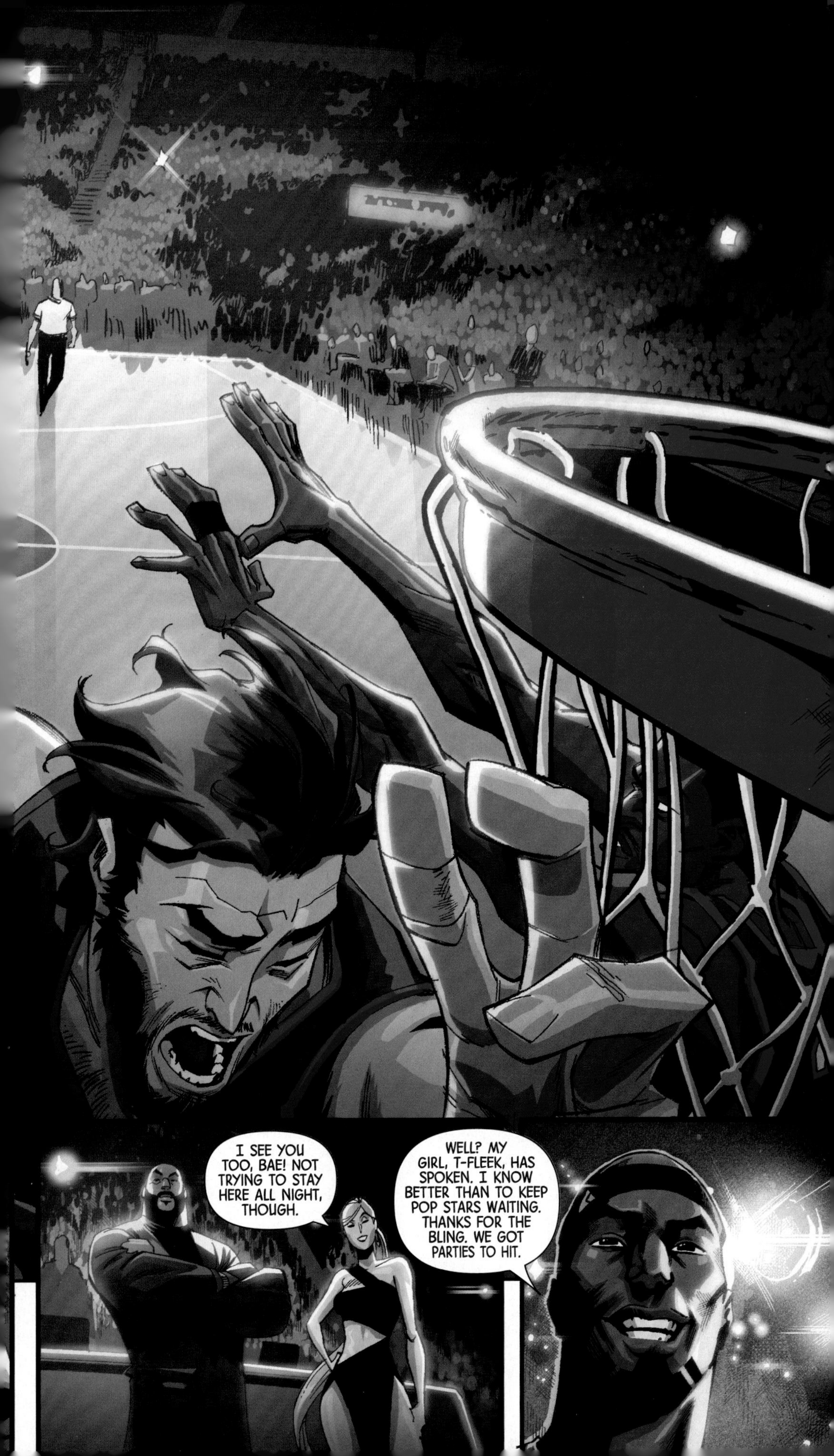

I SEE YOU TOO, BAE! NOT TRYING TO STAY HERE ALL NIGHT, THOUGH.
WELL? MY GIRL, T-FLEEK, HAS SPOKEN. I KNOW BETTER THAN TO KEEP POP STARS WAITING. THANKS FOR THE BLING. WE GOT PARTIES TO HIT.

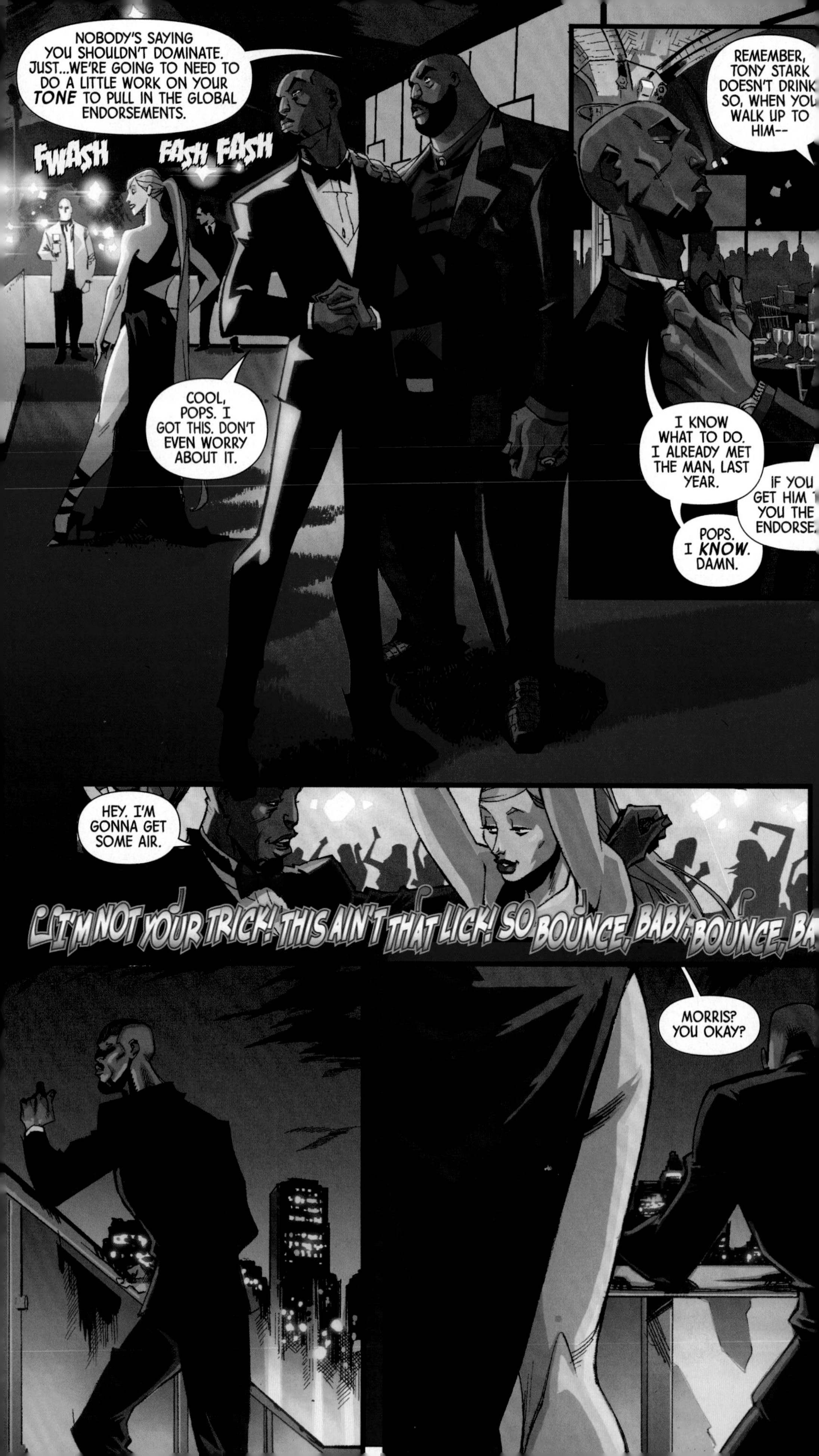
NOBODY'S SAYING YOU SHOULDN'T DOMINATE. JUST...WE'RE GOING TO NEED TO DO A LITTLE WORK ON YOUR *TONE* TO PULL IN THE GLOBAL ENDORSEMENTS.
FWASH
FASH FASH
COOL, POPS. I GOT THIS. DON'T EVEN WORRY ABOUT IT.
REMEMBER, TONY STARK DOESN'T DRINK SO, WHEN YOU WALK UP TO HIM--
I KNOW WHAT TO DO. I ALREADY MET THE MAN, LAST YEAR.
IF YOU GET HIM YOU THE ENDORSE
POPS. I *KNOW*. DAMN.
HEY. I'M GONNA GET SOME AIR.
I'M NOT YOUR TRICK! THIS AIN'T THAT LICK! SO BOUNCE, BABY, BOUNCE, BA
MORRIS? YOU OKAY?

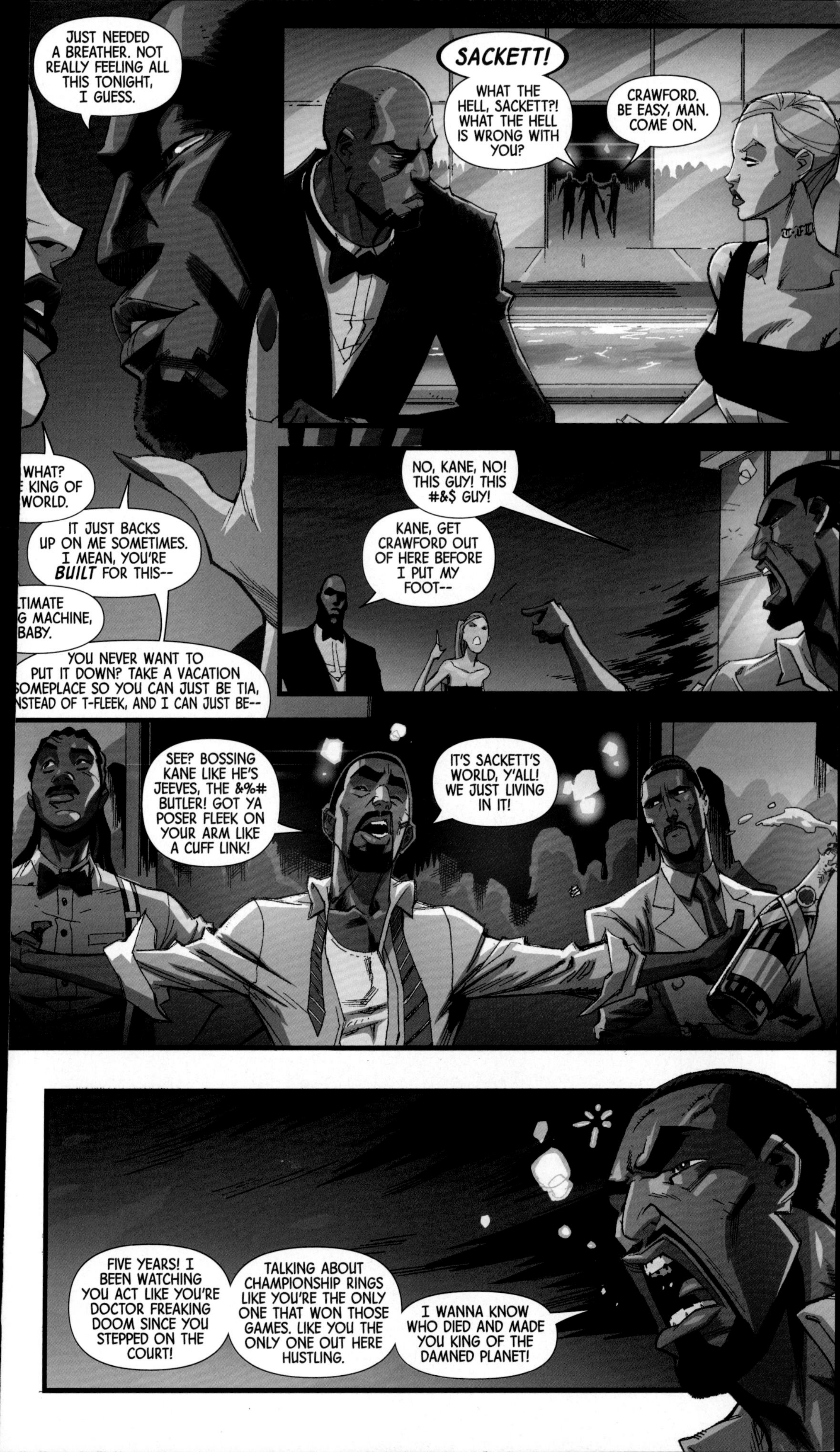
JUST NEEDED A BREATHER. NOT REALLY FEELING ALL THIS TONIGHT, I GUESS.
WHAT? KING OF WORLD.
IT JUST BACKS UP ON ME SOMETIMES. I MEAN, YOU'RE BUILT FOR THIS--
LTIMATE G MACHINE, BABY.
YOU NEVER WANT TO PUT IT DOWN? TAKE A VACATION SOMEPLACE SO YOU CAN JUST BE TIA, NSTEAD OF T-FLEEK, AND I CAN JUST BE--
SACKETT!
WHAT THE HELL, SACKETT?! WHAT THE HELL IS WRONG WITH YOU?
CRAWFORD. BE EASY, MAN. COME ON.
NO, KANE, NO! THIS GUY! THIS #&$ GUY!
KANE, GET CRAWFORD OUT OF HERE BEFORE I PUT MY FOOT--
SEE? BOSSING KANE LIKE HE'S JEEVES, THE &%# BUTLER! GOT YA POSER FLEEK ON YOUR ARM LIKE A CUFF LINK!
IT'S SACKETT'S WORLD, Y'ALL! WE JUST LIVING IN IT!
FIVE YEARS! I BEEN WATCHING YOU ACT LIKE YOU'RE DOCTOR FREAKING DOOM SINCE YOU STEPPED ON THE COURT!
TALKING ABOUT CHAMPIONSHIP RINGS LIKE YOU'RE THE ONLY ONE THAT WON THOSE GAMES. LIKE YOU THE ONLY ONE OUT HERE HUSTLING.
I WANNA KNOW WHO DIED AND MADE YOU KING OF THE DAMNED PLANET!

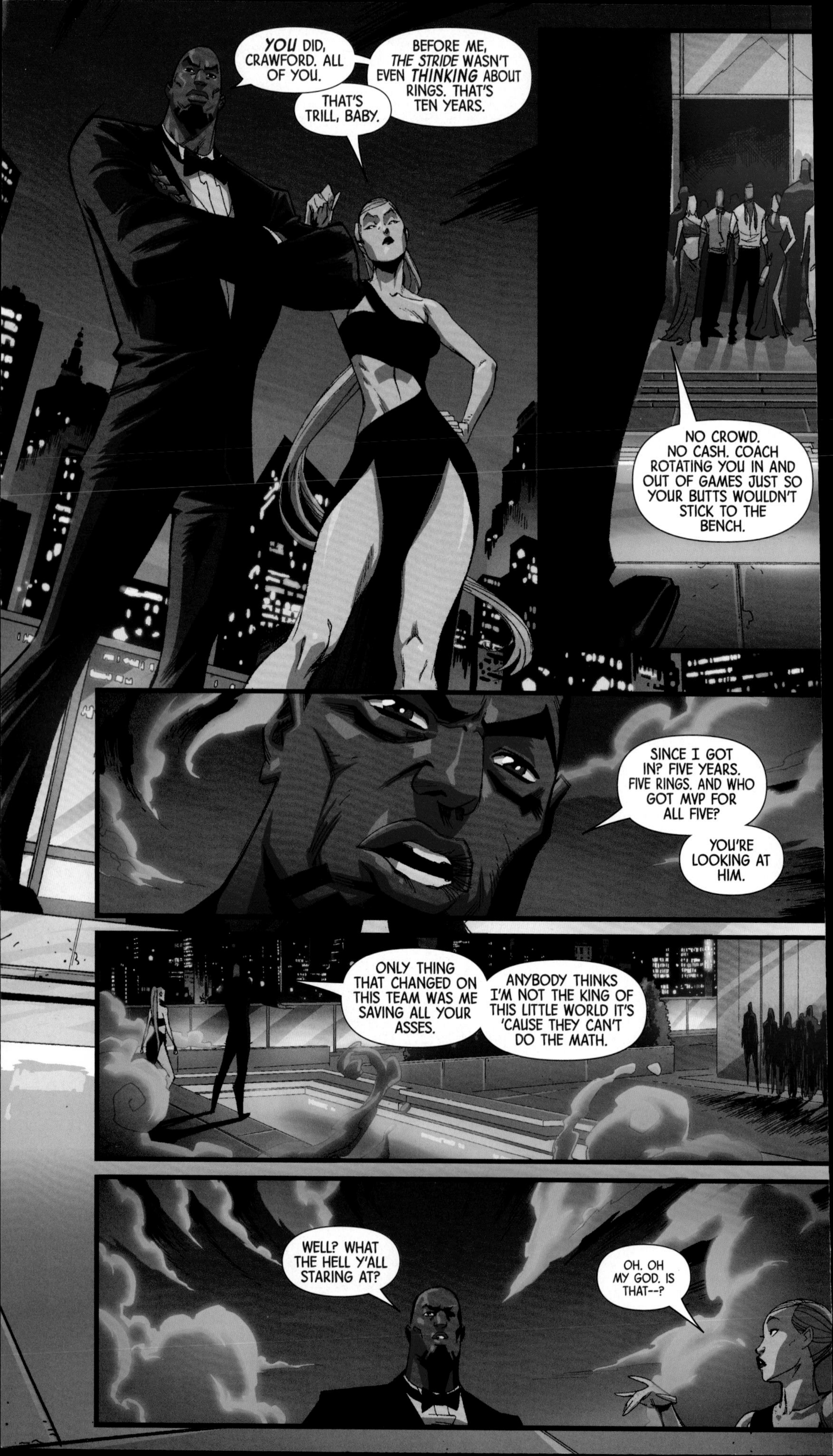
YOU DID, CRAWFORD. ALL OF YOU.
BEFORE ME, THE STRIDE WASN'T EVEN THINKING ABOUT RINGS. THAT'S TEN YEARS.
THAT'S TRILL, BABY.
NO CROWD. NO CASH. COACH ROTATING YOU IN AND OUT OF GAMES JUST SO YOUR BUTTS WOULDN'T STICK TO THE BENCH.
SINCE I GOT IN? FIVE YEARS. FIVE RINGS. AND WHO GOT MVP FOR ALL FIVE?
YOU'RE LOOKING AT HIM.
ONLY THING THAT CHANGED ON THIS TEAM WAS ME SAVING ALL YOUR ASSES.
ANYBODY THINKS I'M NOT THE KING OF THIS LITTLE WORLD IT'S 'CAUSE THEY CAN'T DO THE MATH.
WELL? WHAT THE HELL Y'ALL STARING AT?
OH. OH MY GOD. IS THAT--?

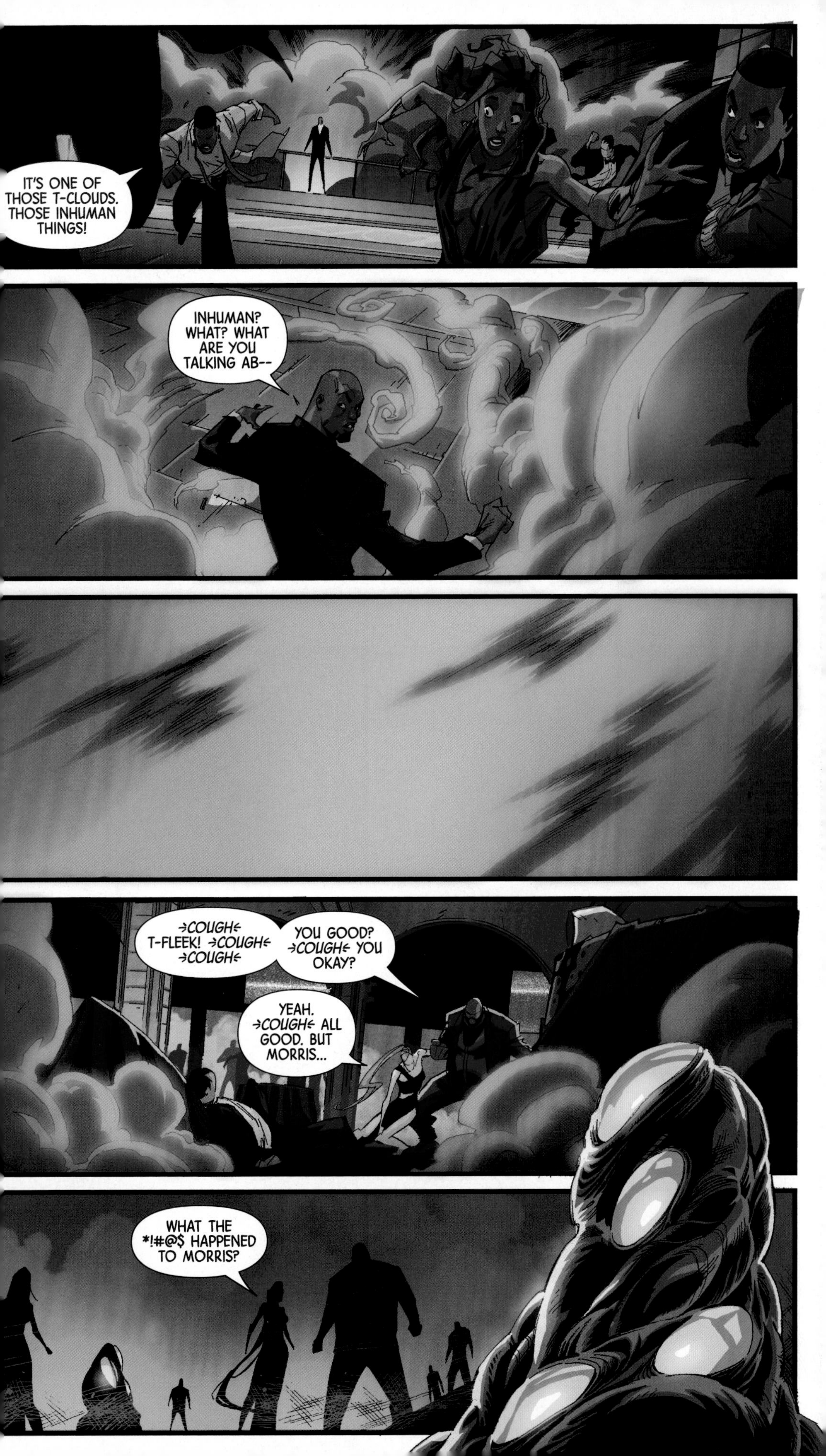
IT'S ONE OF THOSE T-CLOUDS. THOSE INHUMAN THINGS!
INHUMAN? WHAT? WHAT ARE YOU TALKING AB--
→COUGH← T-FLEEK! →COUGH← →COUGH←
YOU GOOD? →COUGH← YOU OKAY?
YEAH. →COUGH← ALL GOOD. BUT MORRIS...
WHAT THE *!#@$ HAPPENED TO MORRIS?

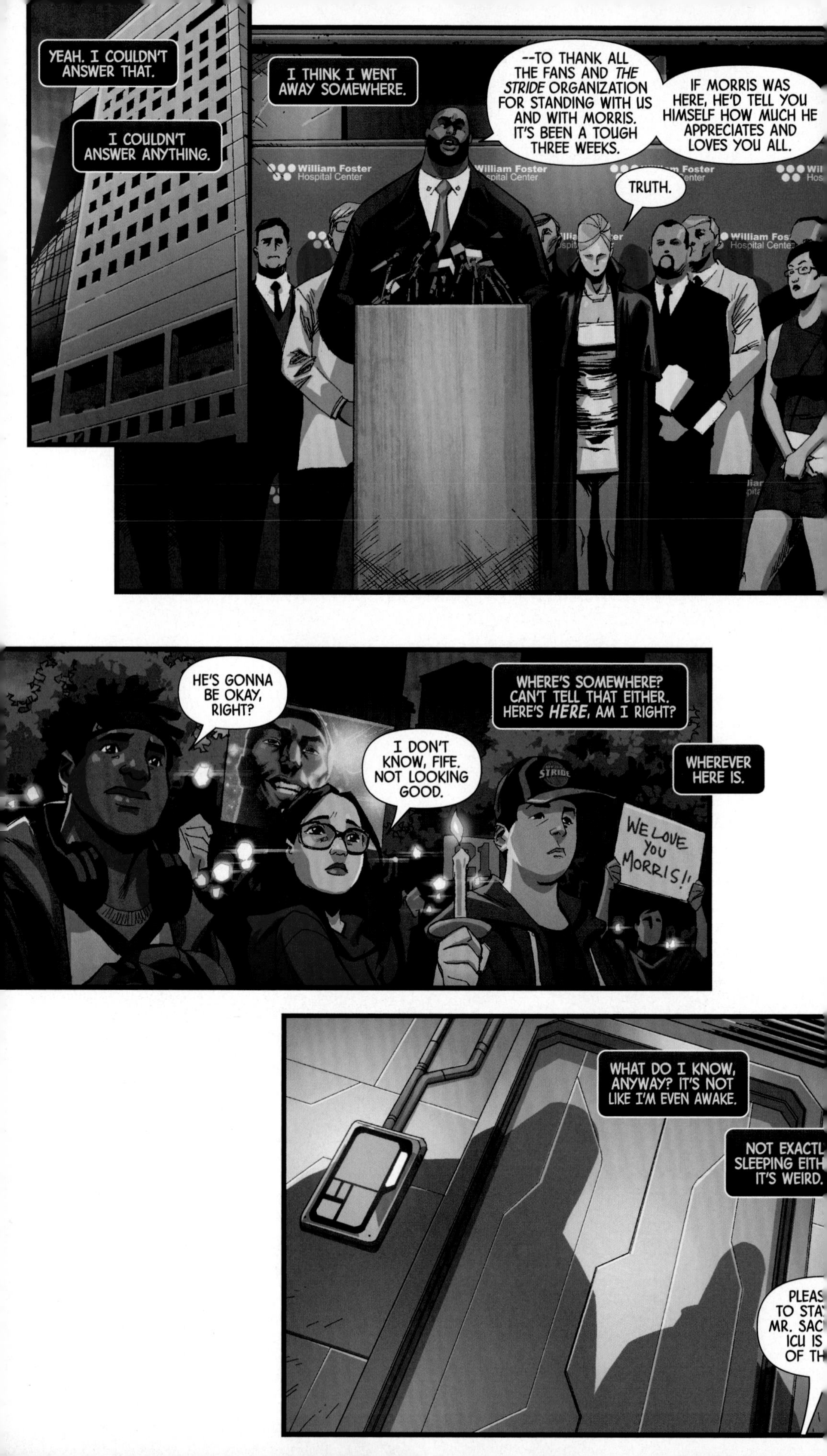

YEAH. I COULDN'T ANSWER THAT.
I COULDN'T ANSWER ANYTHING.
I THINK I WENT AWAY SOMEWHERE.
--TO THANK ALL THE FANS AND *THE STRIDE* ORGANIZATION FOR STANDING WITH US AND WITH MORRIS. IT'S BEEN A TOUGH THREE WEEKS.
IF MORRIS WAS HERE, HE'D TELL YOU HIMSELF HOW MUCH HE APPRECIATES AND LOVES YOU ALL.
TRUTH.
William Foster Hospital Center
HE'S GONNA BE OKAY, RIGHT?
I DON'T KNOW, FIFE. NOT LOOKING GOOD.
WHERE'S SOMEWHERE? CAN'T TELL THAT EITHER. HERE'S *HERE*, AM I RIGHT?
WHEREVER HERE IS.
STRIDE
WE LOVE YOU MORRIS!!
WHAT DO I KNOW, ANYWAY? IT'S NOT LIKE I'M EVEN AWAKE.
NOT EXACTL
SLEEPING EITH
IT'S WEIRD.
PLEAS
TO STA
MR. SAC
ICU IS
OF TH

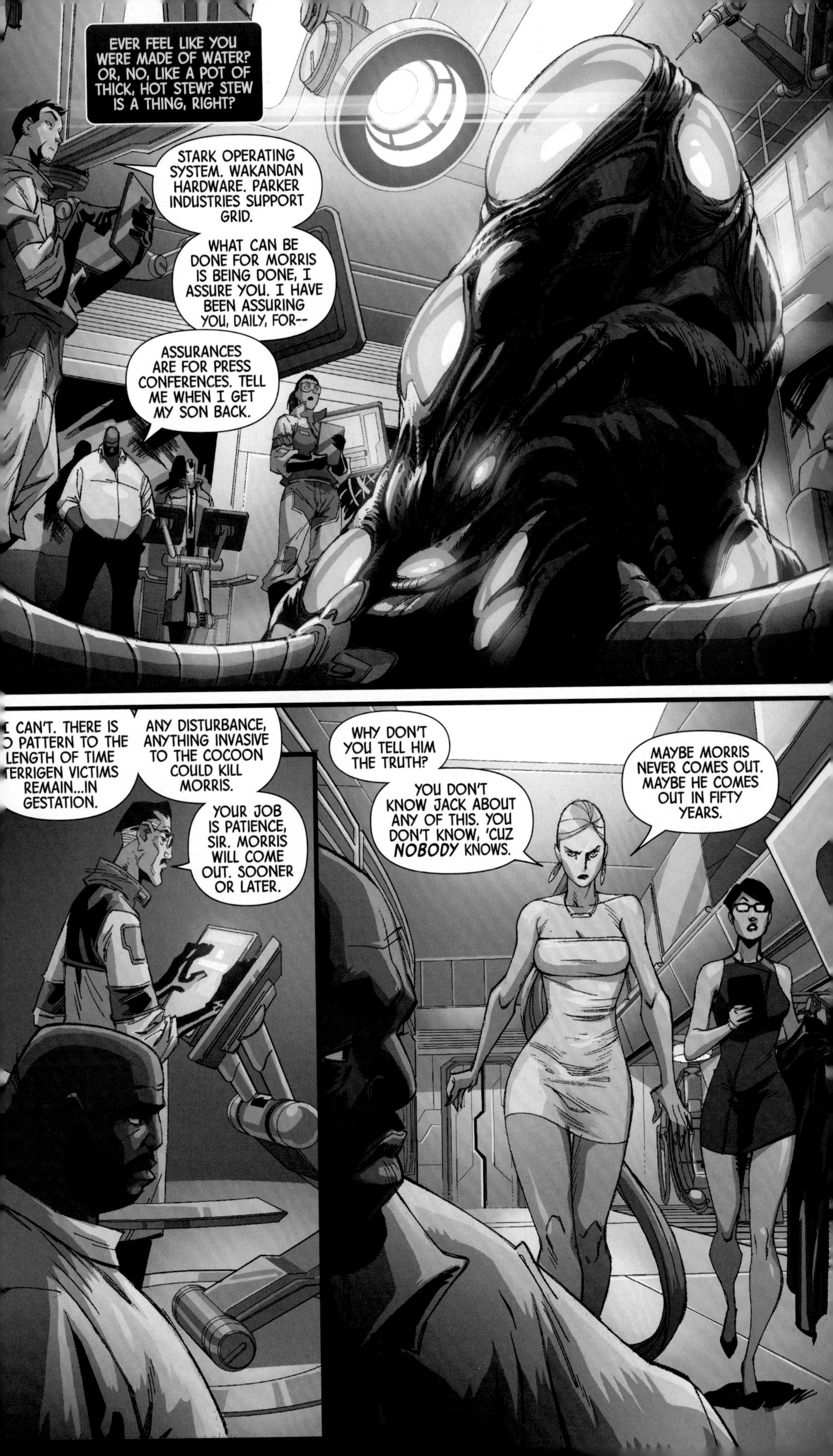

EVER FEEL LIKE YOU WERE MADE OF WATER? OR, NO, LIKE A POT OF THICK, HOT STEW? STEW IS A THING, RIGHT?
STARK OPERATING SYSTEM. WAKANDAN HARDWARE. PARKER INDUSTRIES SUPPORT GRID.
WHAT CAN BE DONE FOR MORRIS IS BEING DONE, I ASSURE YOU. I HAVE BEEN ASSURING YOU, DAILY, FOR--
ASSURANCES ARE FOR PRESS CONFERENCES. TELL ME WHEN I GET MY SON BACK.
I CAN'T. THERE IS NO PATTERN TO THE LENGTH OF TIME TERRIGEN VICTIMS REMAIN...IN GESTATION.
ANY DISTURBANCE, ANYTHING INVASIVE TO THE COCOON COULD KILL MORRIS.
YOUR JOB IS PATIENCE, SIR. MORRIS WILL COME OUT. SOONER OR LATER.
WHY DON'T YOU TELL HIM THE TRUTH?
YOU DON'T KNOW JACK ABOUT ANY OF THIS. YOU DON'T KNOW, 'CUZ *NOBODY* KNOWS.
MAYBE MORRIS NEVER COMES OUT. MAYBE HE COMES OUT IN FIFTY YEARS.

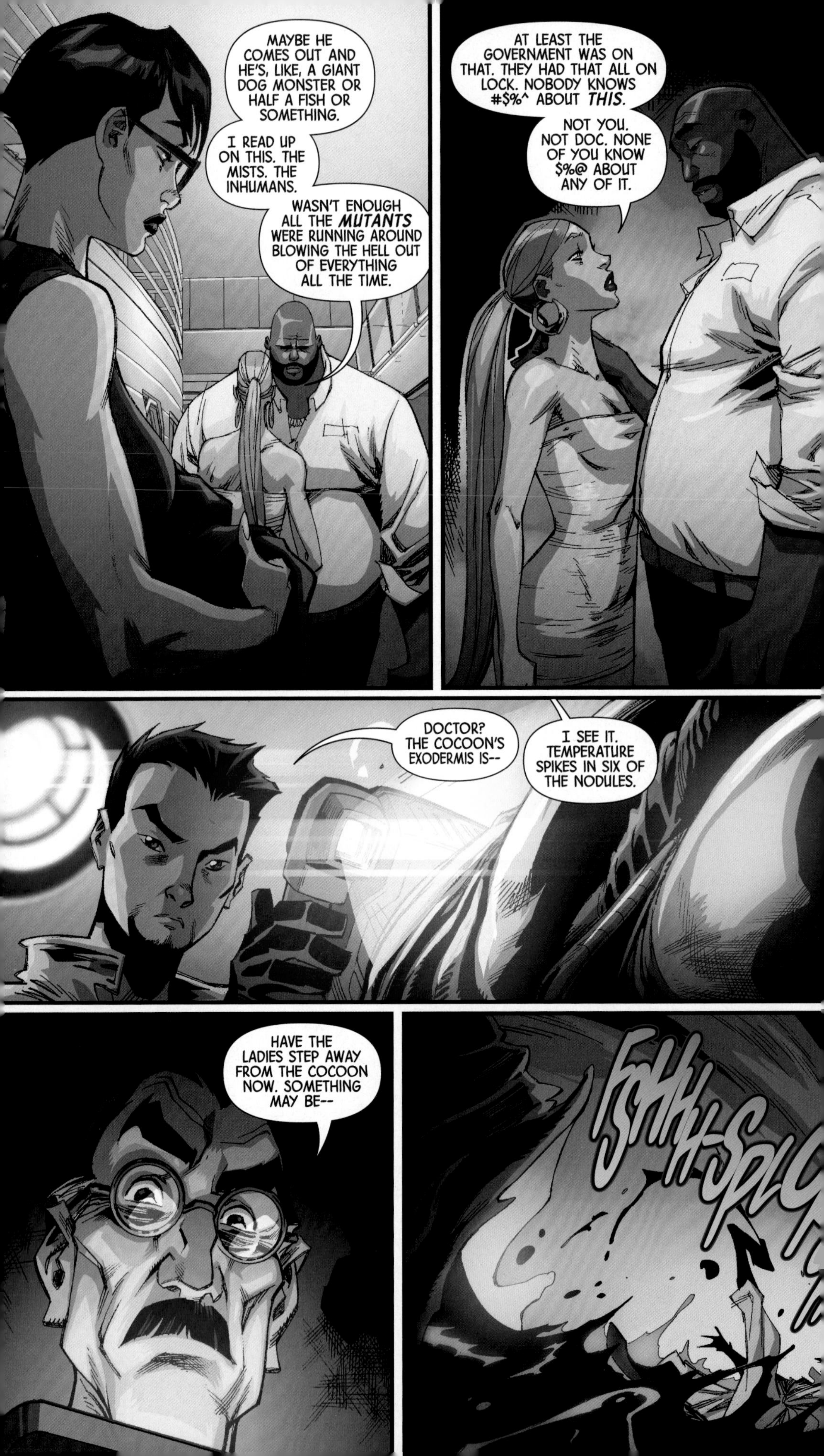

MAYBE HE COMES OUT AND HE'S, LIKE, A GIANT DOG MONSTER OR HALF A FISH OR SOMETHING.
I READ UP ON THIS. THE MISTS. THE INHUMANS.
WASN'T ENOUGH ALL THE *MUTANTS* WERE RUNNING AROUND BLOWING THE HELL OUT OF EVERYTHING ALL THE TIME.
AT LEAST THE GOVERNMENT WAS ON THAT. THEY HAD THAT ALL ON LOCK. NOBODY KNOWS #$%^ ABOUT *THIS*.
NOT YOU. NOT DOC. NONE OF YOU KNOW $%@ ABOUT ANY OF IT.
DOCTOR? THE COCOON'S EXODERMIS IS--
I SEE IT. TEMPERATURE SPIKES IN SIX OF THE NODULES.
HAVE THE LADIES STEP AWAY FROM THE COCOON NOW. SOMETHING MAY BE--

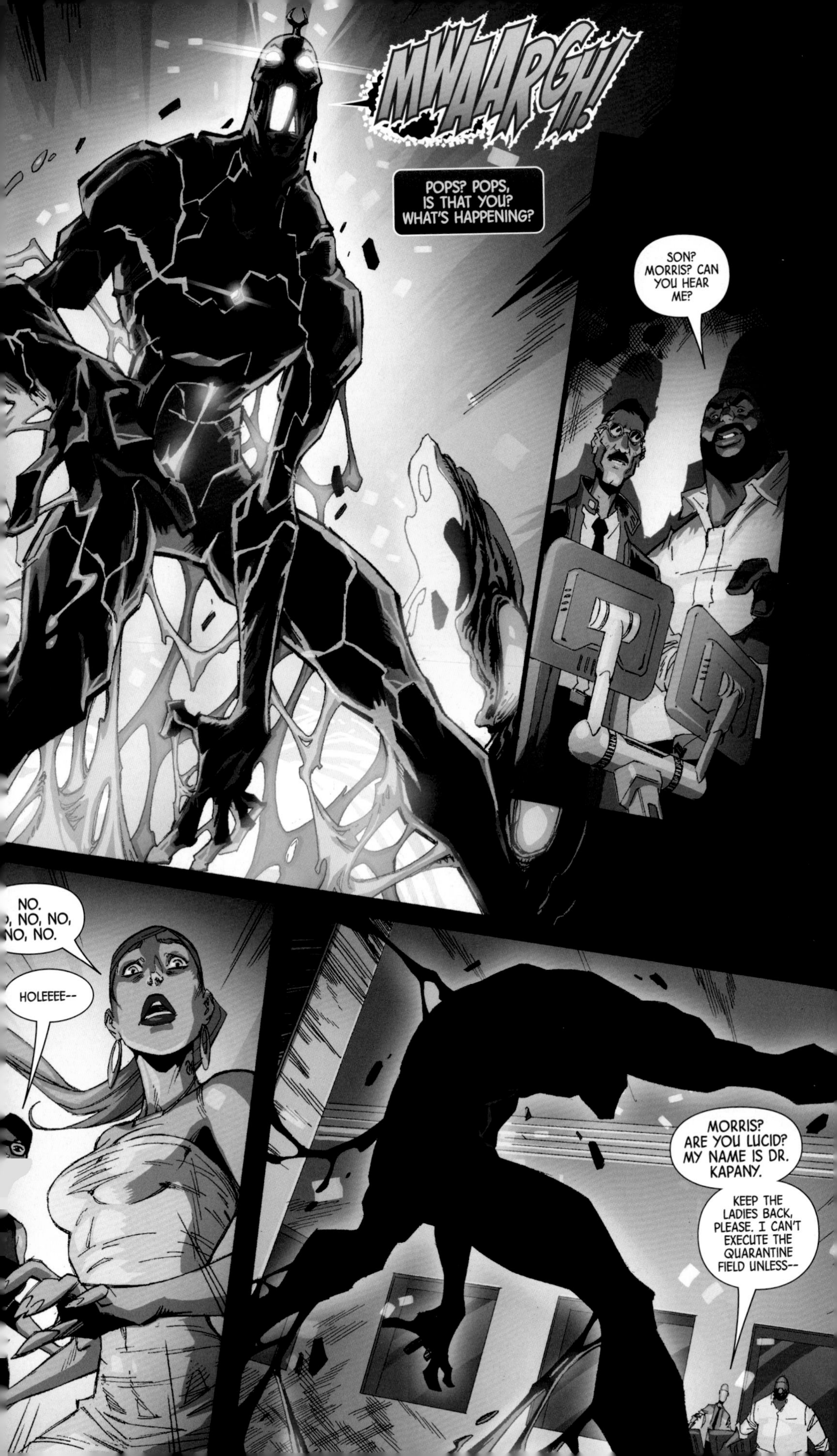
MWAARGH!
POPS? POPS, IS THAT YOU? WHAT'S HAPPENING?
SON? MORRIS? CAN YOU HEAR ME?
NO. NO, NO, NO, NO, NO.
HOLEEEE--
MORRIS? ARE YOU LUCID? MY NAME IS DR. KAPANY.
KEEP THE LADIES BACK, PLEASE. I CAN'T EXECUTE THE QUARANTINE FIELD UNLESS--

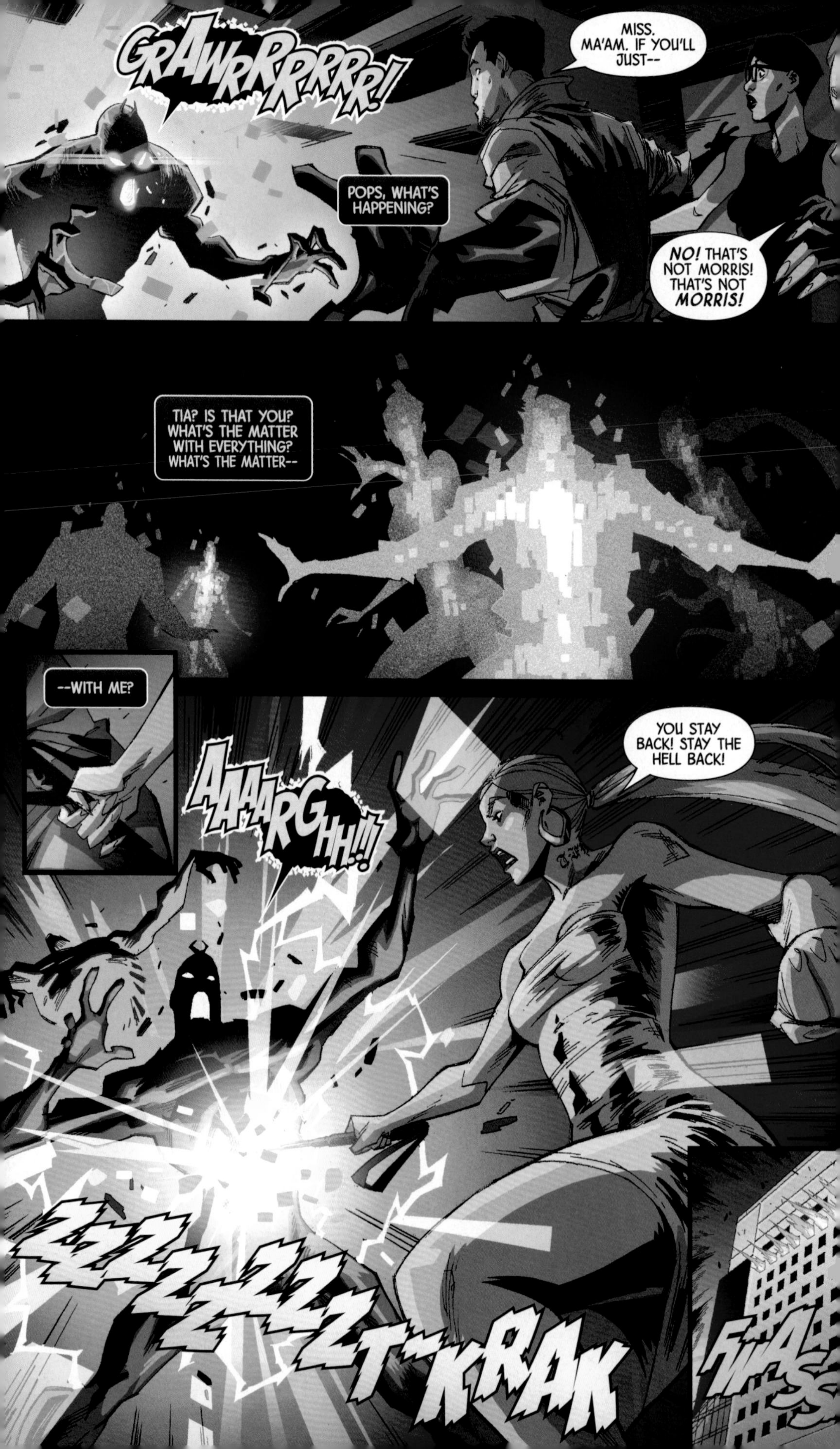
GRAWRRRRRRR!
MISS. MA'AM. IF YOU'LL JUST--
POPS, WHAT'S HAPPENING?
NO! THAT'S NOT MORRIS! THAT'S NOT MORRIS!
TIA? IS THAT YOU? WHAT'S THE MATTER WITH EVERYTHING? WHAT'S THE MATTER--
--WITH ME?
AAAARGHH!!!
YOU STAY BACK! STAY THE HELL BACK!
ZZZZZT-KRAK

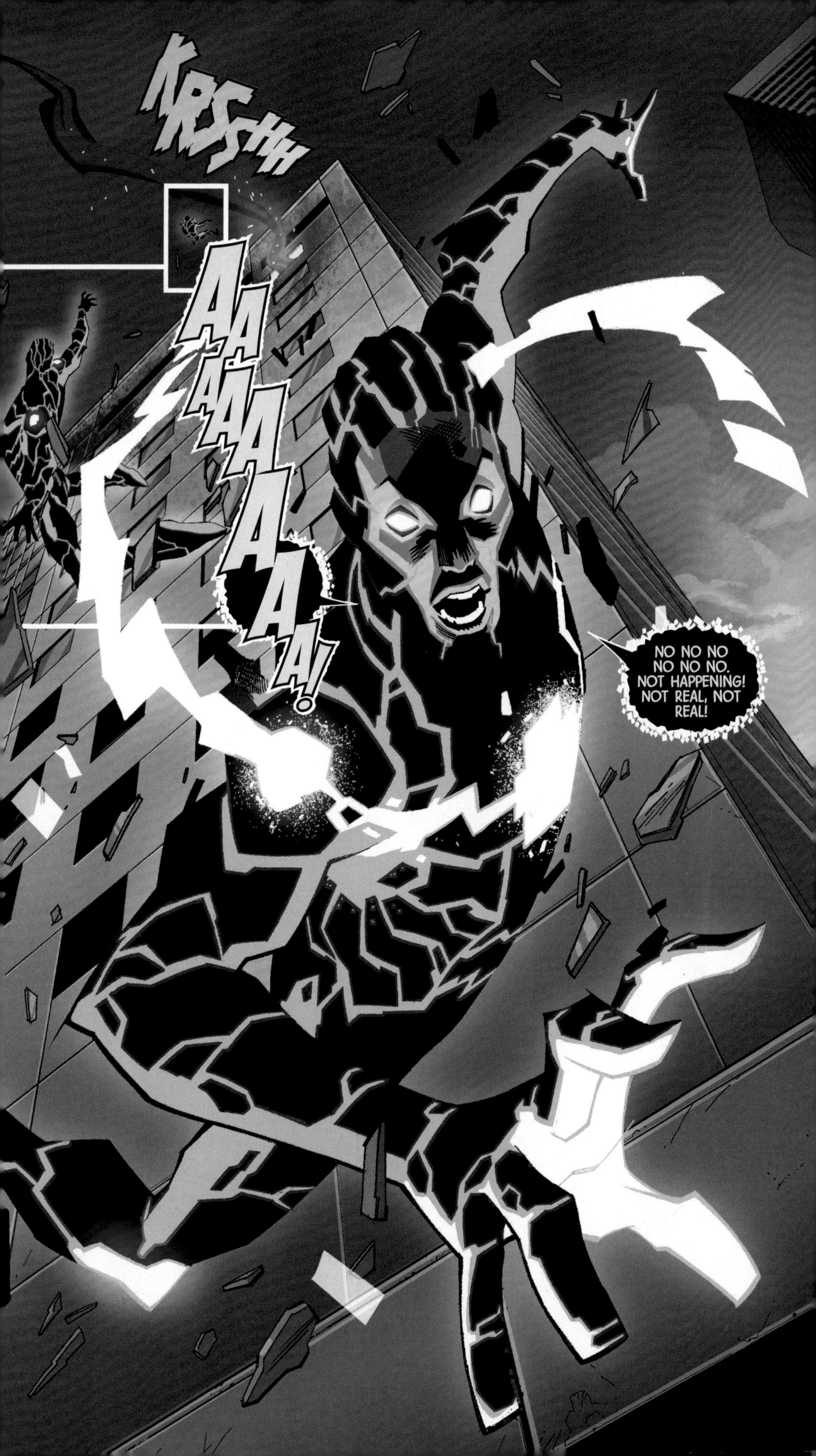
KRSHHH
AAAAAAAAAA!
NO NO NO NO NO NO. NOT HAPPENING! NOT REAL, NOT REAL!

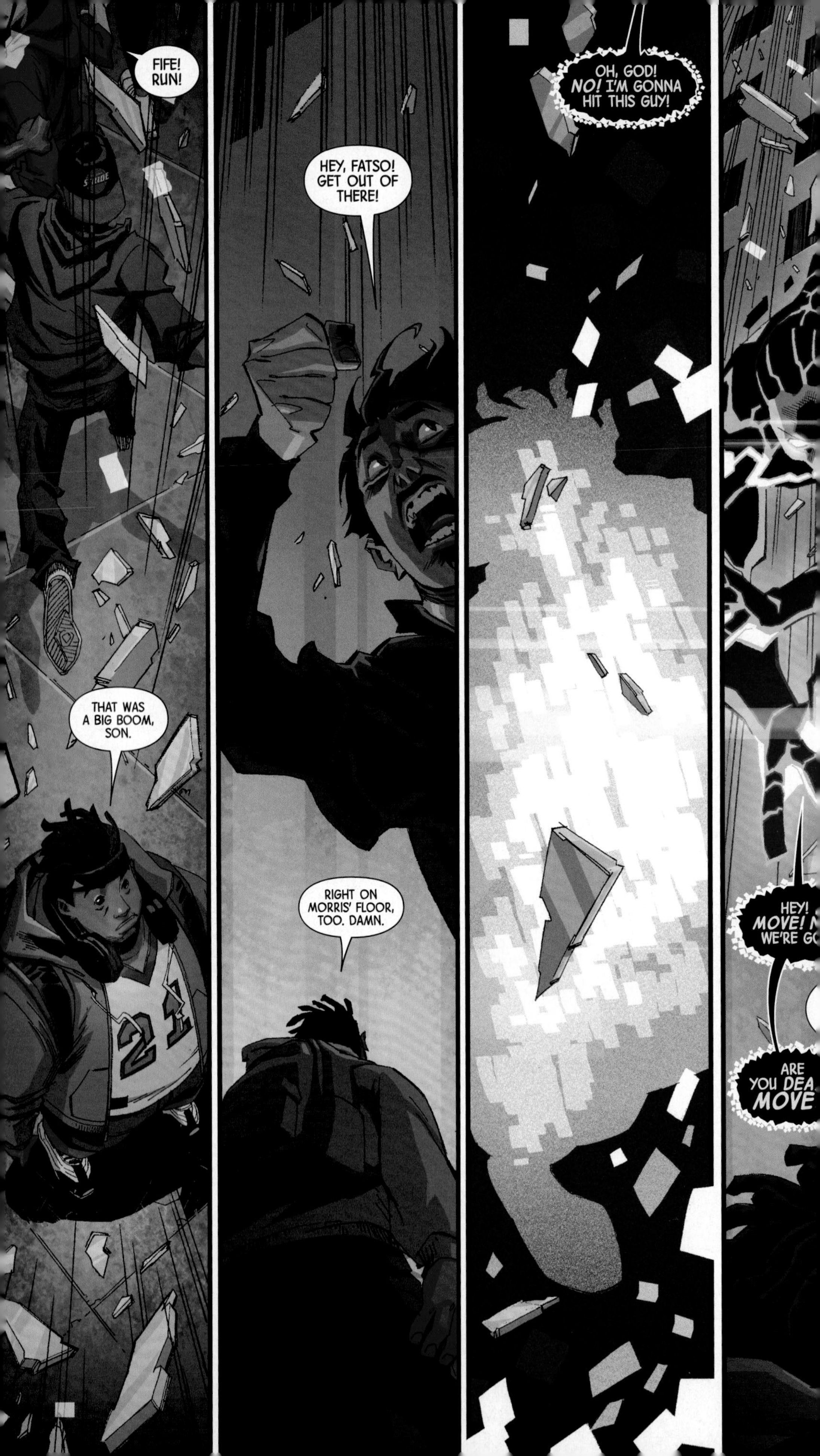
FIFE! RUN!
THAT WAS A BIG BOOM, SON.
HEY, FATSO! GET OUT OF THERE!
RIGHT ON MORRIS' FLOOR, TOO. DAMN.
OH, GOD! NO! I'M GONNA HIT THIS GUY!
HEY! MOVE! N
WE'RE GO
ARE YOU DEA
MOVE

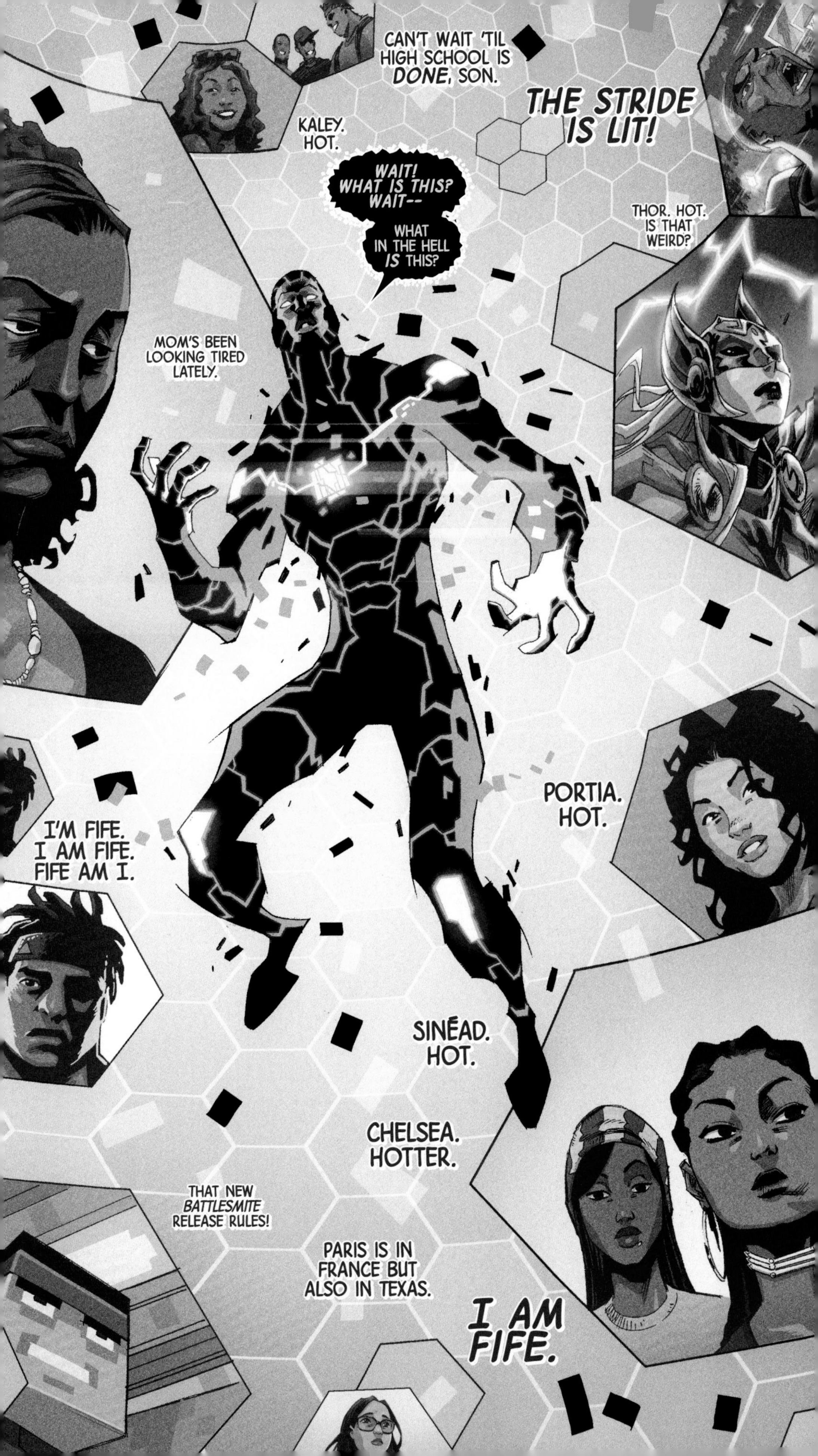
CAN'T WAIT 'TIL HIGH SCHOOL IS DONE, SON.
KALEY. HOT.
THE STRIDE IS LIT!
WAIT! WHAT IS THIS? WAIT--
WHAT IN THE HELL IS THIS?
THOR. HOT. IS THAT WEIRD?
MOM'S BEEN LOOKING TIRED LATELY.
PORTIA. HOT.
I'M FIFE. I AM FIFE. FIFE AM I.
SINÉAD. HOT.
CHELSEA. HOTTER.
THAT NEW BATTLESMITE RELEASE RULES!
PARIS IS IN FRANCE BUT ALSO IN TEXAS.
I AM FIFE.

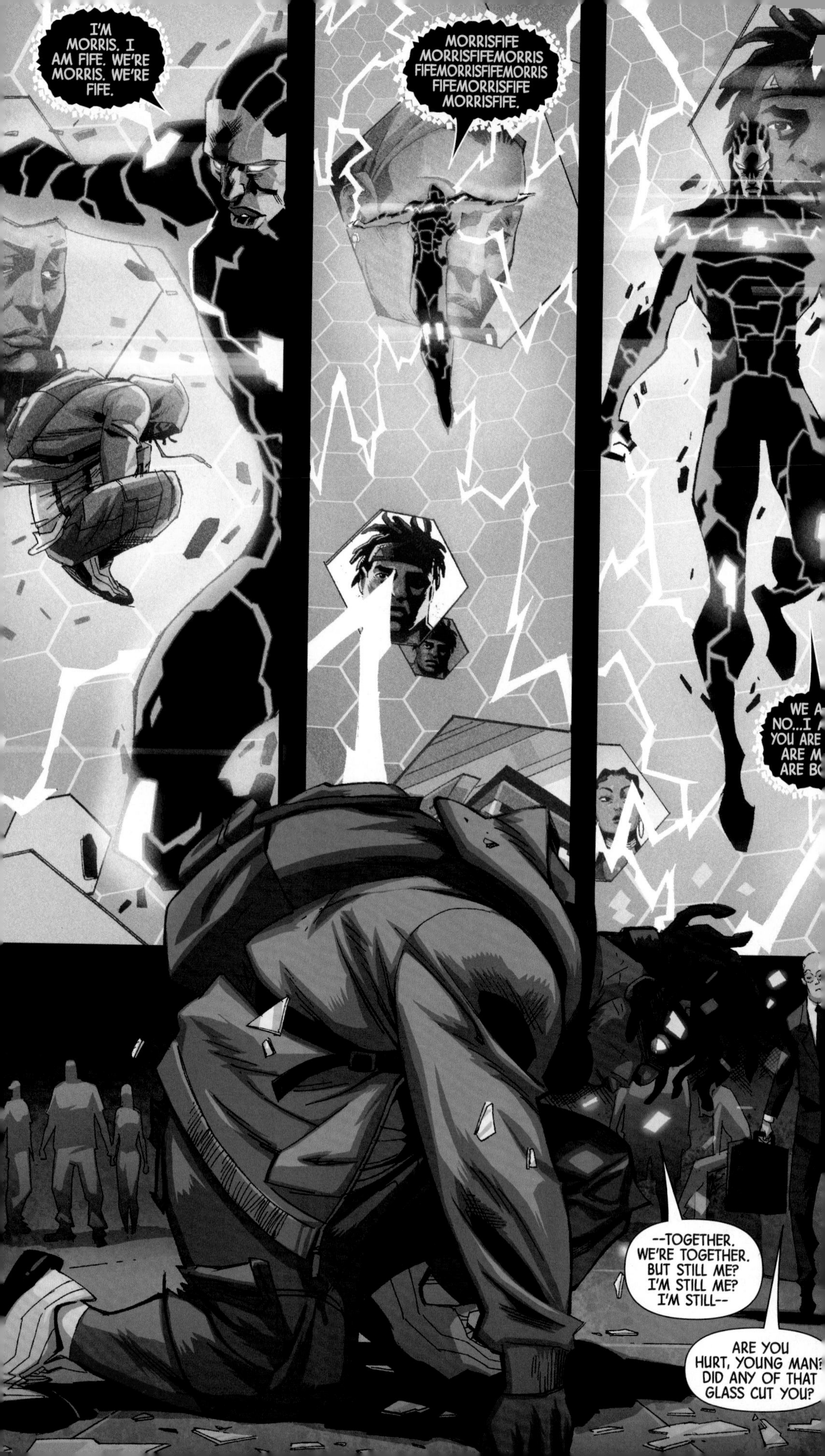
I'M MORRIS. I AM FIFE. WE'RE MORRIS. WE'RE FIFE.
MORRISFIFE MORRISFIFEMORRIS FIFEMORRISFIFEMORRIS FIFEMORRISFIFE MORRISFIFE.
WE A NO...I YOU ARE ARE M ARE BO
--TOGETHER. WE'RE TOGETHER. BUT STILL ME? I'M STILL ME? I'M STILL--
ARE YOU HURT, YOUNG MAN? DID ANY OF THAT GLASS CUT YOU?

NO! IT'S HAPPENING AGAIN! MAKE IT STOP! MAKE IT--

--STOP!

HEY! HE HURT THAT KID!

WE'RE...JAE NOW. AND FIFE? NO. THAT'S NOT RIGHT. NOT EXACTLY.

JAE YU. HERE FROM SEOUL. BANKER. FIFTY BUT SAYS HE'S FORTY-THREE. HE'S ME. WE'RE WE.

AT'D DO TO YOU AK?

WHO, ME? NO, I DIDN'T--IT'S A MISTAKE--

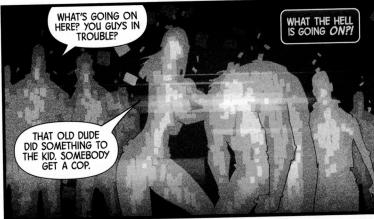

WHAT'S GOING ON HERE? YOU GUYS IN TROUBLE?

WHAT THE HELL IS GOING ON?!

THAT OLD DUDE DID SOMETHING TO THE KID. SOMEBODY GET A COP.

WAIT! NO! GET AWAY!

IT'S NOT MY FAULT!

57 Street Station
N R

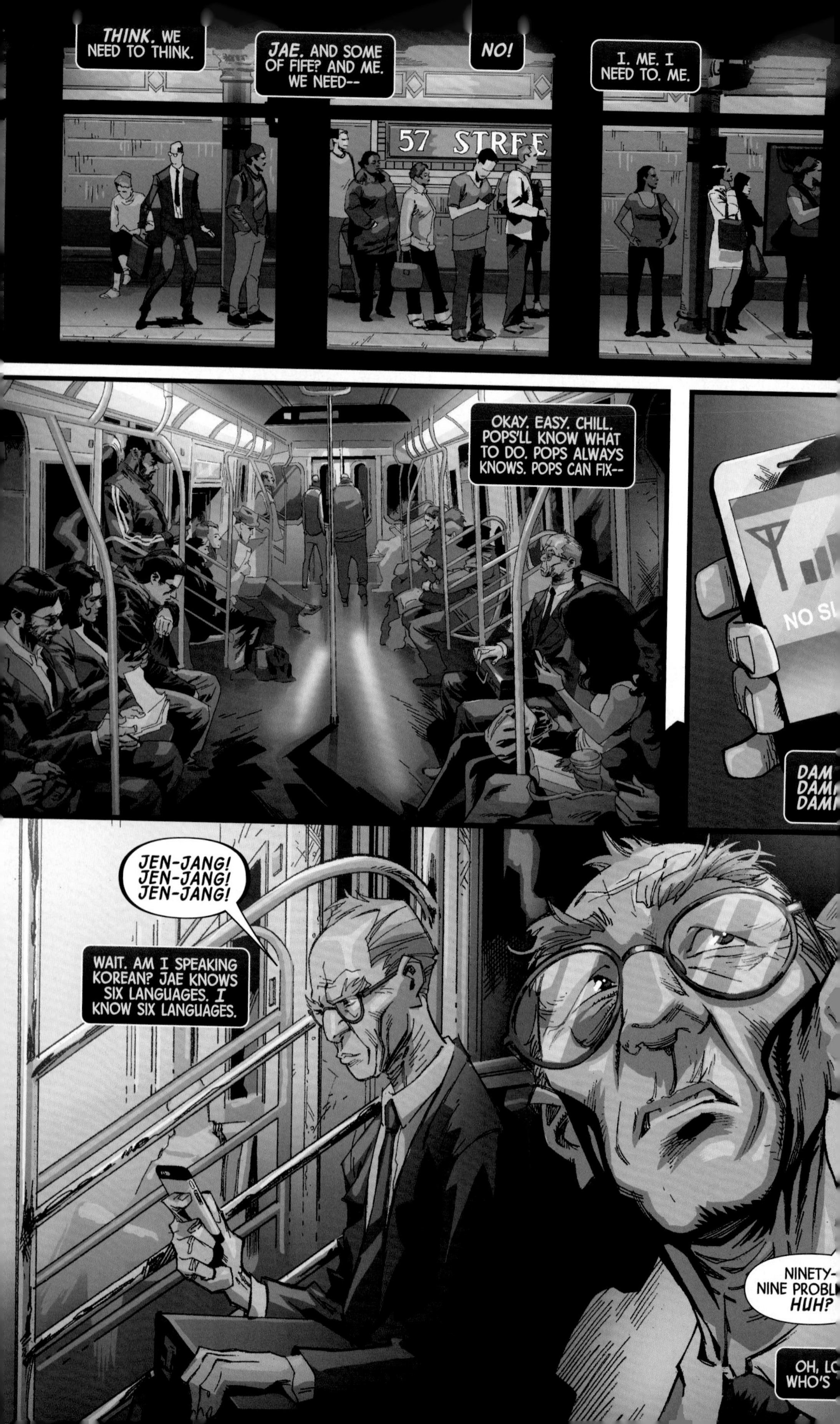

THINK. WE NEED TO THINK.
JAE. AND SOME OF FIFE? AND ME. WE NEED--
NO!
I. ME. I NEED TO. ME.
OKAY. EASY. CHILL. POPS'LL KNOW WHAT TO DO. POPS ALWAYS KNOWS. POPS CAN FIX--
JEN-JANG! JEN-JANG! JEN-JANG!
WAIT. AM I SPEAKING KOREAN? JAE KNOWS SIX LANGUAGES. I KNOW SIX LANGUAGES.

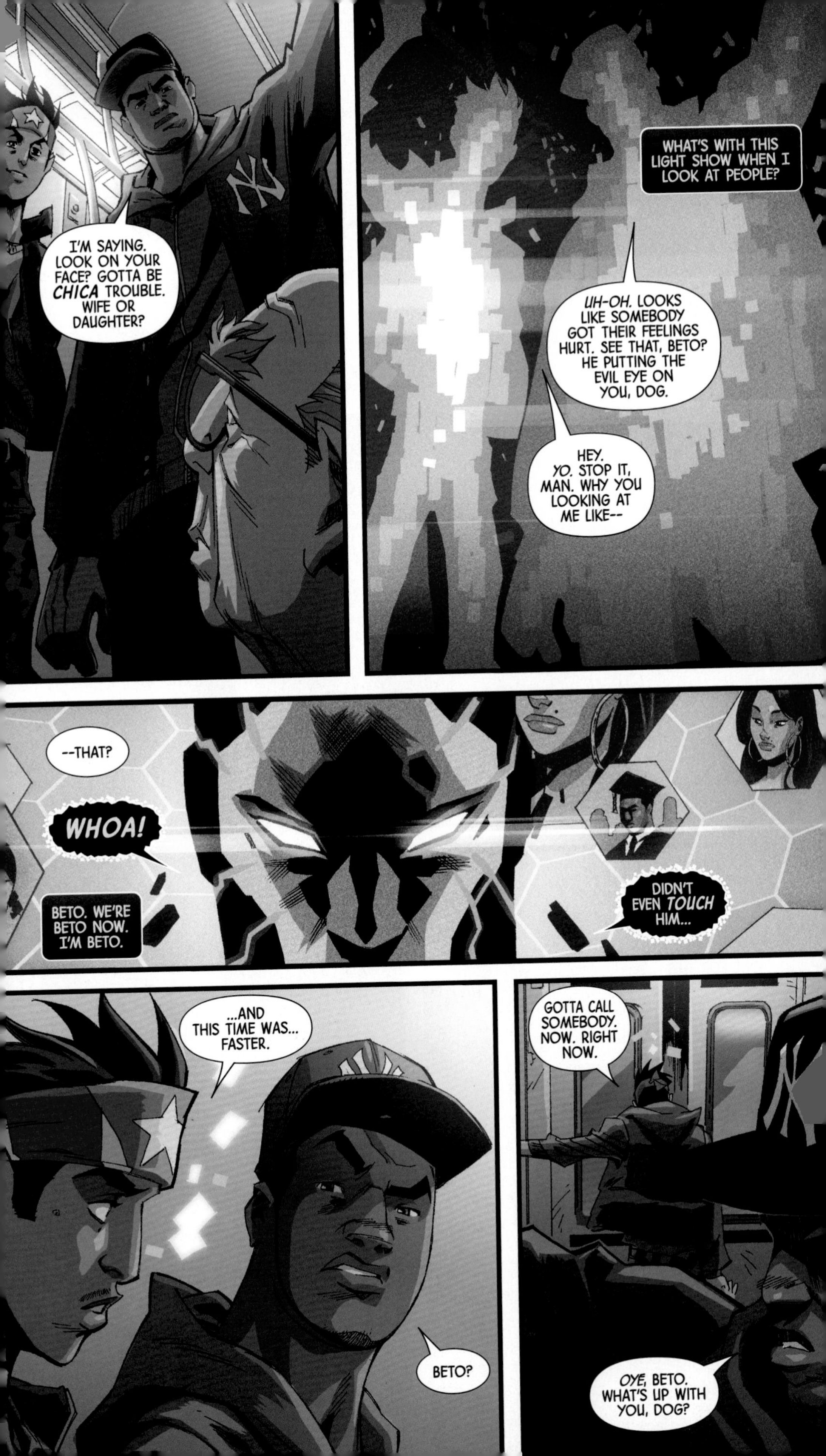

I'M SAYING. LOOK ON YOUR FACE? GOTTA BE *CHICA* TROUBLE. WIFE OR DAUGHTER?
WHAT'S WITH THIS LIGHT SHOW WHEN I LOOK AT PEOPLE?
UH-OH. LOOKS LIKE SOMEBODY GOT THEIR FEELINGS HURT. SEE THAT, BETO? HE PUTTING THE EVIL EYE ON YOU, DOG.
HEY. *YO.* STOP IT, MAN. WHY YOU LOOKING AT ME LIKE--
--THAT?
WHOA!
BETO. WE'RE BETO NOW. I'M BETO.
DIDN'T EVEN *TOUCH* HIM...
...AND THIS TIME WAS... FASTER.
BETO?
GOTTA CALL SOMEBODY. NOW. RIGHT NOW.
OYE, BETO. WHAT'S UP WITH YOU, DOG?

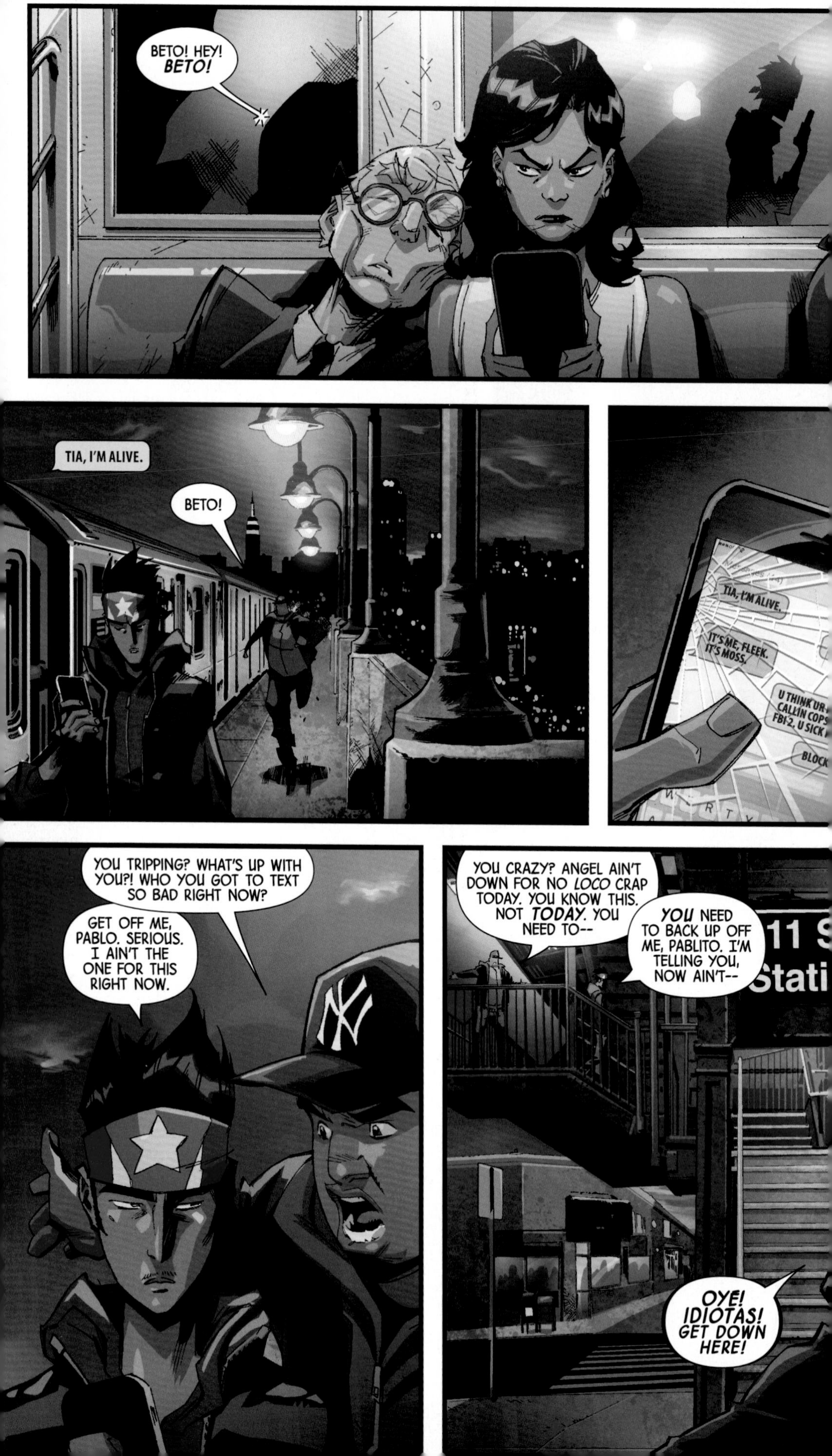
BETO! HEY! BETO!
TIA, I'M ALIVE.
BETO!
TIA, I'M ALIVE.
IT'S ME, FLEEK. IT'S MOSS.
YOU TRIPPING? WHAT'S UP WITH YOU?! WHO YOU GOT TO TEXT SO BAD RIGHT NOW?
GET OFF ME, PABLO. SERIOUS. I AIN'T THE ONE FOR THIS RIGHT NOW.
YOU CRAZY? ANGEL AIN'T DOWN FOR NO LOCO CRAP TODAY. YOU KNOW THIS. NOT TODAY. YOU NEED TO--
YOU NEED TO BACK UP OFF ME, PABLITO. I'M TELLING YOU, NOW AIN'T--
OYE! IDIOTAS! GET DOWN HERE!

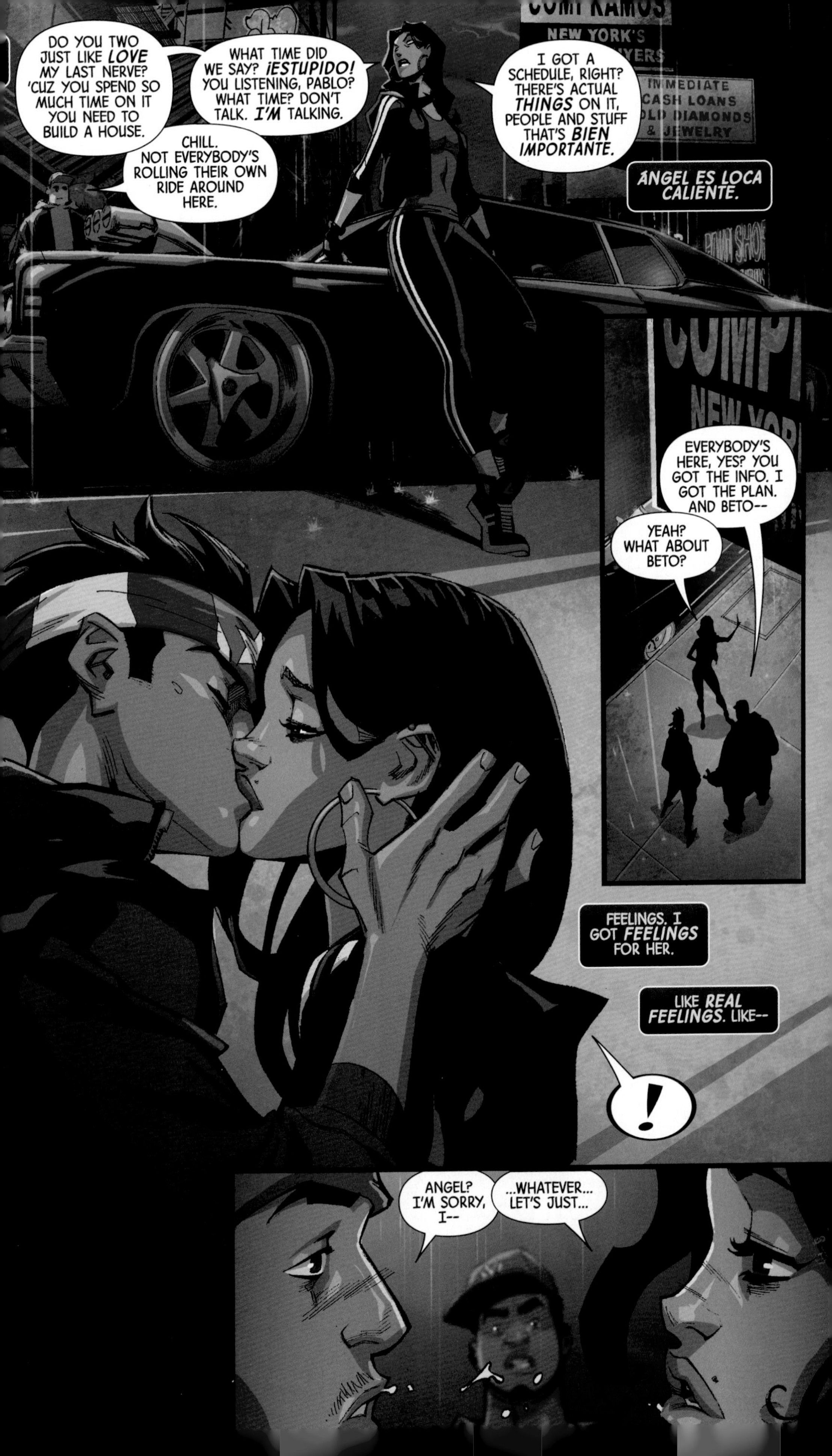

DO YOU TWO JUST LIKE LOVE MY LAST NERVE? 'CUZ YOU SPEND SO MUCH TIME ON IT YOU NEED TO BUILD A HOUSE.
WHAT TIME DID WE SAY? ¡ESTUPIDO! YOU LISTENING, PABLO? WHAT TIME? DON'T TALK. I'M TALKING.
CHILL. NOT EVERYBODY'S ROLLING THEIR OWN RIDE AROUND HERE.
I GOT A SCHEDULE, RIGHT? THERE'S ACTUAL THINGS ON IT, PEOPLE AND STUFF THAT'S BIEN IMPORTANTE.
NEW YORK'S
IMMEDIATE CASH LOANS
& JEWELRY
ÁNGEL ES LOCA CALIENTE.
EVERYBODY'S HERE, YES? YOU GOT THE INFO. I GOT THE PLAN. AND BETO--
YEAH? WHAT ABOUT BETO?
FEELINGS. I GOT FEELINGS FOR HER.
LIKE REAL FEELINGS. LIKE--
!
ANGEL? I'M SORRY, I--
...WHATEVER... LET'S JUST...

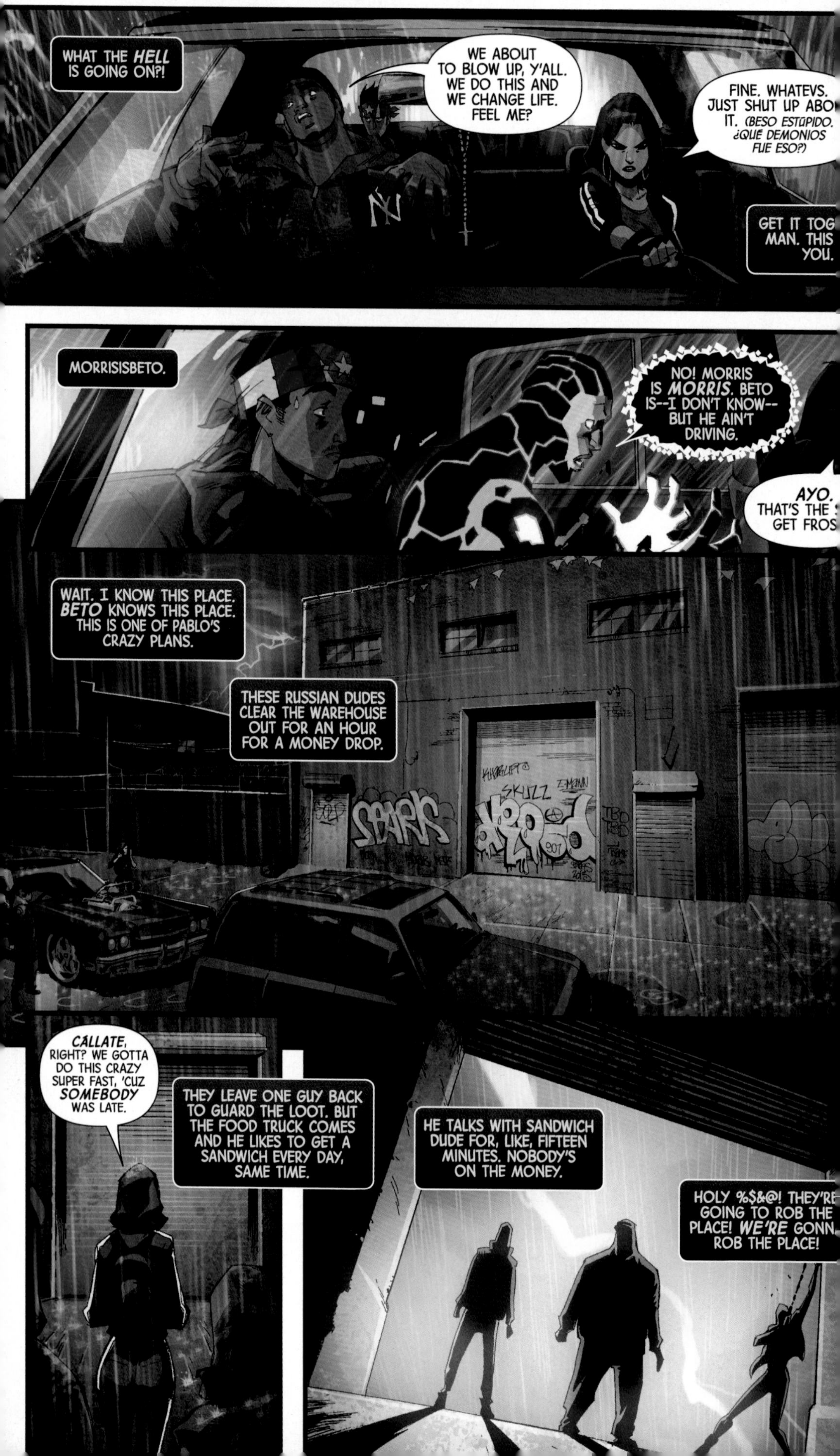

WHAT THE *HELL* IS GOING ON?!
WE ABOUT TO BLOW UP, Y'ALL. WE DO THIS AND WE CHANGE LIFE. FEEL ME?
FINE. WHATEVS. JUST SHUT UP ABO IT. (*BESO ESTÚPIDO. ¿QUÉ DEMONIOS FUE ESO?*)
GET IT TOG MAN. THIS YOU.
MORRISISBETO.
NO! MORRIS IS *MORRIS*. BETO IS--I DON'T KNOW--BUT HE AIN'T DRIVING.
AYO. THAT'S THE GET FROS
WAIT. I KNOW THIS PLACE. *BETO* KNOWS THIS PLACE. THIS IS ONE OF PABLO'S CRAZY PLANS.
THESE RUSSIAN DUDES CLEAR THE WAREHOUSE OUT FOR AN HOUR FOR A MONEY DROP.
CÁLLATE, RIGHT? WE GOTTA DO THIS CRAZY SUPER FAST, 'CUZ *SOMEBODY* WAS LATE.
THEY LEAVE ONE GUY BACK TO GUARD THE LOOT. BUT THE FOOD TRUCK COMES AND HE LIKES TO GET A SANDWICH EVERY DAY, SAME TIME.
HE TALKS WITH SANDWICH DUDE FOR, LIKE, FIFTEEN MINUTES. NOBODY'S ON THE MONEY.
HOLY %$&@! THEY'R GOING TO ROB THE PLACE! *WE'RE* GONN ROB THE PLACE!

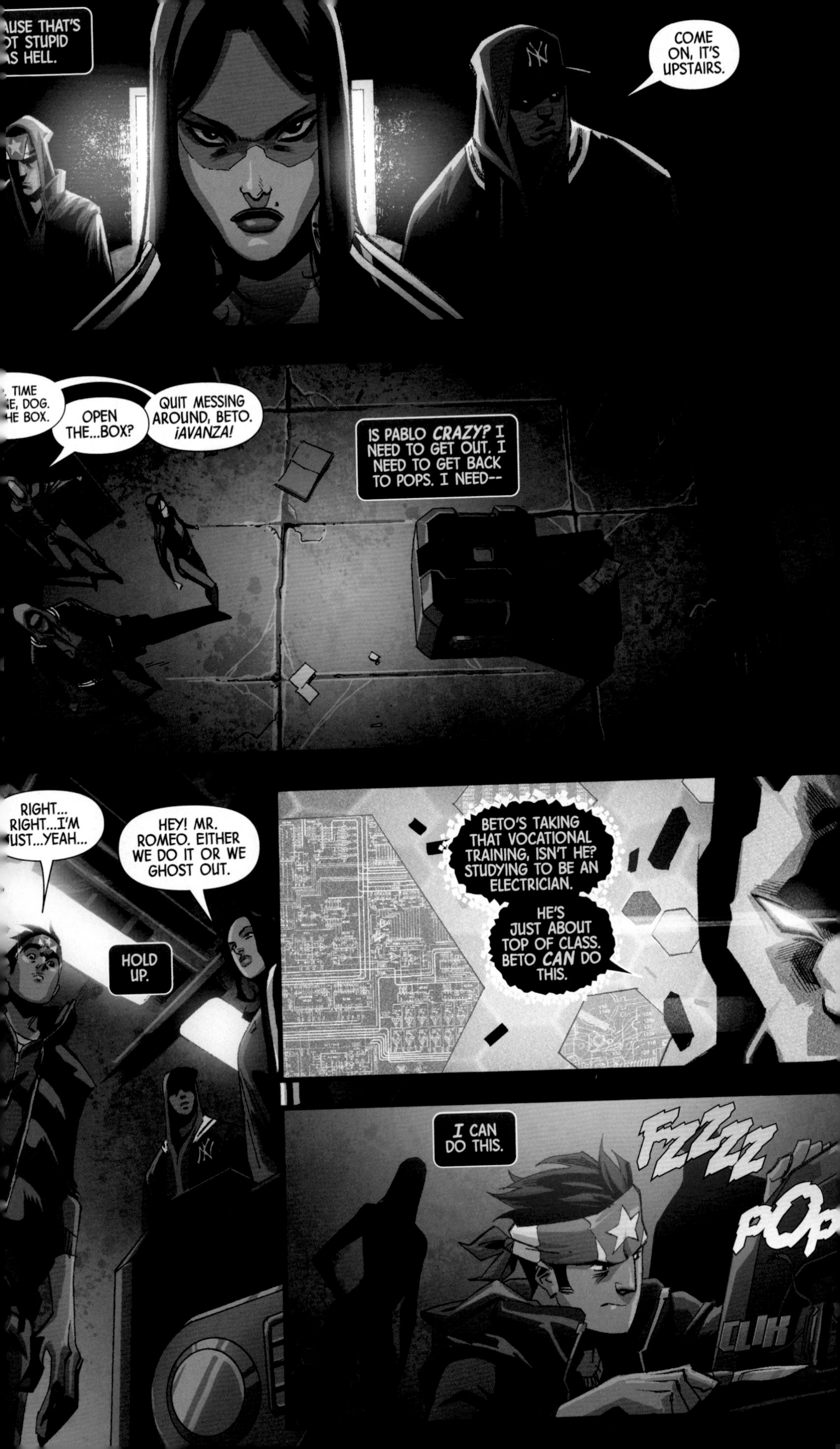

AUSE THAT'S
OT STUPID
AS HELL.
COME ON, IT'S UPSTAIRS.
TIME
E, DOG.
HE BOX.
OPEN THE...BOX?
QUIT MESSING AROUND, BETO. ¡AVANZA!
IS PABLO CRAZY? I NEED TO GET OUT. I NEED TO GET BACK TO POPS. I NEED--
RIGHT... RIGHT...I'M
UST...YEAH...
HEY! MR. ROMEO. EITHER WE DO IT OR WE GHOST OUT.
HOLD UP.
BETO'S TAKING THAT VOCATIONAL TRAINING, ISN'T HE? STUDYING TO BE AN ELECTRICIAN.
HE'S JUST ABOUT TOP OF CLASS. BETO CAN DO THIS.
I CAN DO THIS.
FZZZZ
POP
CLIK

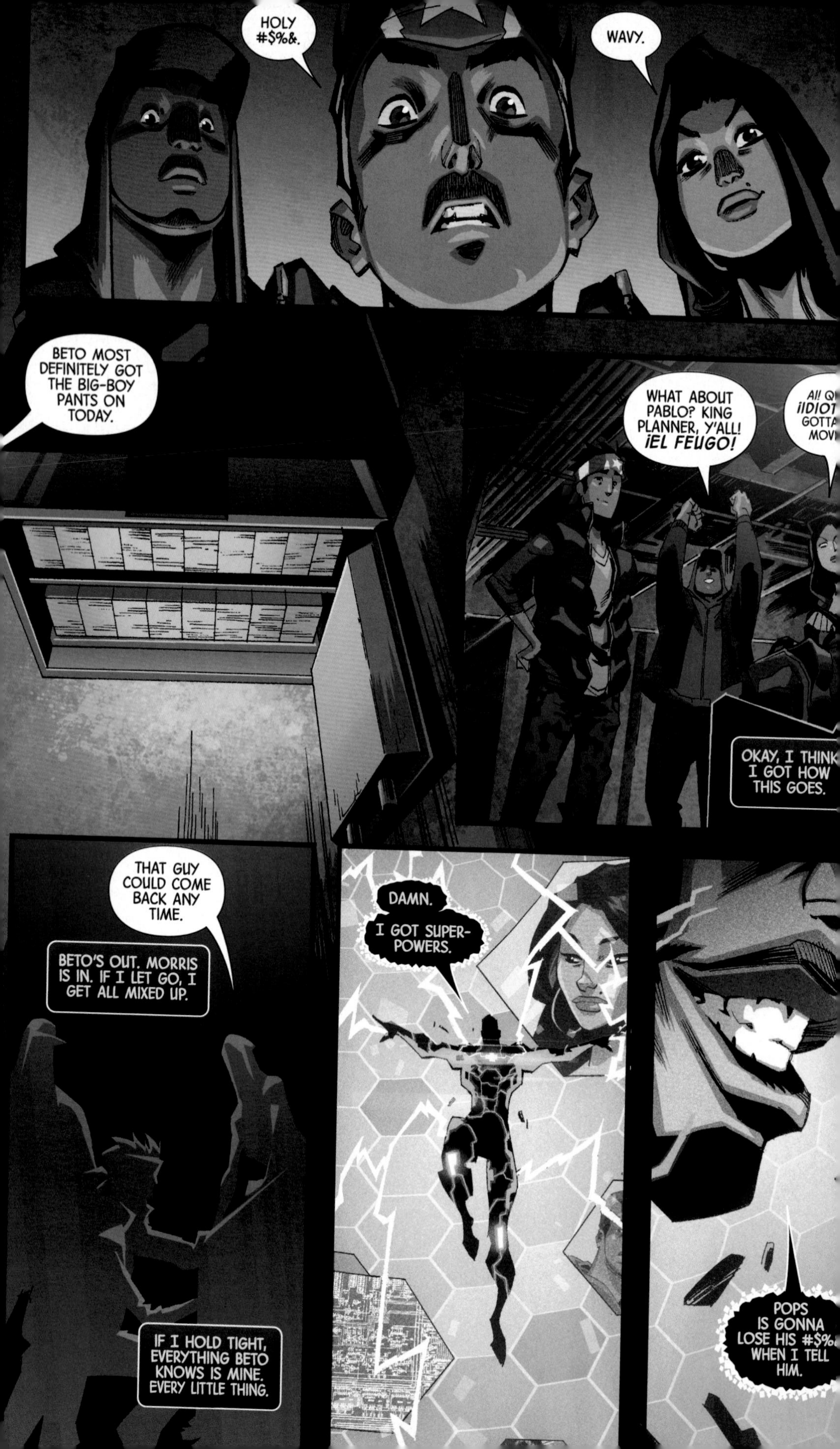
HOLY #$%&.
WAVY.
BETO MOST DEFINITELY GOT THE BIG-BOY PANTS ON TODAY.
WHAT ABOUT PABLO? KING PLANNER, Y'ALL! ¡EL FEUGO!
AI! Q ¡IDIOT GOTTA MOV
OKAY, I THINK I GOT HOW THIS GOES.
THAT GUY COULD COME BACK ANY TIME.
BETO'S OUT. MORRIS IS IN. IF I LET GO, I GET ALL MIXED UP.
IF I HOLD TIGHT, EVERYTHING BETO KNOWS IS MINE. EVERY LITTLE THING.
DAMN.
I GOT SUPER-POWERS.
POPS IS GONNA LOSE HIS #$% WHEN I TELL HIM.

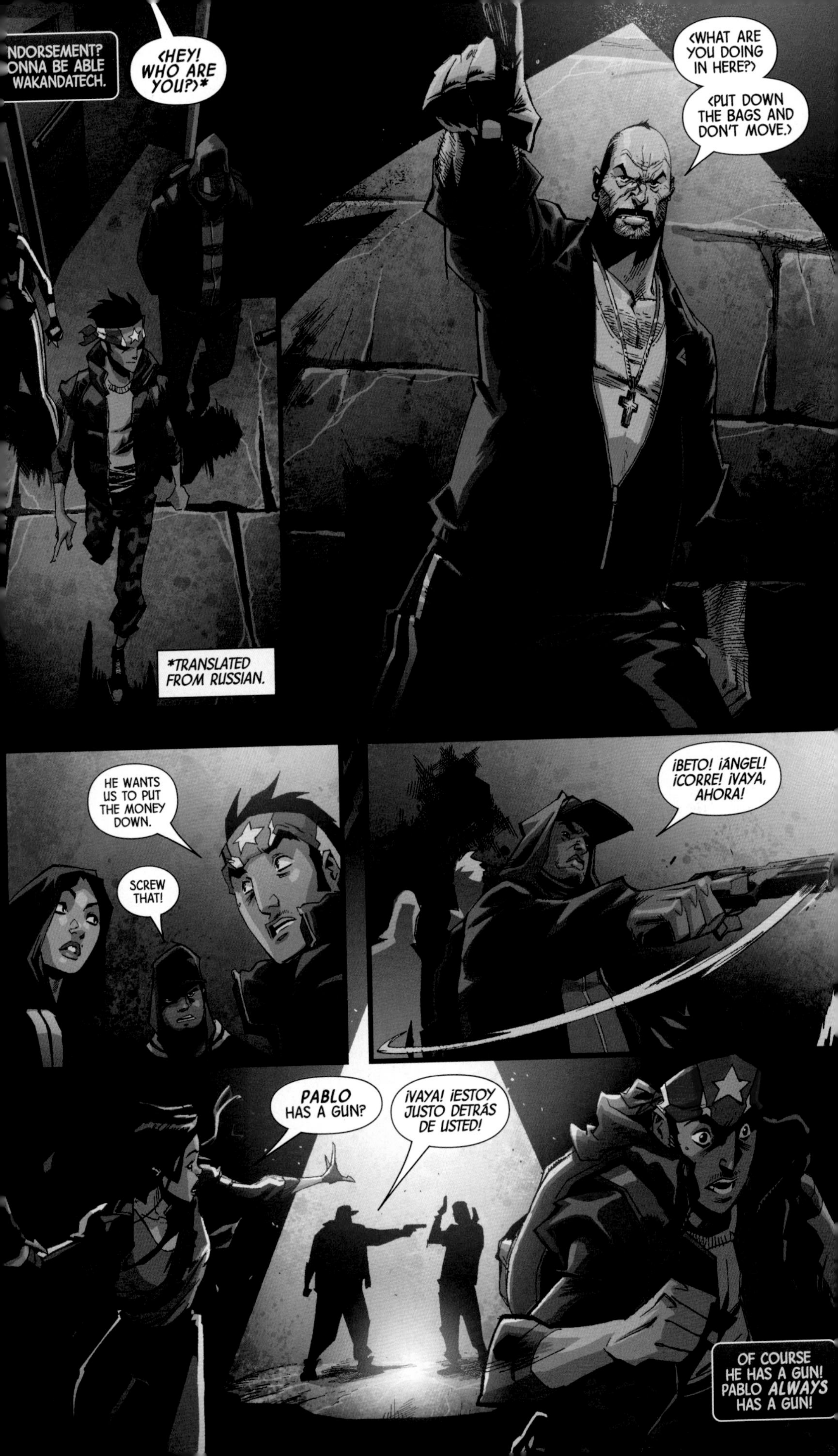
NDORSEMENT?
ONNA BE ABLE
WAKANDATECH.
<HEY! WHO ARE YOU?>*
<WHAT ARE YOU DOING IN HERE?>
<PUT DOWN THE BAGS AND DON'T MOVE.>
*TRANSLATED FROM RUSSIAN.
HE WANTS US TO PUT THE MONEY DOWN.
SCREW THAT!
¡BETO! ¡ÁNGEL! ¡CORRE! ¡VAYA, AHORA!
PABLO HAS A GUN?
¡VAYA! ¡ESTOY JUSTO DETRÁS DE USTED!
OF COURSE HE HAS A GUN! PABLO ALWAYS HAS A GUN!

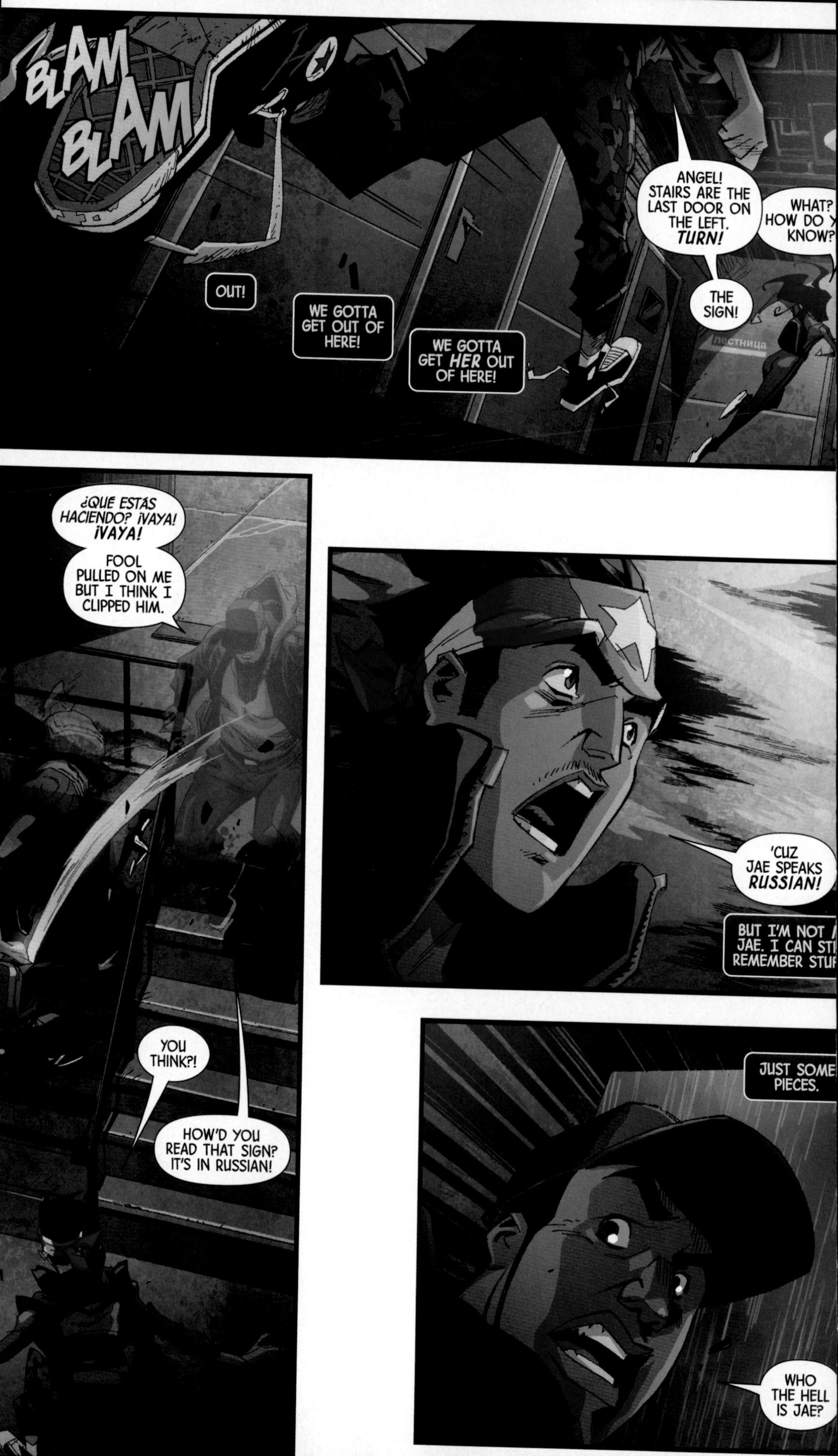
BLAM
BLAM
BLAM
OUT!
WE GOTTA GET OUT OF HERE!
WE GOTTA GET *HER* OUT OF HERE!
ANGEL! STAIRS ARE THE LAST DOOR ON THE LEFT. *TURN!*
WHAT? HOW DO Y KNOW?
THE SIGN!
лестница
¿QUÉ ESTÁS HACIENDO? ¡VAYA! *¡VAYA!*
FOOL PULLED ON ME BUT I THINK I CLIPPED HIM.
YOU THINK?!
HOW'D YOU READ THAT SIGN? IT'S IN RUSSIAN!
'CUZ JAE SPEAKS *RUSSIAN!*
BUT I'M NOT JAE. I CAN STI REMEMBER STUF
JUST SOME PIECES.
WHO THE HELL IS JAE?

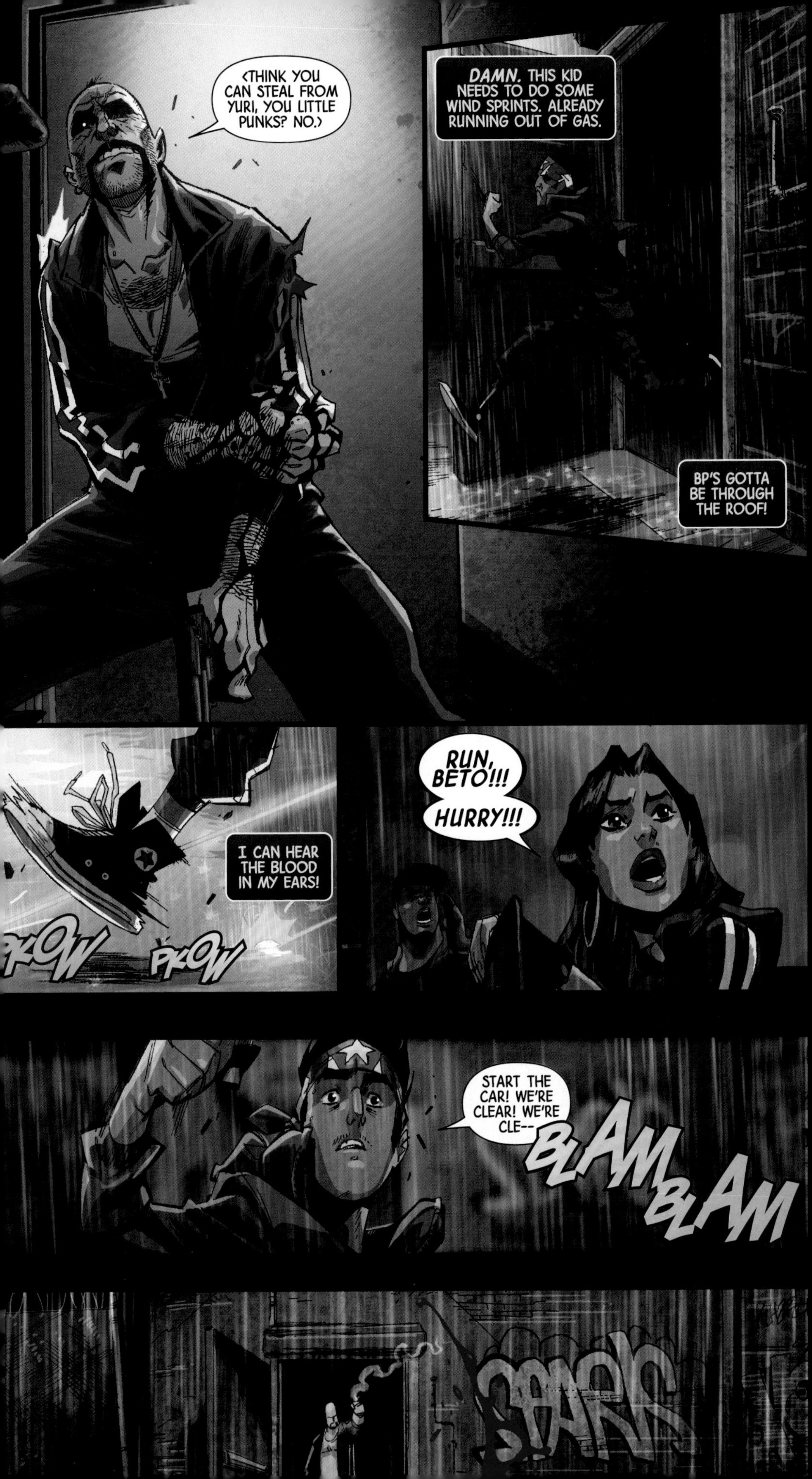

<THINK YOU CAN STEAL FROM YURI, YOU LITTLE PUNKS? NO.>
DAMN. THIS KID NEEDS TO DO SOME WIND SPRINTS. ALREADY RUNNING OUT OF GAS.
BP'S GOTTA BE THROUGH THE ROOF!
I CAN HEAR THE BLOOD IN MY EARS!
PKOW
PKOW
RUN, BETO!!!
HURRY!!!
START THE CAR! WE'RE CLEAR! WE'RE CLE--
BLAM
BLAM

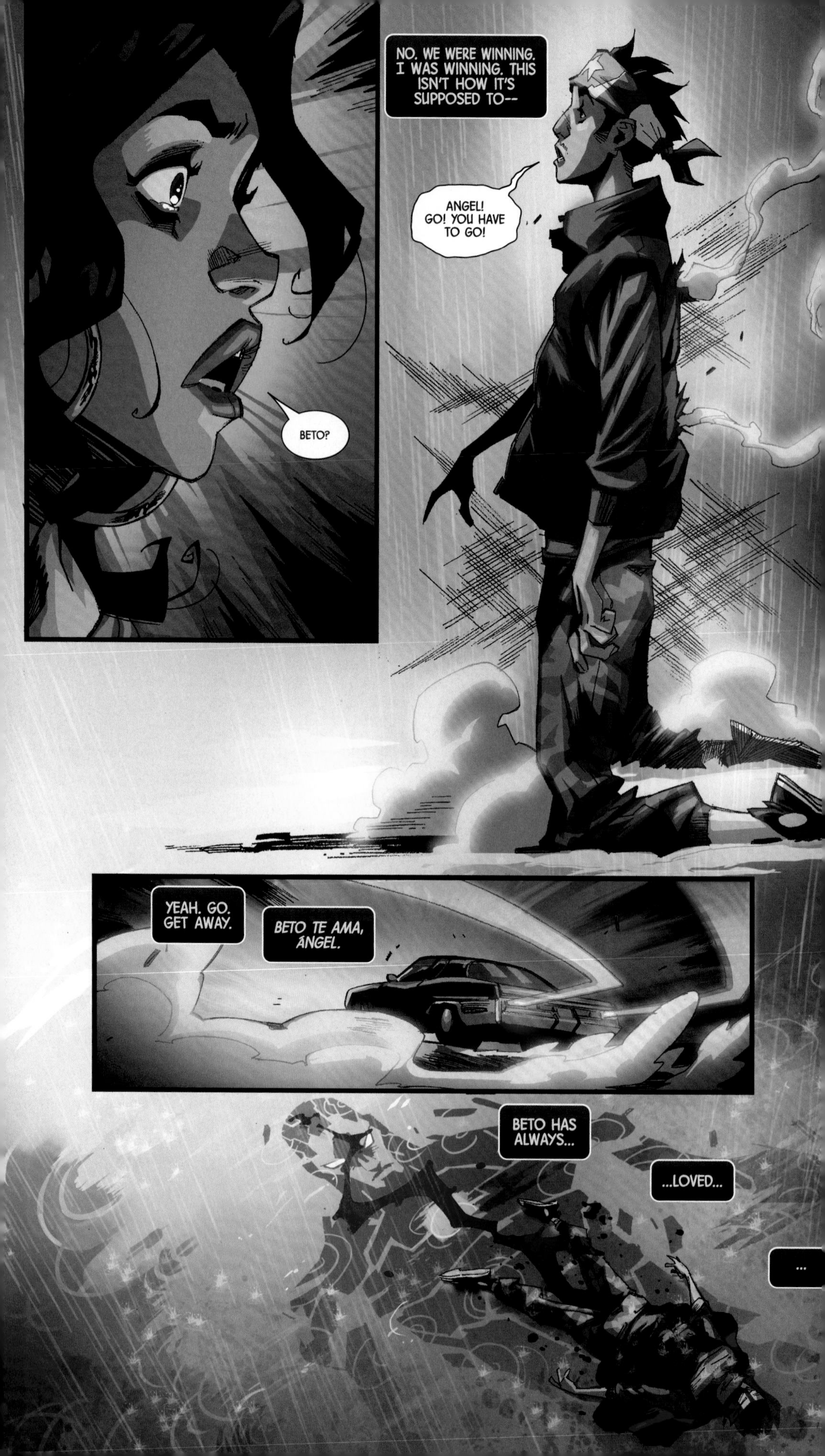
NO. WE WERE WINNING. I WAS WINNING. THIS ISN'T HOW IT'S SUPPOSED TO--
BETO?
ANGEL! GO! YOU HAVE TO GO!
YEAH. GO. GET AWAY.
BETO TE AMA, ÁNGEL.
BETO HAS ALWAYS...
...LOVED...
...

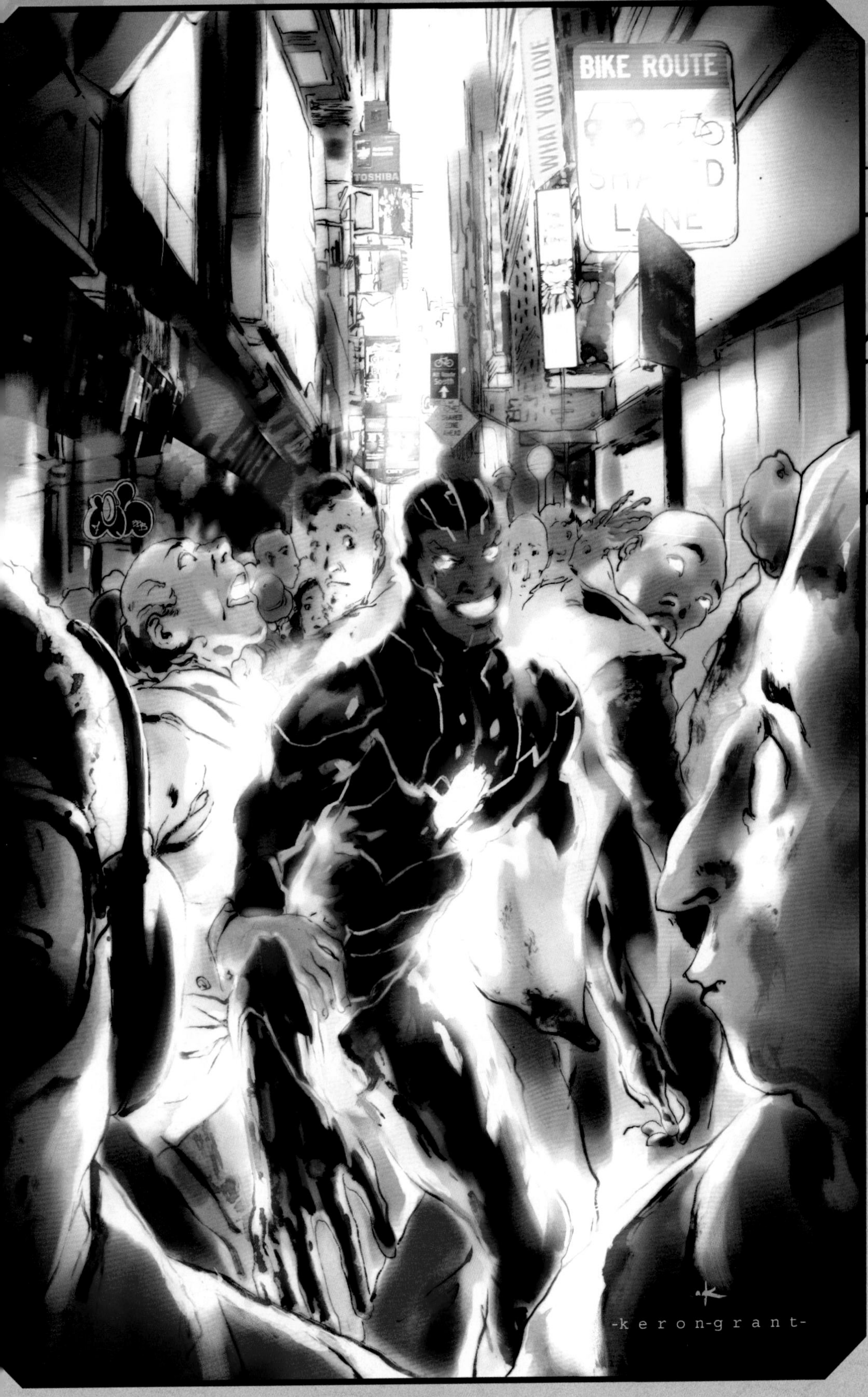
BIKE ROUTE
SHARED LANE
WHAT YOU LOVE
TOSHIBA
-keron-grant-

SOUL ON ICE

2

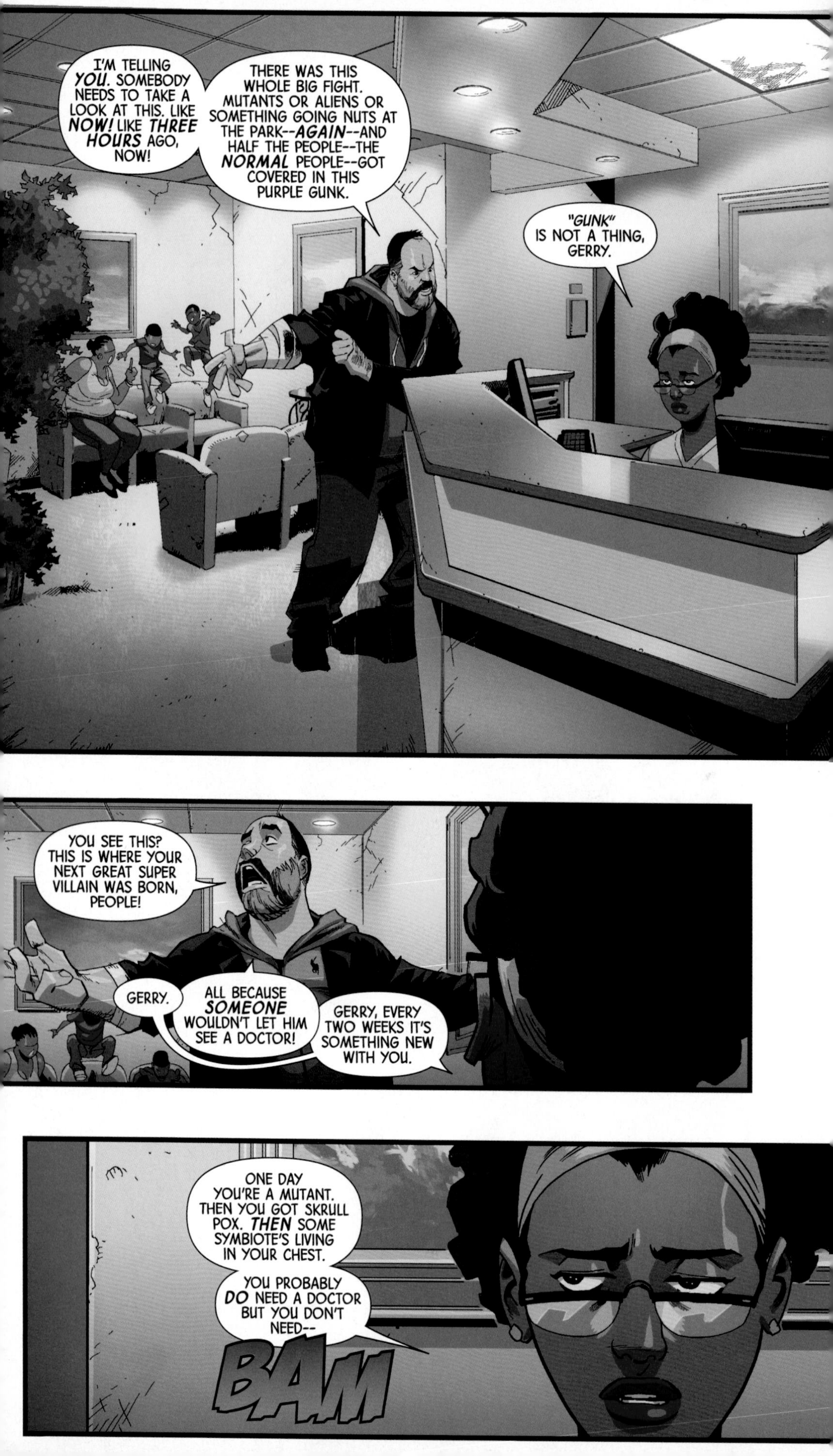
I'M TELLING YOU. SOMEBODY NEEDS TO TAKE A LOOK AT THIS. LIKE NOW! LIKE THREE HOURS AGO, NOW!
THERE WAS THIS WHOLE BIG FIGHT. MUTANTS OR ALIENS OR SOMETHING GOING NUTS AT THE PARK--AGAIN--AND HALF THE PEOPLE--THE NORMAL PEOPLE--GOT COVERED IN THIS PURPLE GUNK.
"GUNK" IS NOT A THING, GERRY.
YOU SEE THIS? THIS IS WHERE YOUR NEXT GREAT SUPER VILLAIN WAS BORN, PEOPLE!
GERRY.
ALL BECAUSE SOMEONE WOULDN'T LET HIM SEE A DOCTOR!
GERRY, EVERY TWO WEEKS IT'S SOMETHING NEW WITH YOU.
ONE DAY YOU'RE A MUTANT. THEN YOU GOT SKRULL POX. THEN SOME SYMBIOTE'S LIVING IN YOUR CHEST.
YOU PROBABLY DO NEED A DOCTOR BUT YOU DON'T NEED--
BAM

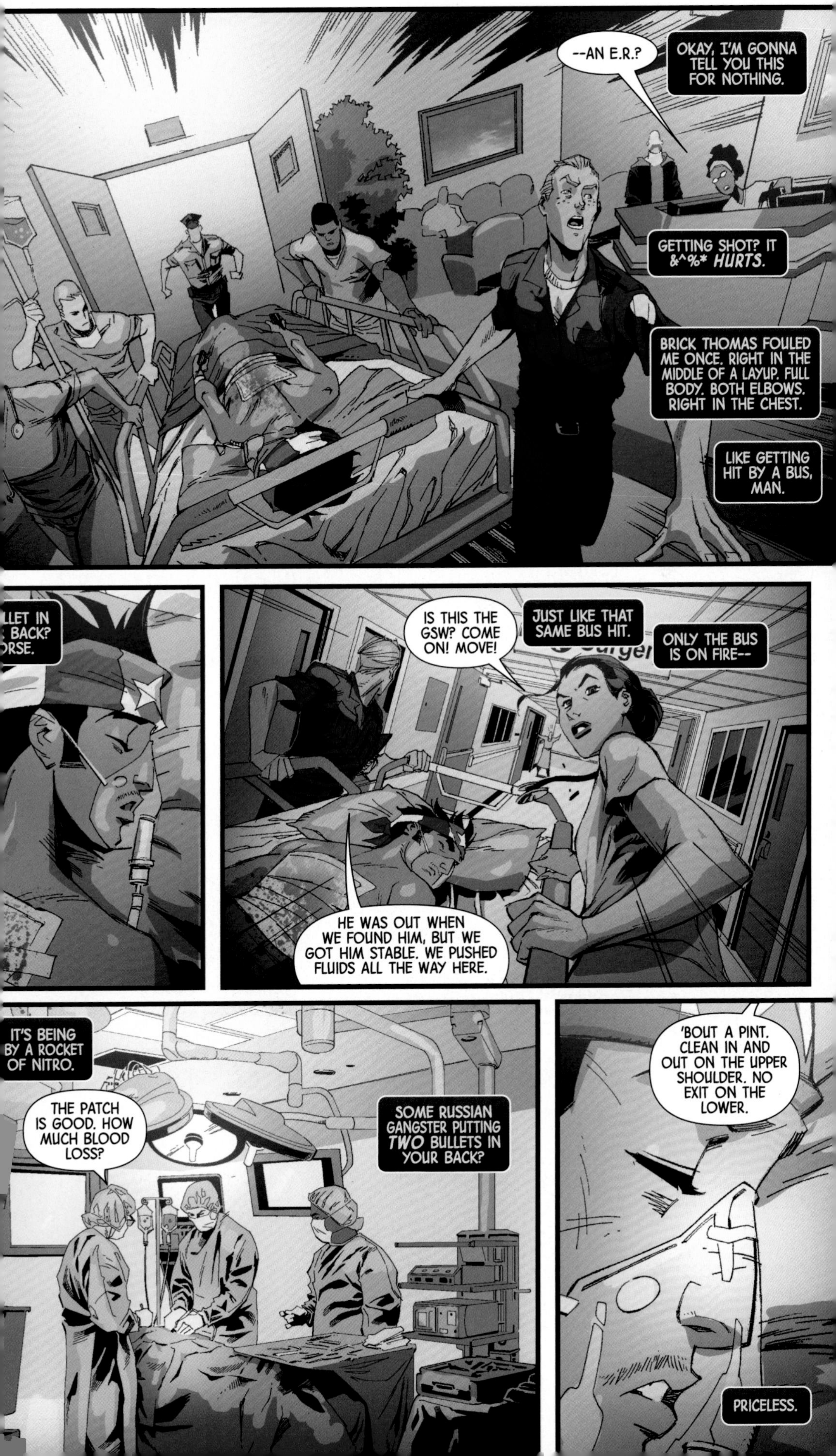
--AN E.R.?
OKAY, I'M GONNA TELL YOU THIS FOR NOTHING.
GETTING SHOT? IT &^%* *HURTS.*
BRICK THOMAS FOULED ME ONCE. RIGHT IN THE MIDDLE OF A LAYUP. FULL BODY. BOTH ELBOWS. RIGHT IN THE CHEST.
LIKE GETTING HIT BY A BUS, MAN.
LLET IN BACK? RSE.
IS THIS THE GSW? COME ON! MOVE!
JUST LIKE THAT SAME BUS HIT.
ONLY THE BUS IS ON FIRE--
HE WAS OUT WHEN WE FOUND HIM, BUT WE GOT HIM STABLE. WE PUSHED FLUIDS ALL THE WAY HERE.
IT'S BEING BY A ROCKET OF NITRO.
THE PATCH IS GOOD. HOW MUCH BLOOD LOSS?
SOME RUSSIAN GANGSTER PUTTING *TWO* BULLETS IN YOUR BACK?
'BOUT A PINT. CLEAN IN AND OUT ON THE UPPER SHOULDER. NO EXIT ON THE LOWER.
PRICELESS.

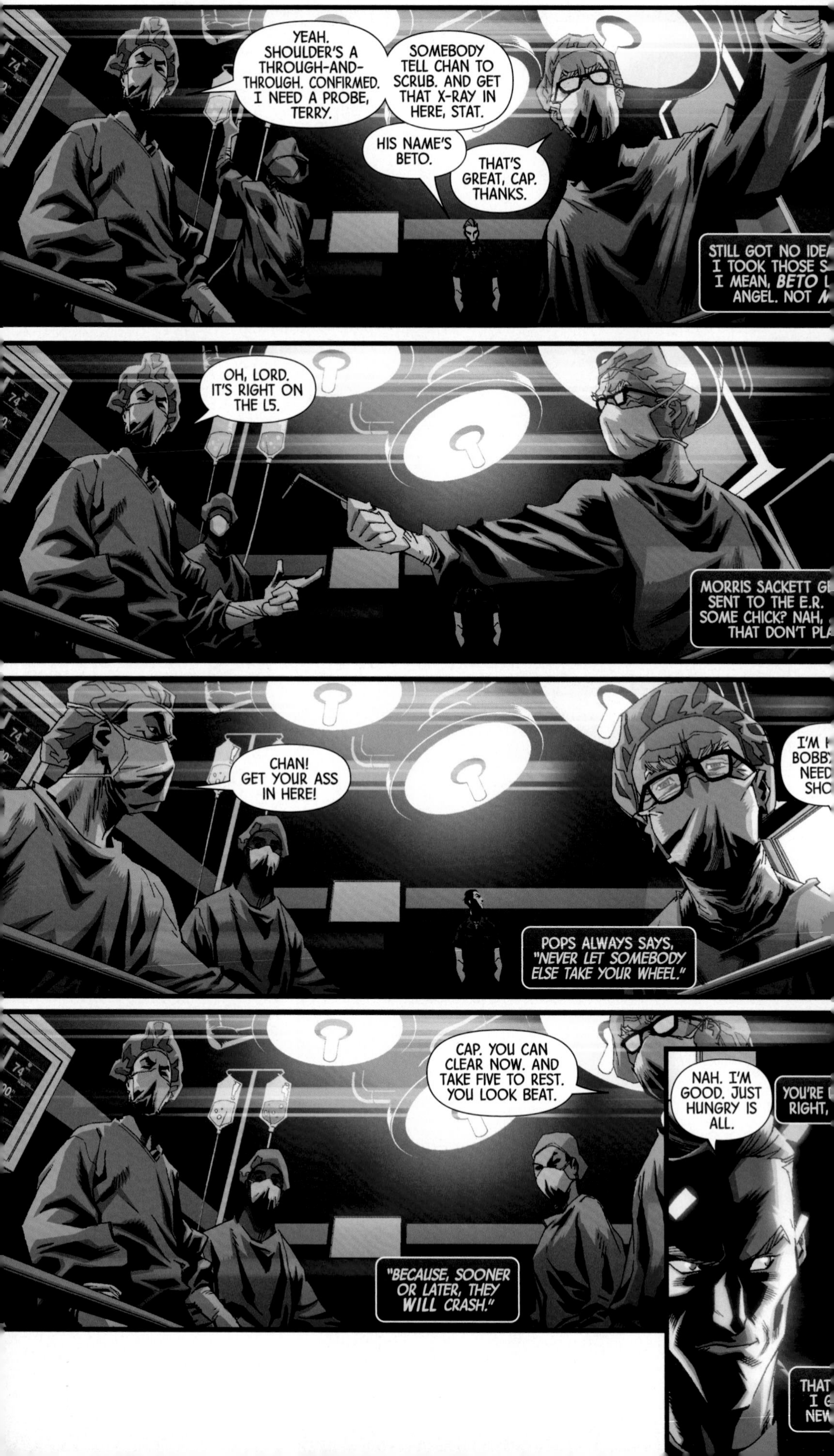
YEAH. SHOULDER'S A THROUGH-AND-THROUGH. CONFIRMED. I NEED A PROBE, TERRY.
SOMEBODY TELL CHAN TO SCRUB. AND GET THAT X-RAY IN HERE, STAT.
HIS NAME'S BETO.
THAT'S GREAT, CAP. THANKS.
STILL GOT NO IDE
I TOOK THOSE S
I MEAN, BETO
ANGEL. NOT
OH, LORD. IT'S RIGHT ON THE L5.
MORRIS SACKETT G
SENT TO THE E.R.
SOME CHICK? NAH,
THAT DON'T PL
CHAN! GET YOUR ASS IN HERE!
I'M
BOBB
NEED
SHO
POPS ALWAYS SAYS, "NEVER LET SOMEBODY ELSE TAKE YOUR WHEEL."
CAP. YOU CAN CLEAR NOW. AND TAKE FIVE TO REST. YOU LOOK BEAT.
NAH. I'M GOOD. JUST HUNGRY IS ALL.
YOU'RE
RIGHT,
"BECAUSE, SOONER OR LATER, THEY WILL CRASH."
THAT
NEW

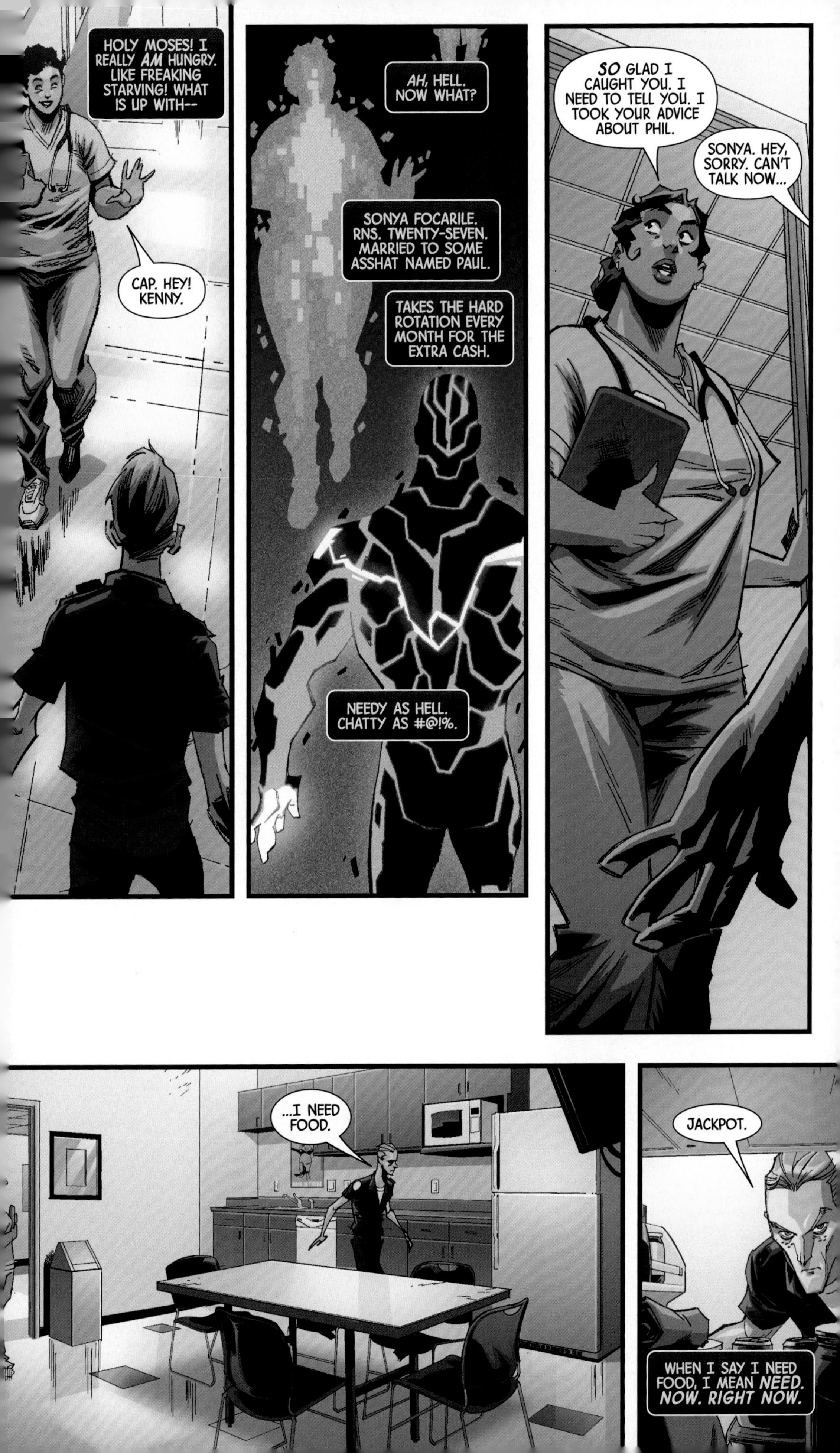
HOLY MOSES! I REALLY AM HUNGRY. LIKE FREAKING STARVING! WHAT IS UP WITH--
CAP. HEY! KENNY.
AH, HELL. NOW WHAT?
SONYA FOCARILE. RNS. TWENTY-SEVEN. MARRIED TO SOME ASSHAT NAMED PAUL.
TAKES THE HARD ROTATION EVERY MONTH FOR THE EXTRA CASH.
NEEDY AS HELL. CHATTY AS #@!%.
SO GLAD I CAUGHT YOU. I NEED TO TELL YOU. I TOOK YOUR ADVICE ABOUT PHIL.
SONYA. HEY, SORRY. CAN'T TALK NOW...
...I NEED FOOD.
JACKPOT.
WHEN I SAY I NEED FOOD, I MEAN NEED. NOW. RIGHT NOW.

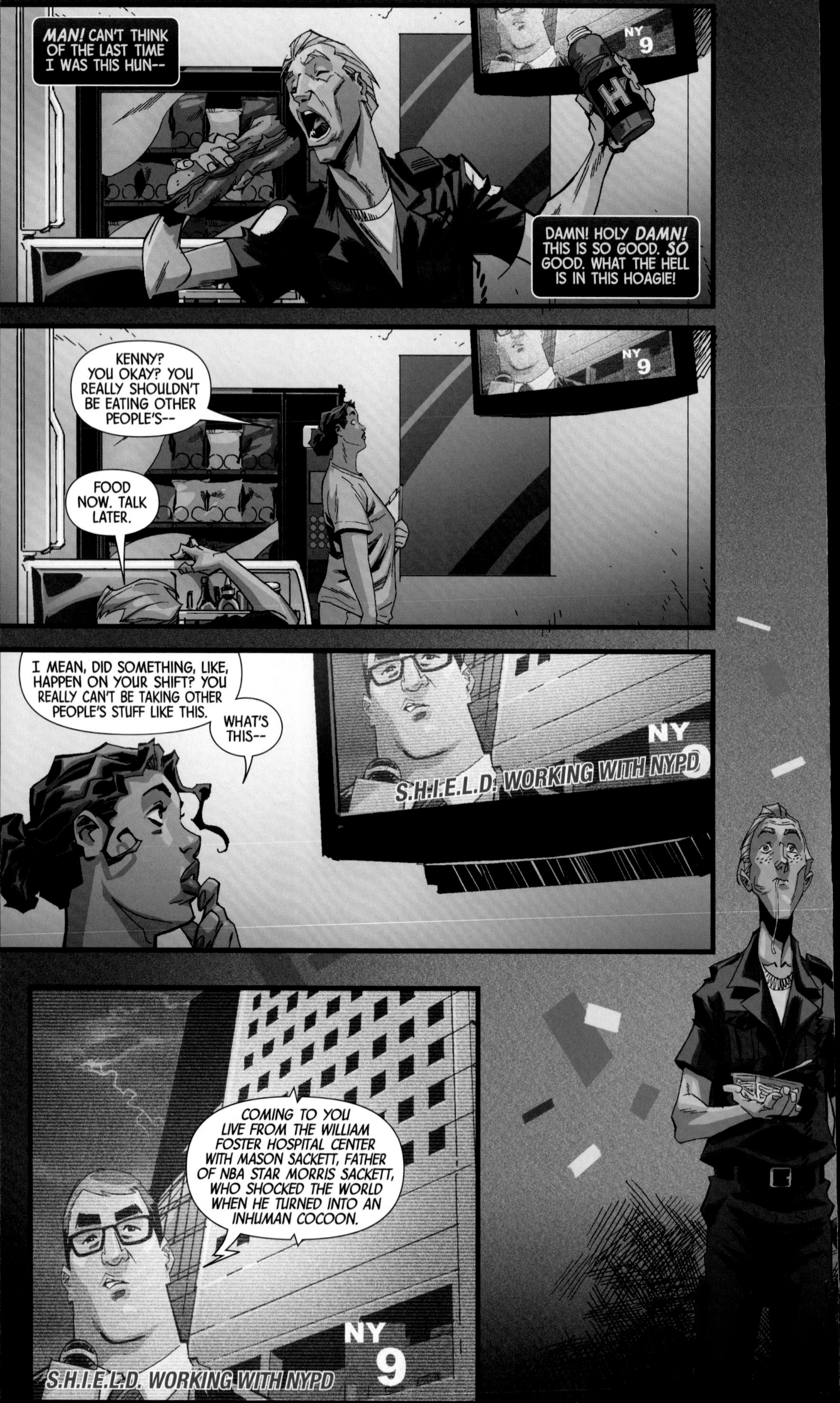
MAN! CAN'T THINK OF THE LAST TIME I WAS THIS HUN--
NY 9
DAMN! HOLY DAMN! THIS IS SO GOOD. SO GOOD. WHAT THE HELL IS IN THIS HOAGIE!
NY 9
KENNY? YOU OKAY? YOU REALLY SHOULDN'T BE EATING OTHER PEOPLE'S--
FOOD NOW. TALK LATER.
I MEAN, DID SOMETHING, LIKE, HAPPEN ON YOUR SHIFT? YOU REALLY CAN'T BE TAKING OTHER PEOPLE'S STUFF LIKE THIS.
WHAT'S THIS--
NY
S.H.I.E.L.D. WORKING WITH NYPD
COMING TO YOU LIVE FROM THE WILLIAM FOSTER HOSPITAL CENTER WITH MASON SACKETT, FATHER OF NBA STAR MORRIS SACKETT, WHO SHOCKED THE WORLD WHEN HE TURNED INTO AN INHUMAN COCOON.
NY 9
S.H.I.E.L.D. WORKING WITH NYPD

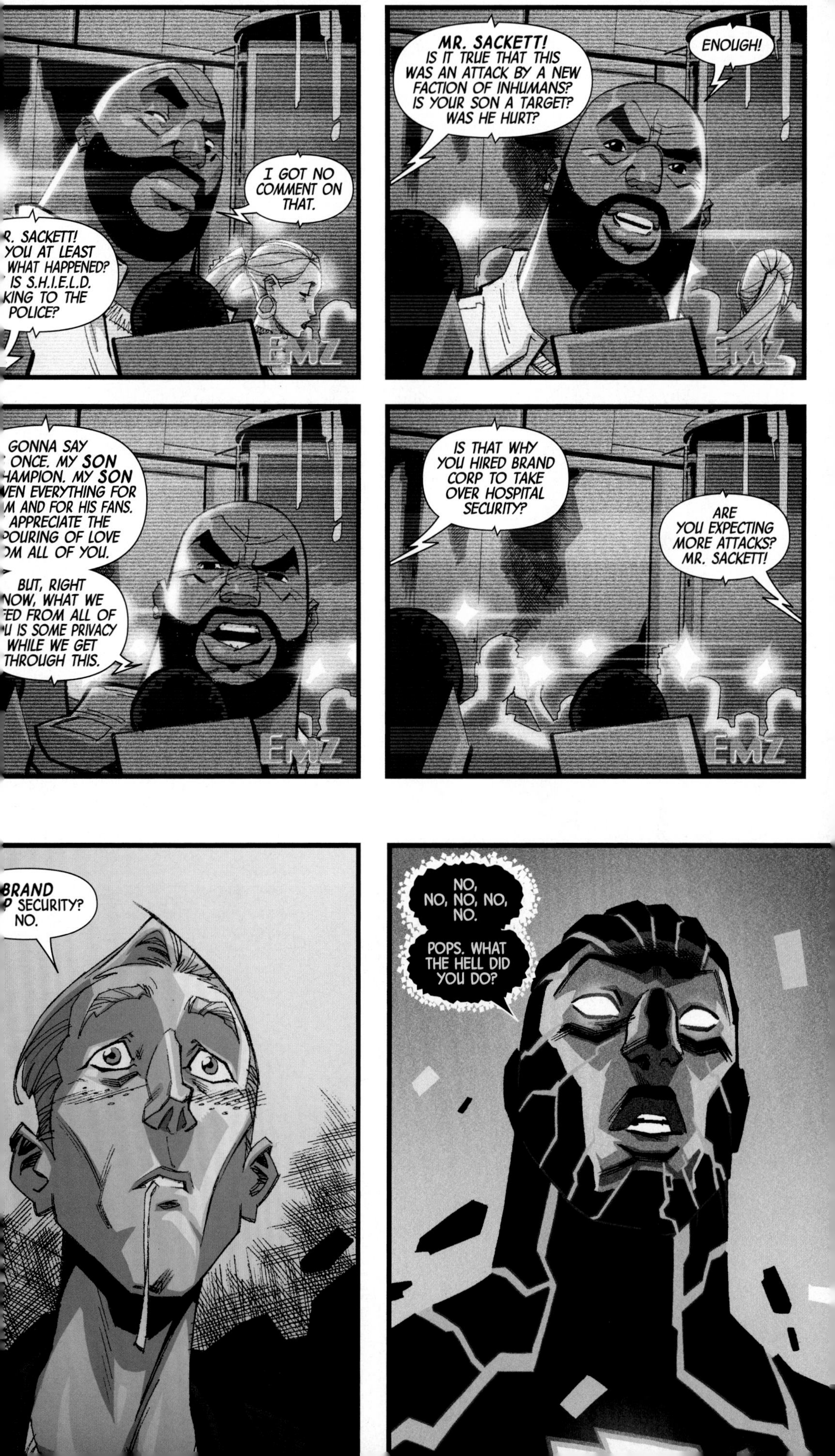
R. SACKETT! YOU AT LEAST WHAT HAPPENED? IS S.H.I.E.L.D. KING TO THE POLICE?
I GOT NO COMMENT ON THAT.
EMZ
MR. SACKETT! IS IT TRUE THAT THIS WAS AN ATTACK BY A NEW FACTION OF INHUMANS? IS YOUR SON A TARGET? WAS HE HURT?
ENOUGH!
EMZ
GONNA SAY ONCE. MY SON HAMPION. MY SON IVEN EVERYTHING FOR M AND FOR HIS FANS. APPRECIATE THE POURING OF LOVE OM ALL OF YOU.
BUT, RIGHT NOW, WHAT WE ED FROM ALL OF U IS SOME PRIVACY WHILE WE GET THROUGH THIS.
EMZ
IS THAT WHY YOU HIRED BRAND CORP TO TAKE OVER HOSPITAL SECURITY?
ARE YOU EXPECTING MORE ATTACKS? MR. SACKETT!
EMZ
BRAND SECURITY? NO.
NO, NO, NO, NO, NO.
POPS. WHAT THE HELL DID YOU DO?

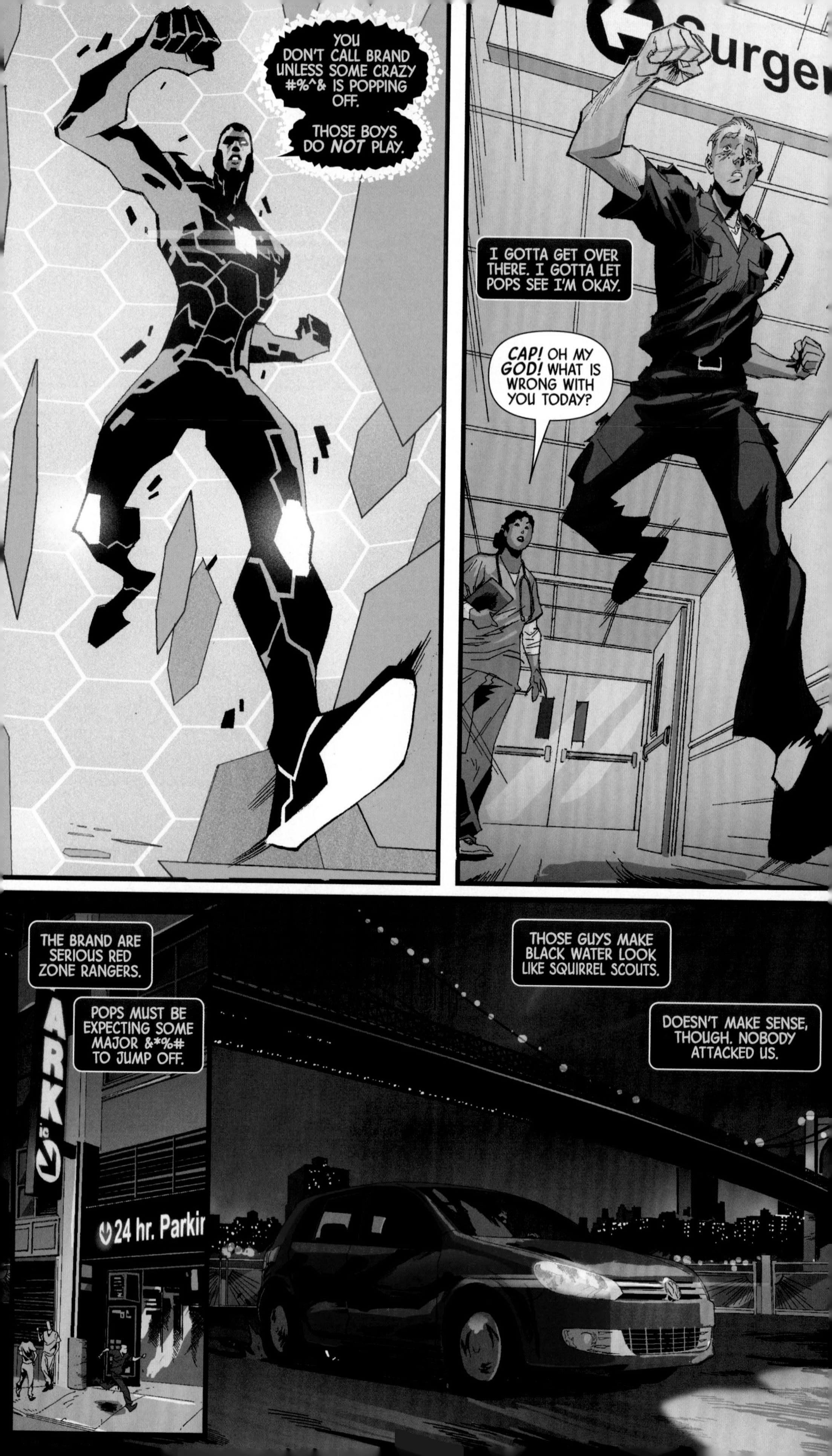

YOU DON'T CALL BRAND UNLESS SOME CRAZY #%^& IS POPPING OFF.
THOSE BOYS DO NOT PLAY.
Surger
I GOTTA GET OVER THERE. I GOTTA LET POPS SEE I'M OKAY.
CAP! OH MY GOD! WHAT IS WRONG WITH YOU TODAY?
THE BRAND ARE SERIOUS RED ZONE RANGERS.
POPS MUST BE EXPECTING SOME MAJOR &*%# TO JUMP OFF.
THOSE GUYS MAKE BLACK WATER LOOK LIKE SQUIRREL SCOUTS.
DOESN'T MAKE SENSE, THOUGH. NOBODY ATTACKED US.
ARK
24 hr. Parkir

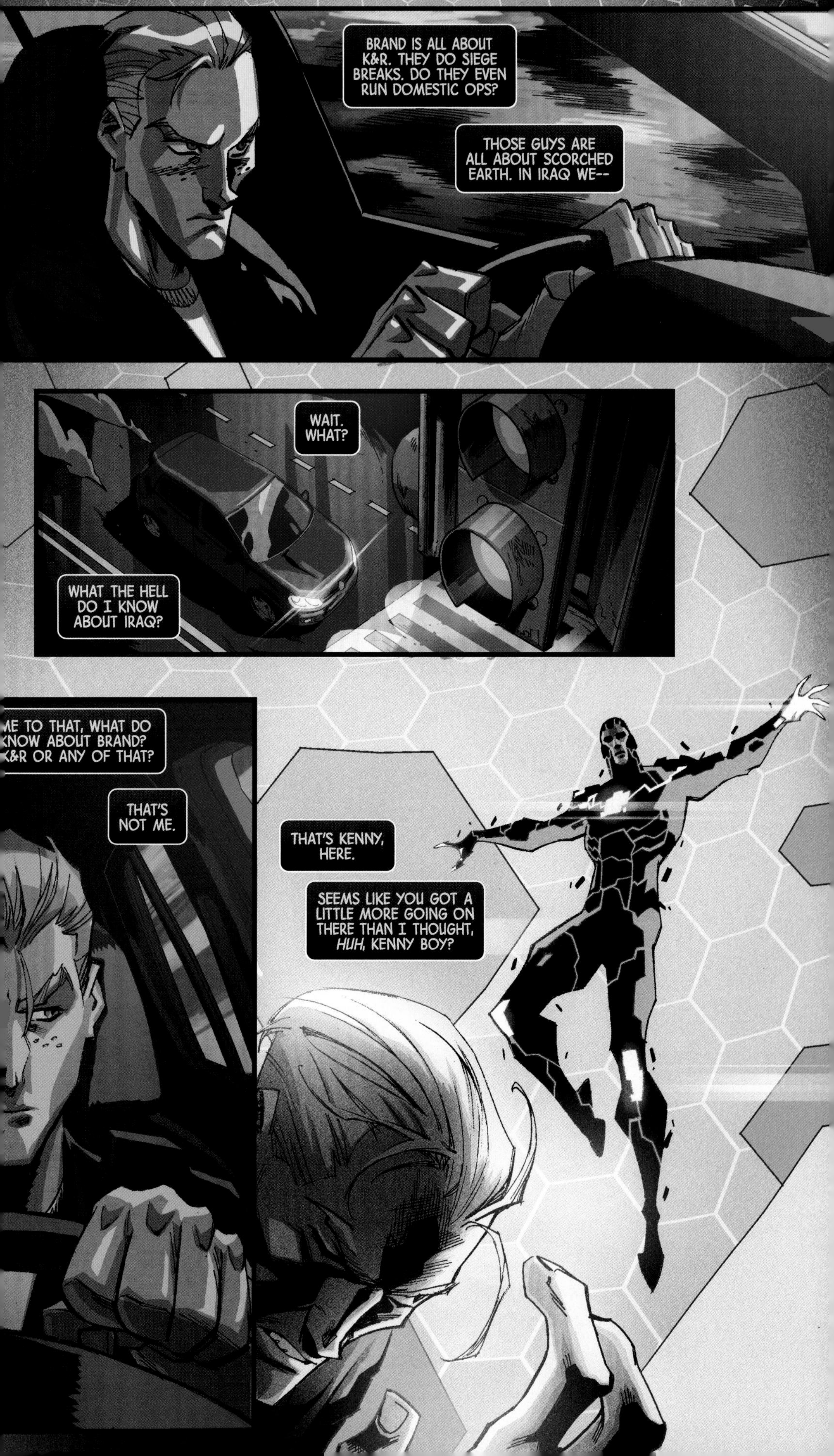
BRAND IS ALL ABOUT K&R. THEY DO SIEGE BREAKS. DO THEY EVEN RUN DOMESTIC OPS?
THOSE GUYS ARE ALL ABOUT SCORCHED EARTH. IN IRAQ WE--
WAIT. WHAT?
WHAT THE HELL DO I KNOW ABOUT IRAQ?
ME TO THAT, WHAT DO KNOW ABOUT BRAND? K&R OR ANY OF THAT?
THAT'S NOT ME.
THAT'S KENNY, HERE.
SEEMS LIKE YOU GOT A LITTLE MORE GOING ON THERE THAN I THOUGHT, *HUH*, KENNY BOY?

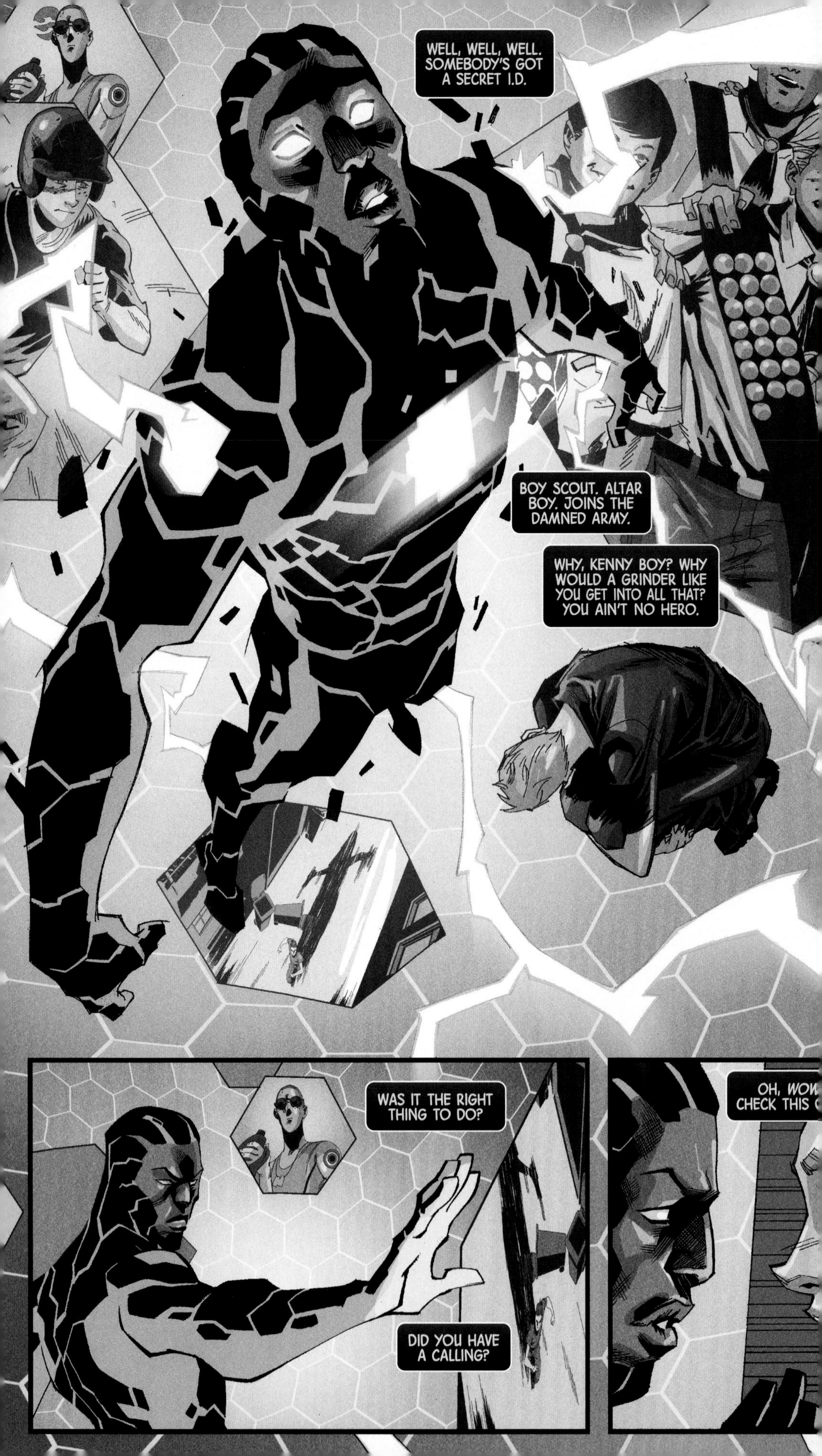
WELL, WELL, WELL. SOMEBODY'S GOT A SECRET I.D.
BOY SCOUT. ALTAR BOY. JOINS THE DAMNED ARMY.
WHY, KENNY BOY? WHY WOULD A GRINDER LIKE YOU GET INTO ALL THAT? YOU AIN'T NO HERO.
WAS IT THE RIGHT THING TO DO?
DID YOU HAVE A CALLING?
OH, WOW
CHECK THIS

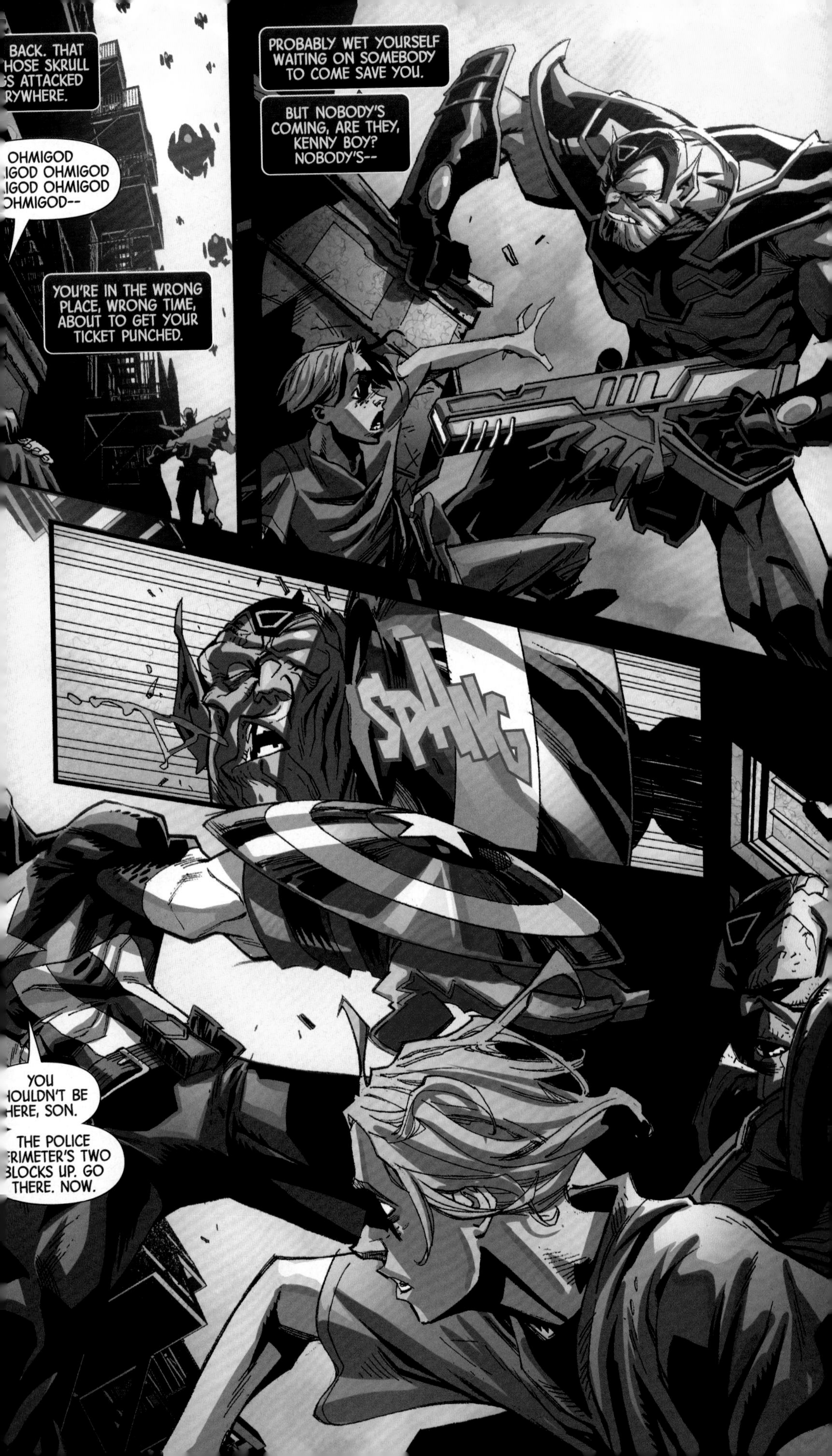
BACK. THAT
HOSE SKRULL
S ATTACKED
RYWHERE.
OHMIGOD
IGOD OHMIGOD
IGOD OHMIGOD
OHMIGOD--
YOU'RE IN THE WRONG PLACE, WRONG TIME, ABOUT TO GET YOUR TICKET PUNCHED.
PROBABLY WET YOURSELF WAITING ON SOMEBODY TO COME SAVE YOU.
BUT NOBODY'S COMING, ARE THEY, KENNY BOY? NOBODY'S--
SPANG
YOU
HOULDN'T BE
HERE, SON.
THE POLICE
RIMETER'S TWO
BLOCKS UP. GO
THERE. NOW.

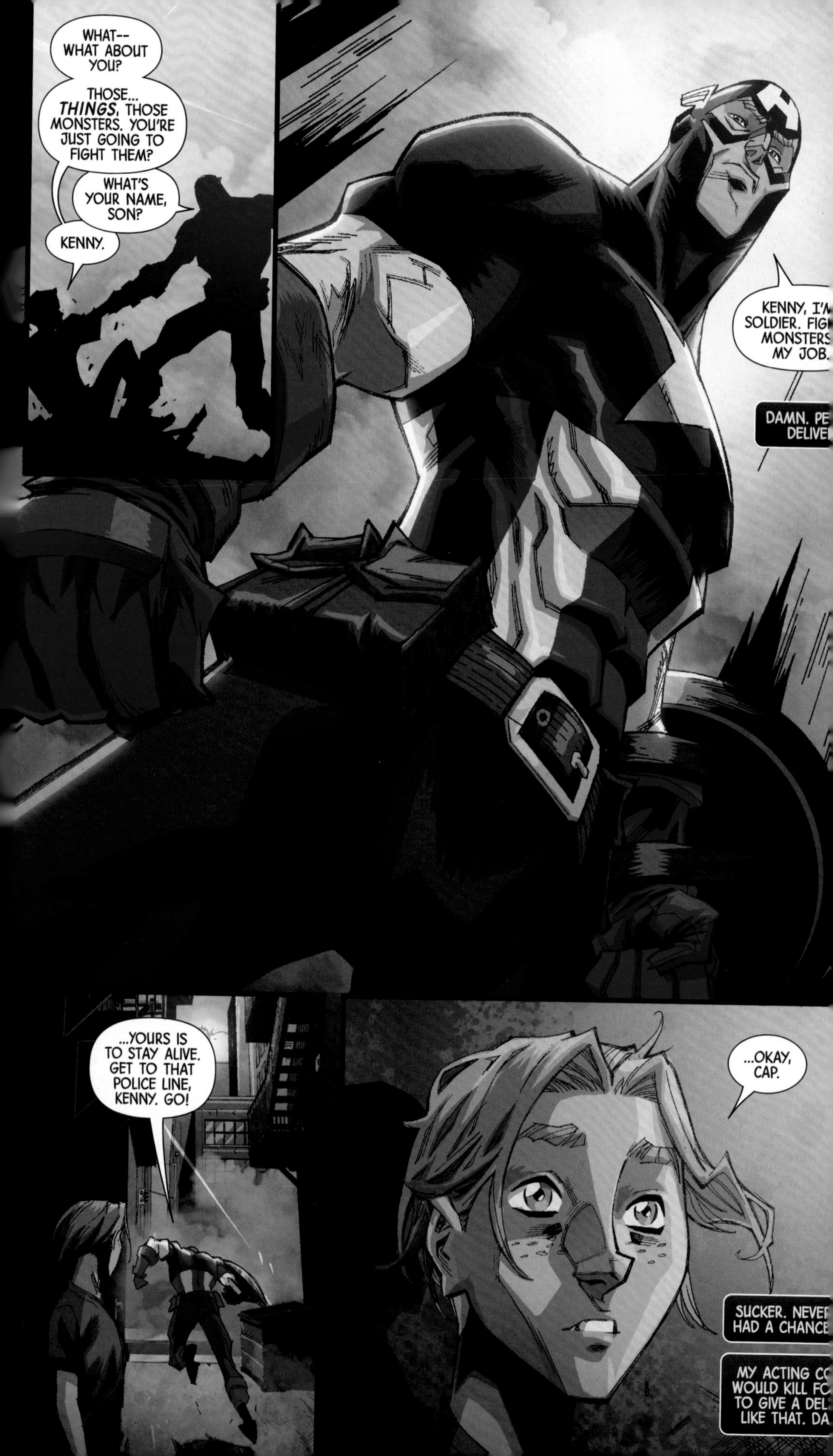
WHAT-- WHAT ABOUT YOU?
THOSE... *THINGS*, THOSE MONSTERS. YOU'RE JUST GOING TO FIGHT THEM?
WHAT'S YOUR NAME, SON?
KENNY.
KENNY, I' SOLDIER. FIG MONSTERS MY JOB.
DAMN. PE DELIVE
...YOURS IS TO STAY ALIVE. GET TO THAT POLICE LINE, KENNY. GO!
...OKAY, CAP.
SUCKER. NEVE HAD A CHANCE
MY ACTING C WOULD KILL F TO GIVE A DE LIKE THAT. DA

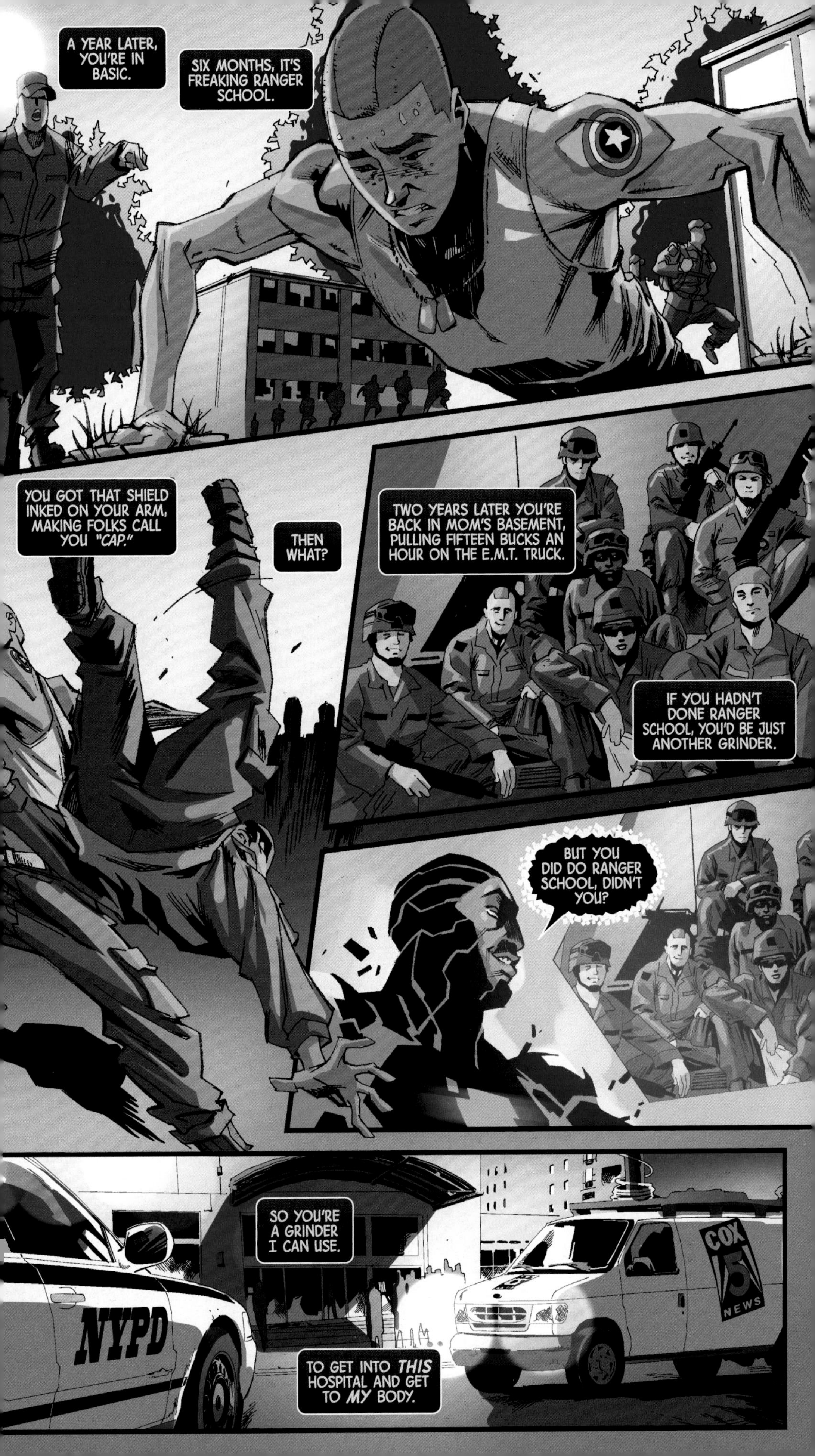

A YEAR LATER, YOU'RE IN BASIC.
SIX MONTHS, IT'S FREAKING RANGER SCHOOL.
YOU GOT THAT SHIELD INKED ON YOUR ARM, MAKING FOLKS CALL YOU "CAP."
THEN WHAT?
TWO YEARS LATER YOU'RE BACK IN MOM'S BASEMENT, PULLING FIFTEEN BUCKS AN HOUR ON THE E.M.T. TRUCK.
IF YOU HADN'T DONE RANGER SCHOOL, YOU'D BE JUST ANOTHER GRINDER.
BUT YOU DID DO RANGER SCHOOL, DIDN'T YOU?
SO YOU'RE A GRINDER I CAN USE.
NYPD
COX 5 NEWS
TO GET INTO THIS HOSPITAL AND GET TO MY BODY.

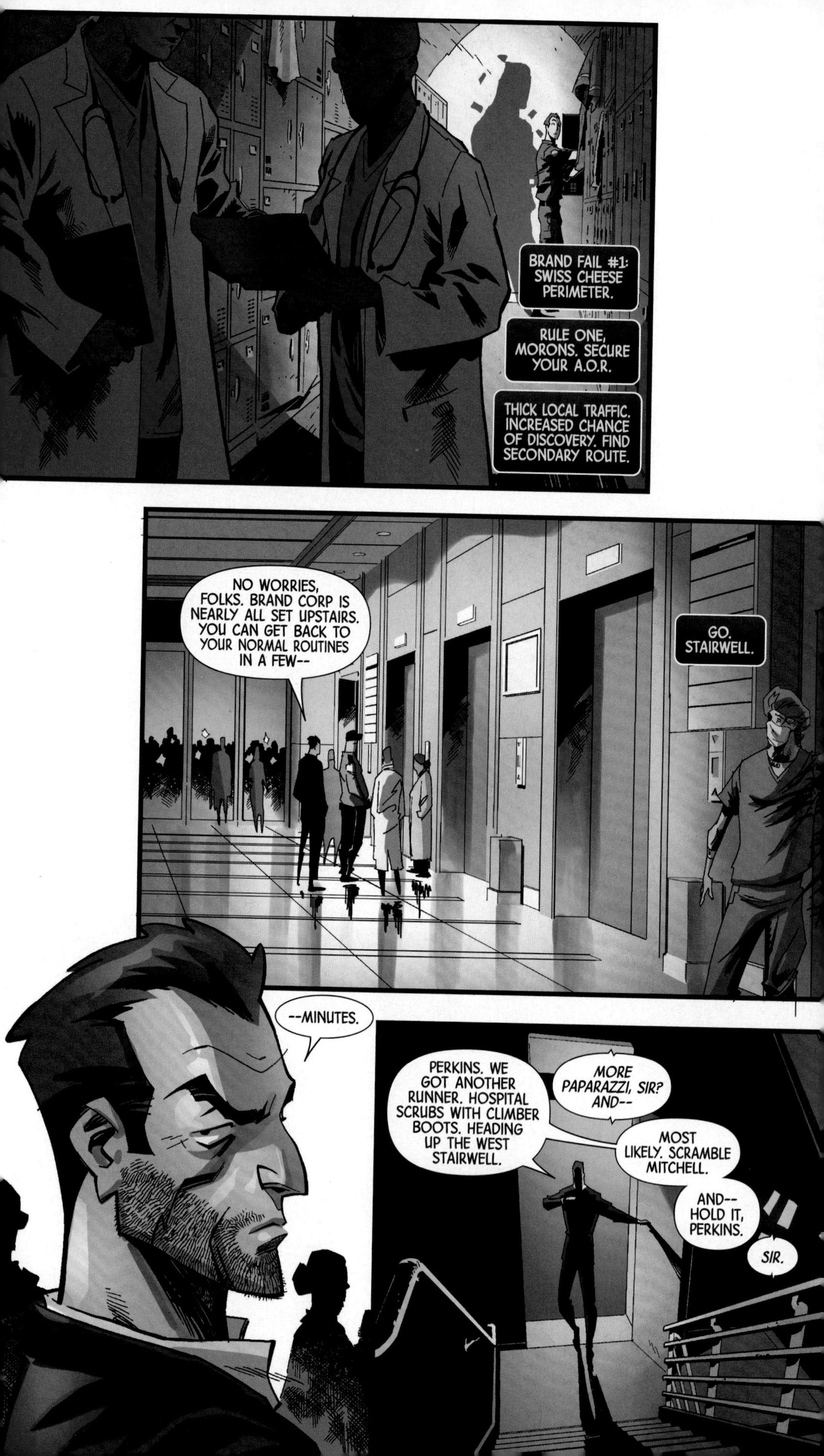
BRAND FAIL #1: SWISS CHEESE PERIMETER.
RULE ONE, MORONS. SECURE YOUR A.O.R.
THICK LOCAL TRAFFIC. INCREASED CHANCE OF DISCOVERY. FIND SECONDARY ROUTE.
NO WORRIES, FOLKS. BRAND CORP IS NEARLY ALL SET UPSTAIRS. YOU CAN GET BACK TO YOUR NORMAL ROUTINES IN A FEW--
GO. STAIRWELL.
--MINUTES.
PERKINS. WE GOT ANOTHER RUNNER. HOSPITAL SCRUBS WITH CLIMBER BOOTS. HEADING UP THE WEST STAIRWELL.
MORE PAPARAZZI, SIR? AND--
MOST LIKELY. SCRAMBLE MITCHELL.
AND-- HOLD IT, PERKINS.
SIR.

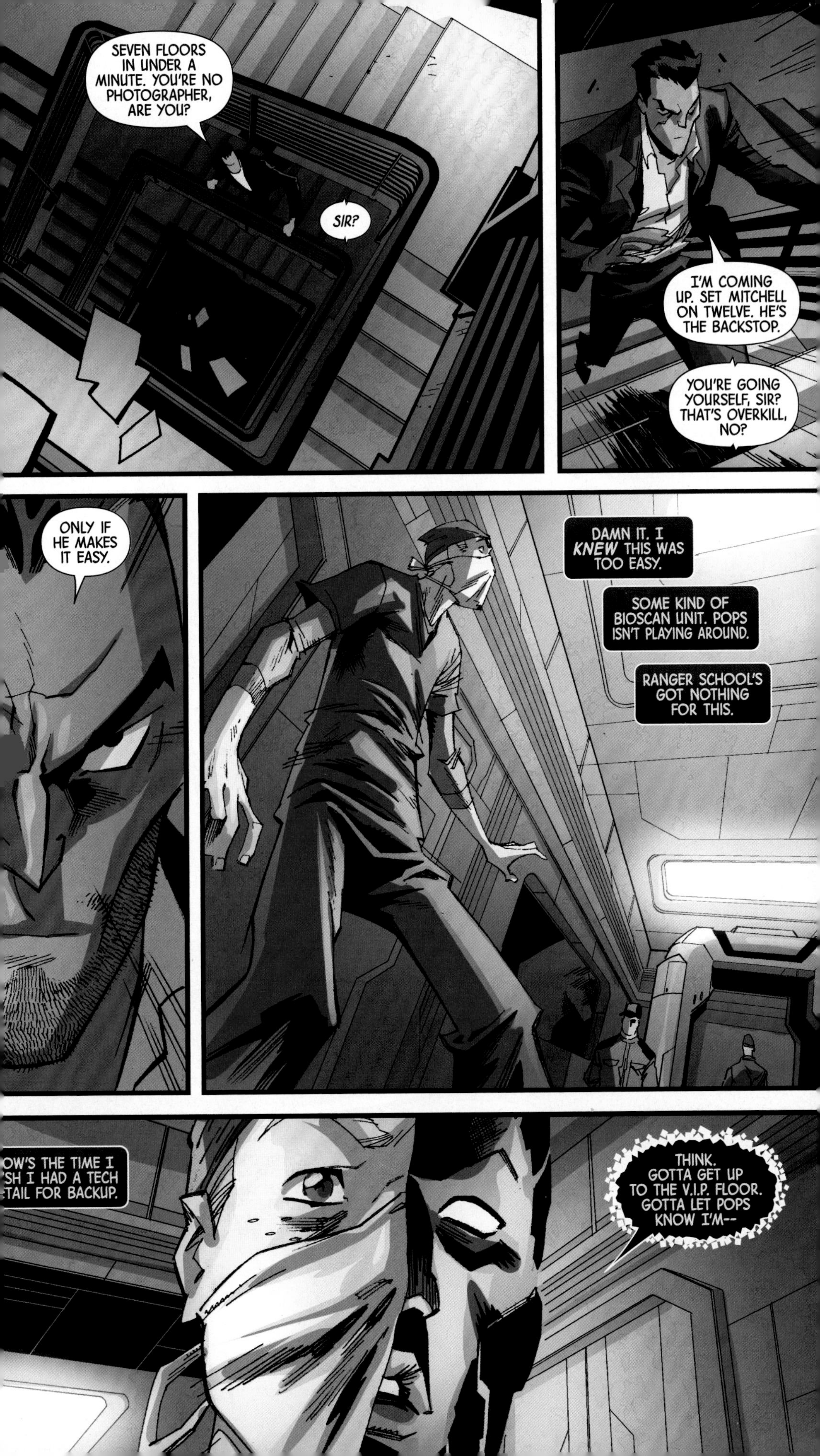
SEVEN FLOORS IN UNDER A MINUTE. YOU'RE NO PHOTOGRAPHER, ARE YOU?
SIR?
I'M COMING UP. SET MITCHELL ON TWELVE. HE'S THE BACKSTOP.
YOU'RE GOING YOURSELF, SIR? THAT'S OVERKILL, NO?
ONLY IF HE MAKES IT EASY.
DAMN IT. I *KNEW* THIS WAS TOO EASY.
SOME KIND OF BIOSCAN UNIT. POPS ISN'T PLAYING AROUND.
RANGER SCHOOL'S GOT NOTHING FOR THIS.
OW'S THE TIME I SH I HAD A TECH TAIL FOR BACKUP.
THINK. GOTTA GET UP TO THE V.I.P. FLOOR. GOTTA LET POPS KNOW I'M--

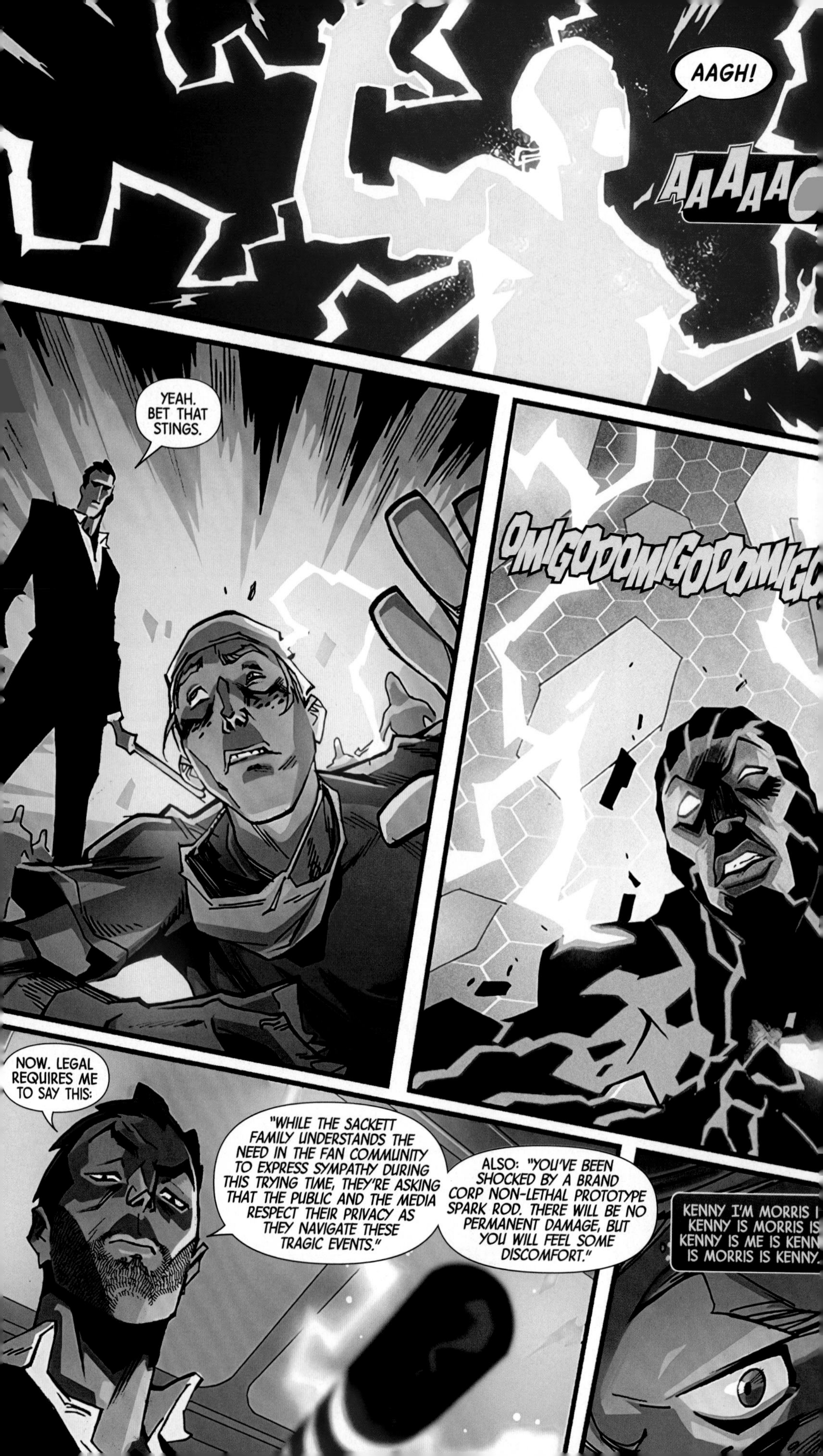

AAGH!
AAAAAG
YEAH. BET THAT STINGS.
OMIGODOMIGODOMIGO
NOW. LEGAL REQUIRES ME TO SAY THIS:
"WHILE THE SACKETT FAMILY UNDERSTANDS THE NEED IN THE FAN COMMUNITY TO EXPRESS SYMPATHY DURING THIS TRYING TIME, THEY'RE ASKING THAT THE PUBLIC AND THE MEDIA RESPECT THEIR PRIVACY AS THEY NAVIGATE THESE TRAGIC EVENTS."
ALSO: "YOU'VE BEEN SHOCKED BY A BRAND CORP NON-LETHAL PROTOTYPE SPARK ROD. THERE WILL BE NO PERMANENT DAMAGE, BUT YOU WILL FEEL SOME DISCOMFORT."
KENNY I'M MORRIS I KENNY IS MORRIS IS KENNY IS ME IS KENN IS MORRIS IS KENNY.

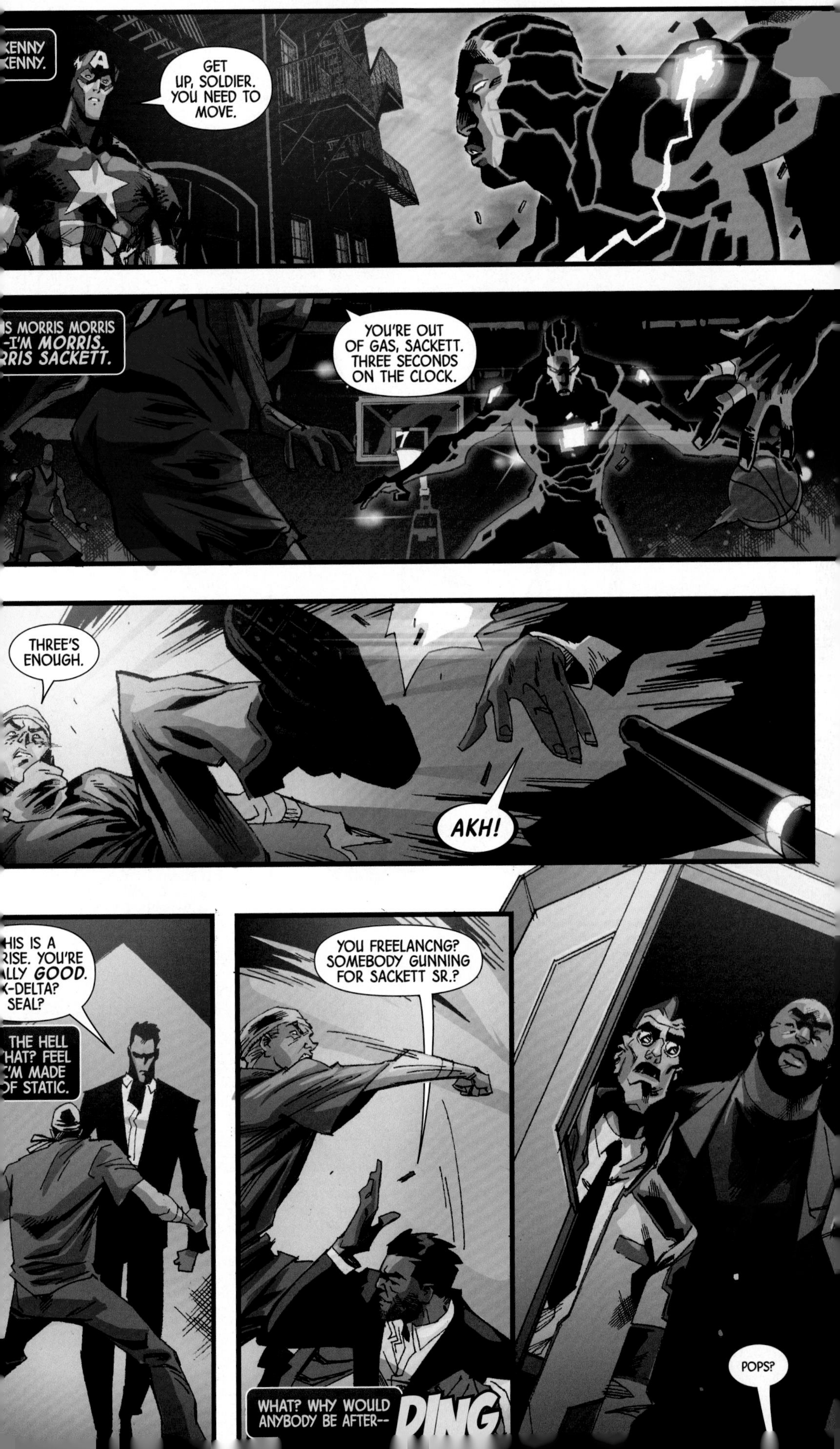
ENNY
ENNY.
GET UP, SOLDIER. YOU NEED TO MOVE.
S MORRIS MORRIS -I'M *MORRIS.* RRIS SACKETT.
YOU'RE OUT OF GAS, SACKETT. THREE SECONDS ON THE CLOCK.
THREE'S ENOUGH.
AKH!
HIS IS A RISE. YOU'RE LLY *GOOD.* -DELTA? SEAL?
THE HELL HAT? FEEL 'M MADE F STATIC.
YOU FREELANCNG? SOMEBODY GUNNING FOR SACKETT SR.?
WHAT? WHY WOULD ANYBODY BE AFTER--
DING
POPS?

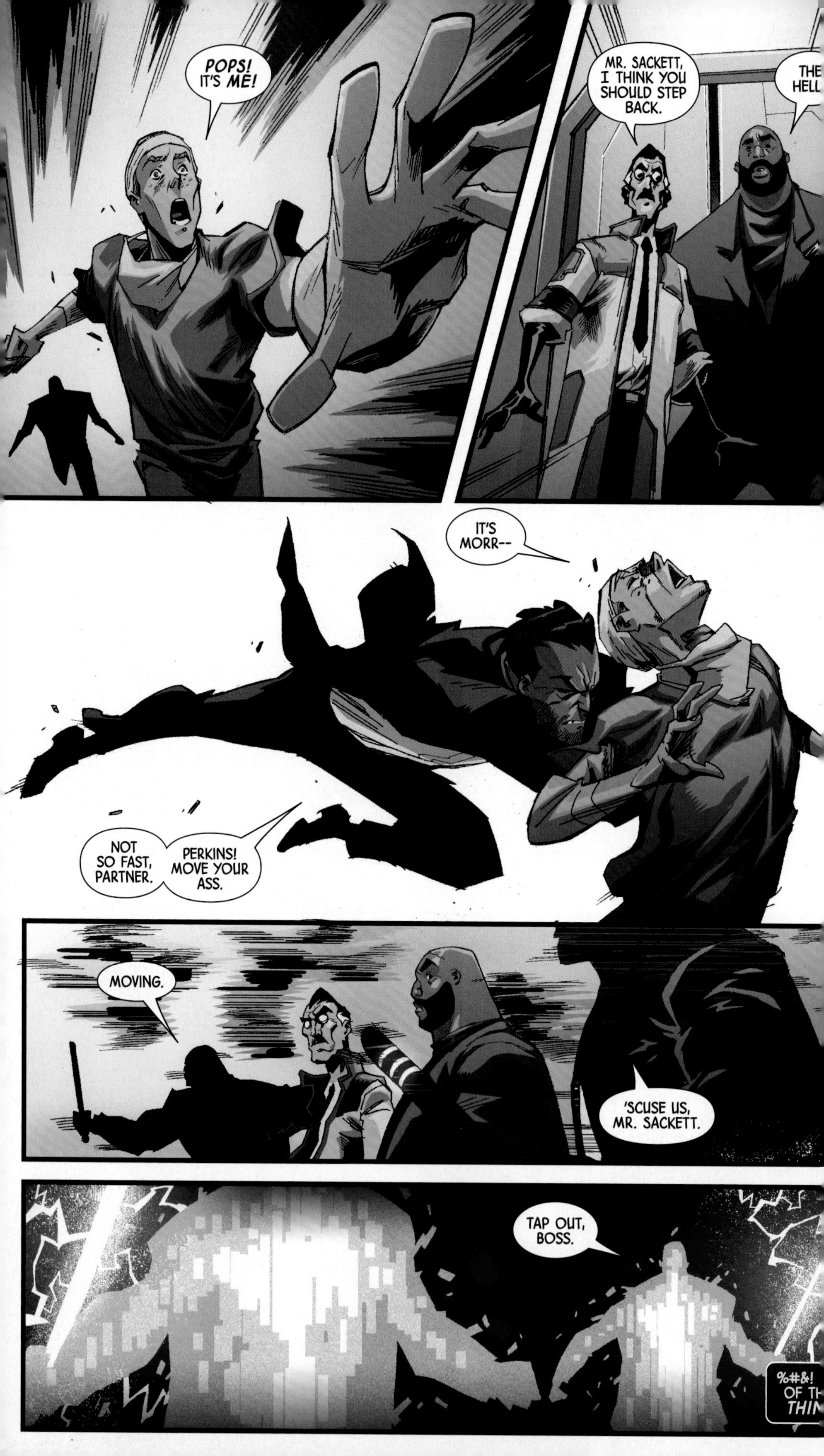
POPS! IT'S ME!
MR. SACKETT, I THINK YOU SHOULD STEP BACK.
THE HELL
IT'S MORR--
NOT SO FAST, PARTNER.
PERKINS! MOVE YOUR ASS.
MOVING.
'SCUSE US, MR. SACKETT.
TAP OUT, BOSS.
%#&! OF TH THIN

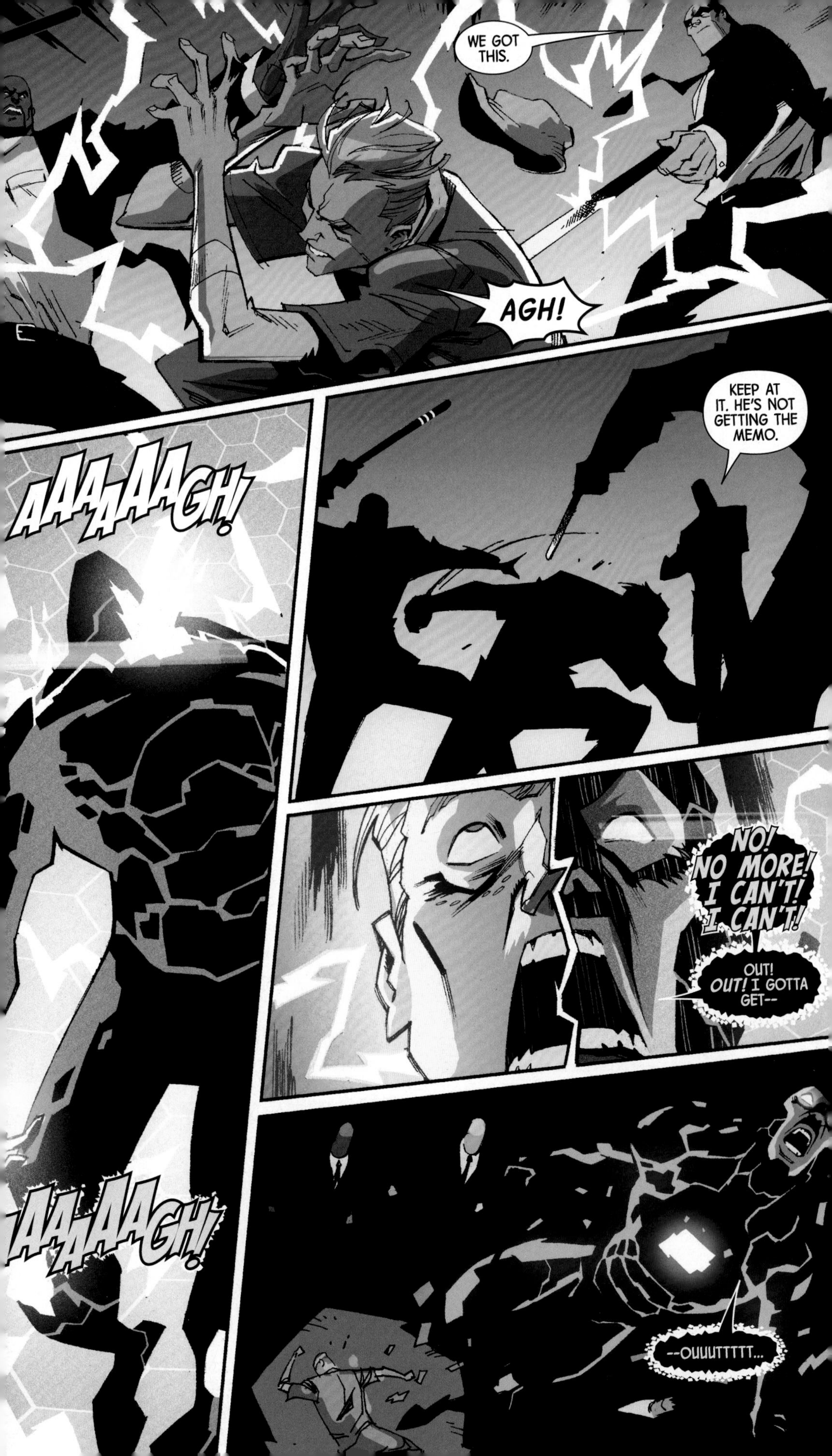
WE GOT THIS.
AGH!
KEEP AT IT. HE'S NOT GETTING THE MEMO.
AAAAAAGH!
NO! NO MORE! I CAN'T! I CAN'T!
OUT! OUT! I GOTTA GET--
AAAAAGH!
--OUUUTTTTT...

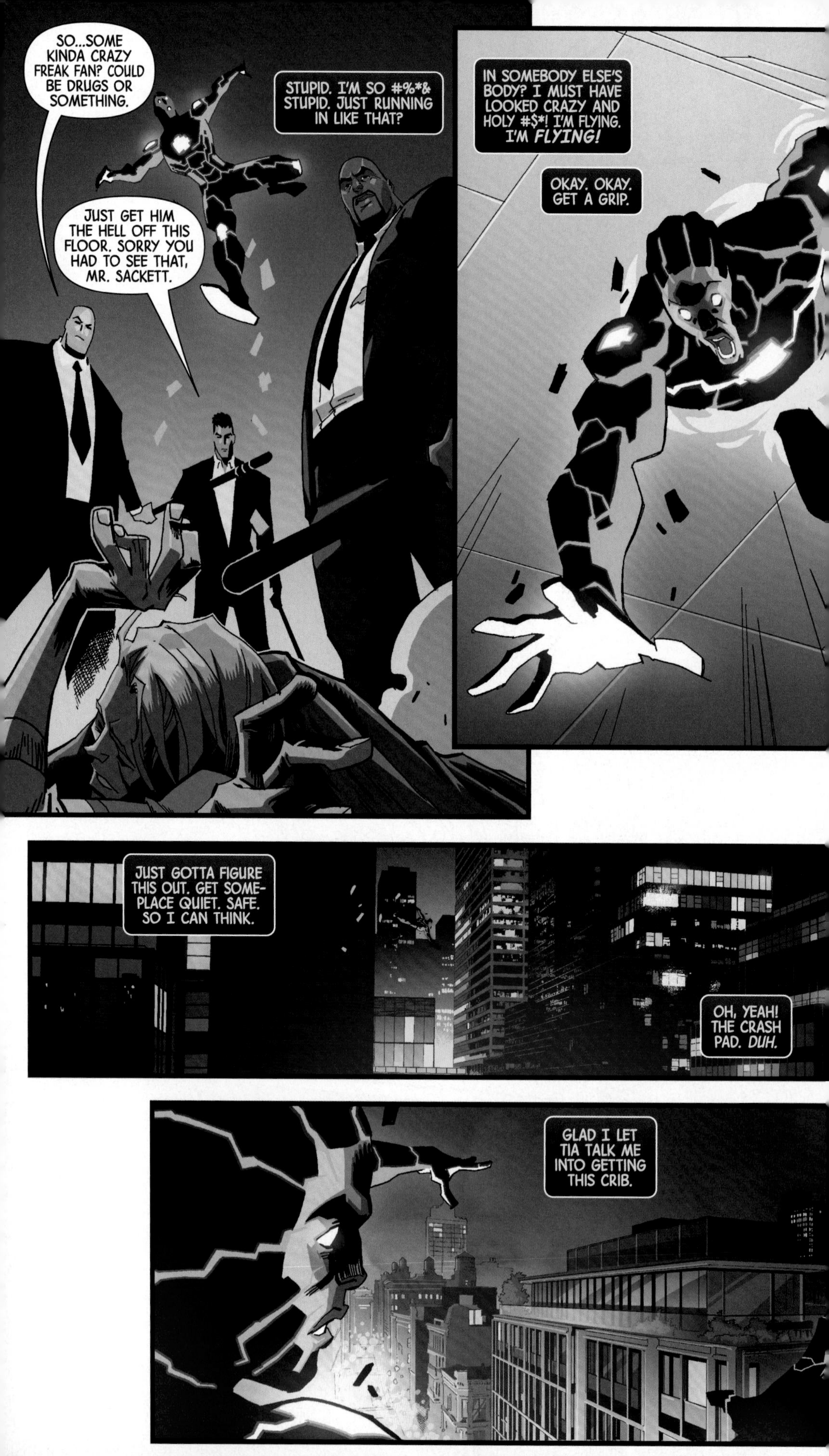
SO...SOME KINDA CRAZY FREAK FAN? COULD BE DRUGS OR SOMETHING.
JUST GET HIM THE HELL OFF THIS FLOOR. SORRY YOU HAD TO SEE THAT, MR. SACKETT.
STUPID. I'M SO #%*& STUPID. JUST RUNNING IN LIKE THAT?
IN SOMEBODY ELSE'S BODY? I MUST HAVE LOOKED CRAZY AND HOLY #$*! I'M FLYING. I'M *FLYING!*
OKAY. OKAY. GET A GRIP.
JUST GOTTA FIGURE THIS OUT. GET SOME-PLACE QUIET. SAFE. SO I CAN THINK.
OH, YEAH! THE CRASH PAD. *DUH.*
GLAD I LET TIA TALK ME INTO GETTING THIS CRIB.

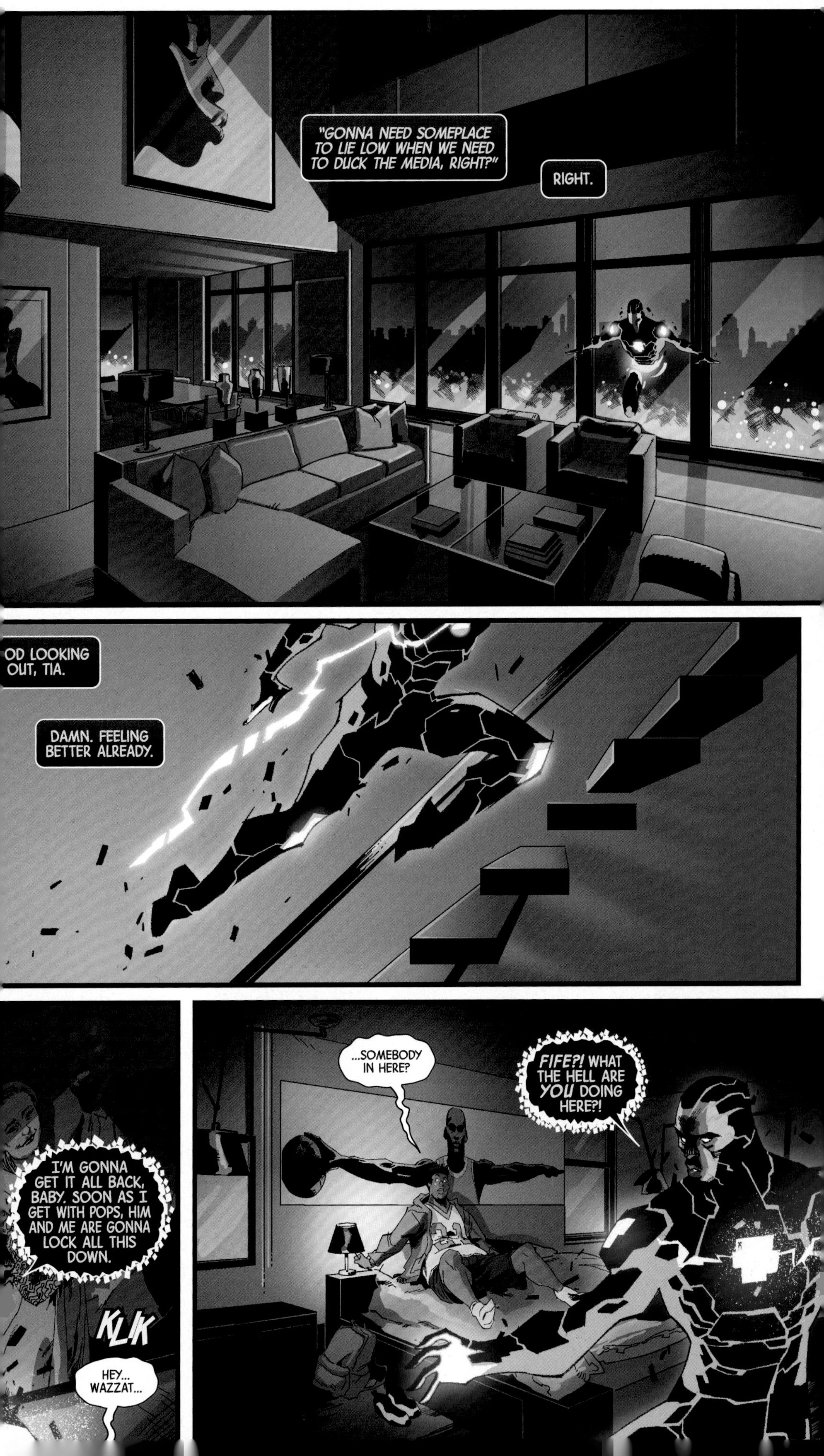
"GONNA NEED SOMEPLACE TO LIE LOW WHEN WE NEED TO DUCK THE MEDIA, RIGHT?"
RIGHT.
OD LOOKING OUT, TIA.
DAMN. FEELING BETTER ALREADY.
I'M GONNA GET IT ALL BACK, BABY. SOON AS I GET WITH POPS, HIM AND ME ARE GONNA LOCK ALL THIS DOWN.
KLIK
HEY... WAZZAT...
...SOMEBODY IN HERE?
FIFE?! WHAT THE HELL ARE YOU DOING HERE?!

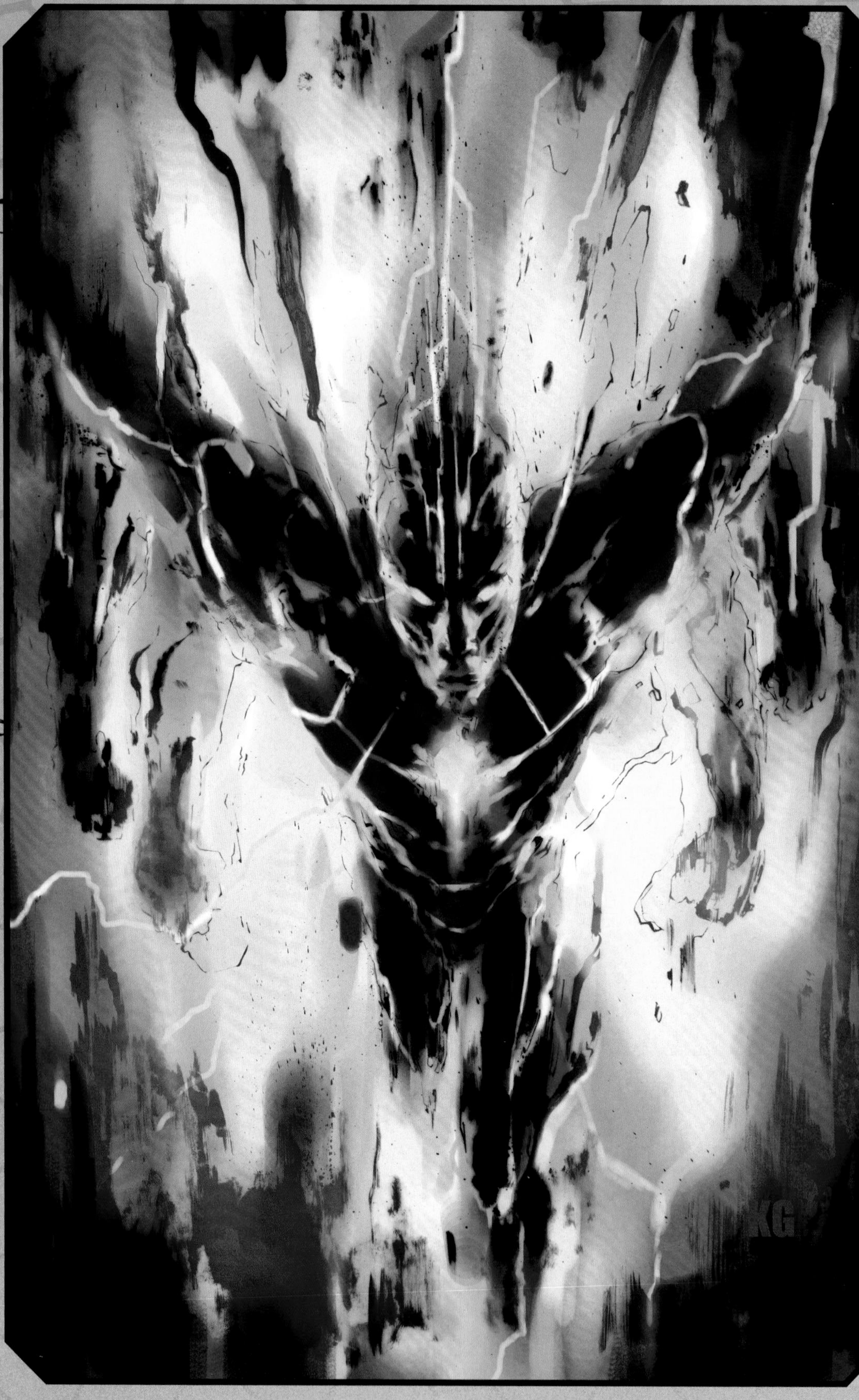
KG

PARABLE OF THE SOWER

3

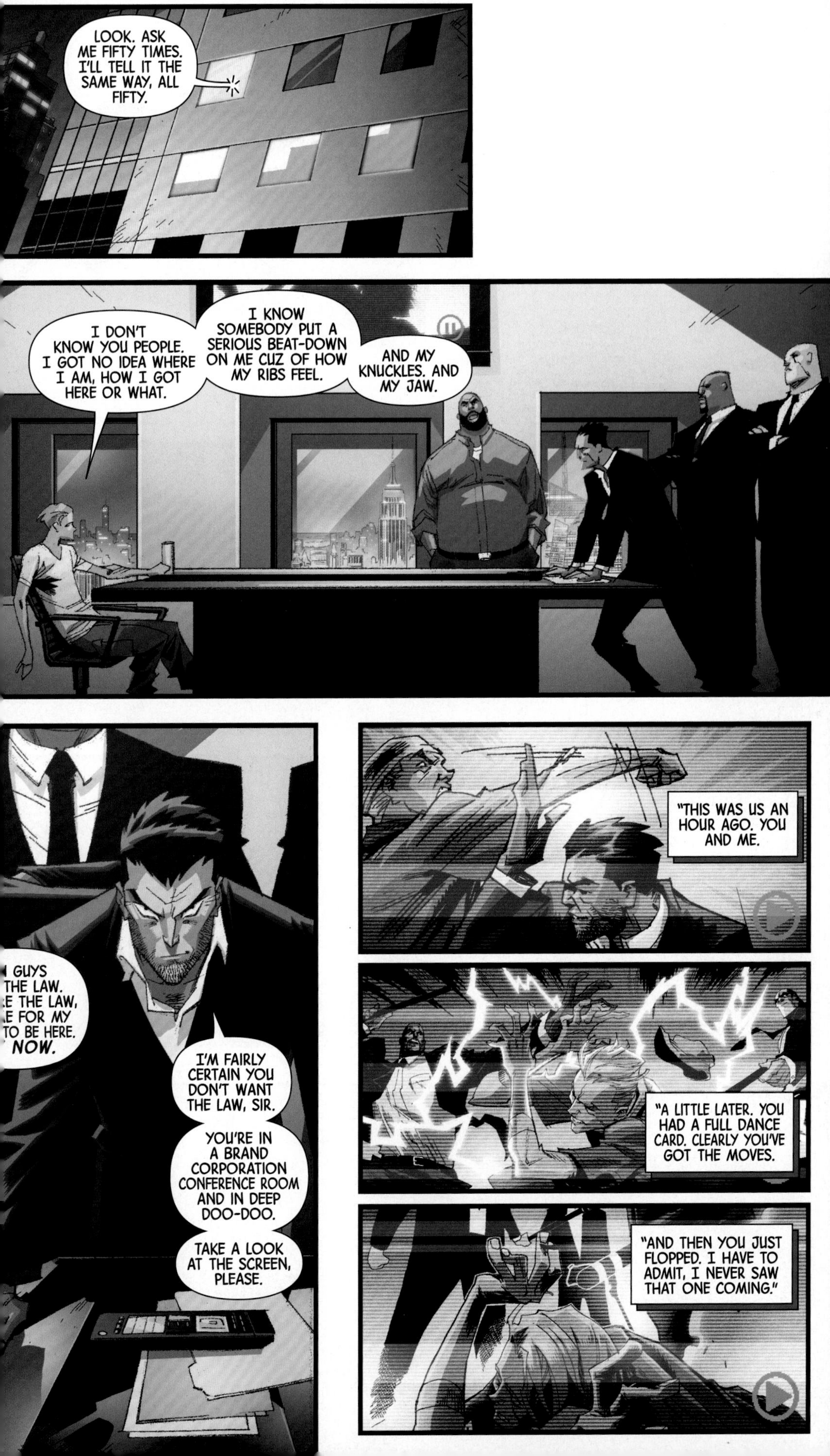
LOOK. ASK ME FIFTY TIMES. I'LL TELL IT THE SAME WAY, ALL FIFTY.
I DON'T KNOW YOU PEOPLE. I GOT NO IDEA WHERE I AM, HOW I GOT HERE OR WHAT.
I KNOW SOMEBODY PUT A SERIOUS BEAT-DOWN ON ME CUZ OF HOW MY RIBS FEEL.
AND MY KNUCKLES. AND MY JAW.
GUYS THE LAW. THE LAW, FOR MY TO BE HERE. NOW.
I'M FAIRLY CERTAIN YOU DON'T WANT THE LAW, SIR.
YOU'RE IN A BRAND CORPORATION CONFERENCE ROOM AND IN DEEP DOO-DOO.
TAKE A LOOK AT THE SCREEN, PLEASE.
"THIS WAS US AN HOUR AGO. YOU AND ME.
"A LITTLE LATER. YOU HAD A FULL DANCE CARD. CLEARLY YOU'VE GOT THE MOVES.
"AND THEN YOU JUST FLOPPED. I HAVE TO ADMIT, I NEVER SAW THAT ONE COMING."

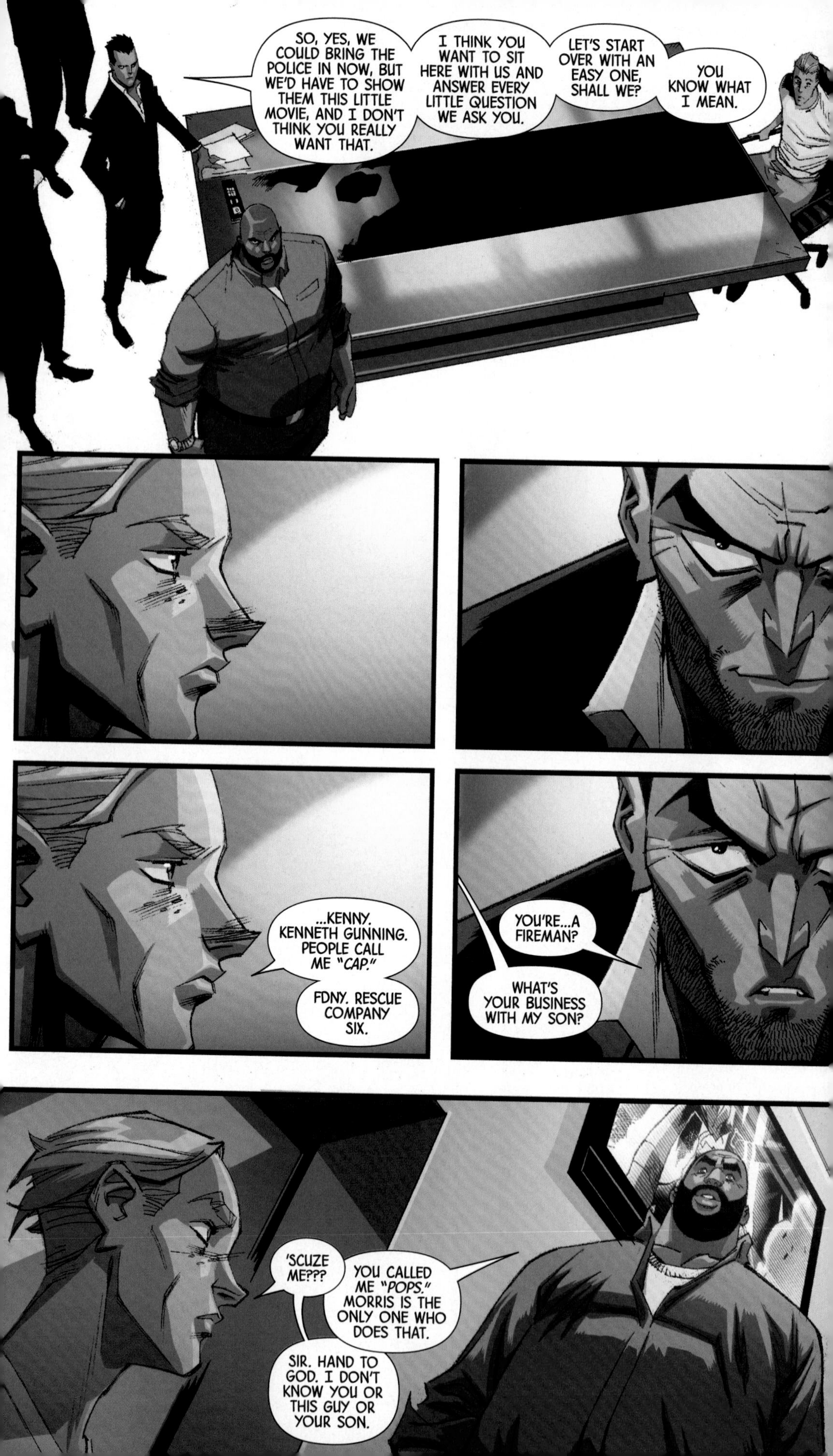
SO, YES, WE COULD BRING THE POLICE IN NOW, BUT WE'D HAVE TO SHOW THEM THIS LITTLE MOVIE, AND I DON'T THINK YOU REALLY WANT THAT.
I THINK YOU WANT TO SIT HERE WITH US AND ANSWER EVERY LITTLE QUESTION WE ASK YOU.
LET'S START OVER WITH AN EASY ONE, SHALL WE?
YOU KNOW WHAT I MEAN.
...KENNY. KENNETH GUNNING. PEOPLE CALL ME "CAP."
FDNY. RESCUE COMPANY SIX.
YOU'RE...A FIREMAN?
WHAT'S YOUR BUSINESS WITH MY SON?
'SCUZE ME???
YOU CALLED ME "POPS." MORRIS IS THE ONLY ONE WHO DOES THAT.
SIR. HAND TO GOD. I DON'T KNOW YOU OR THIS GUY OR YOUR SON.

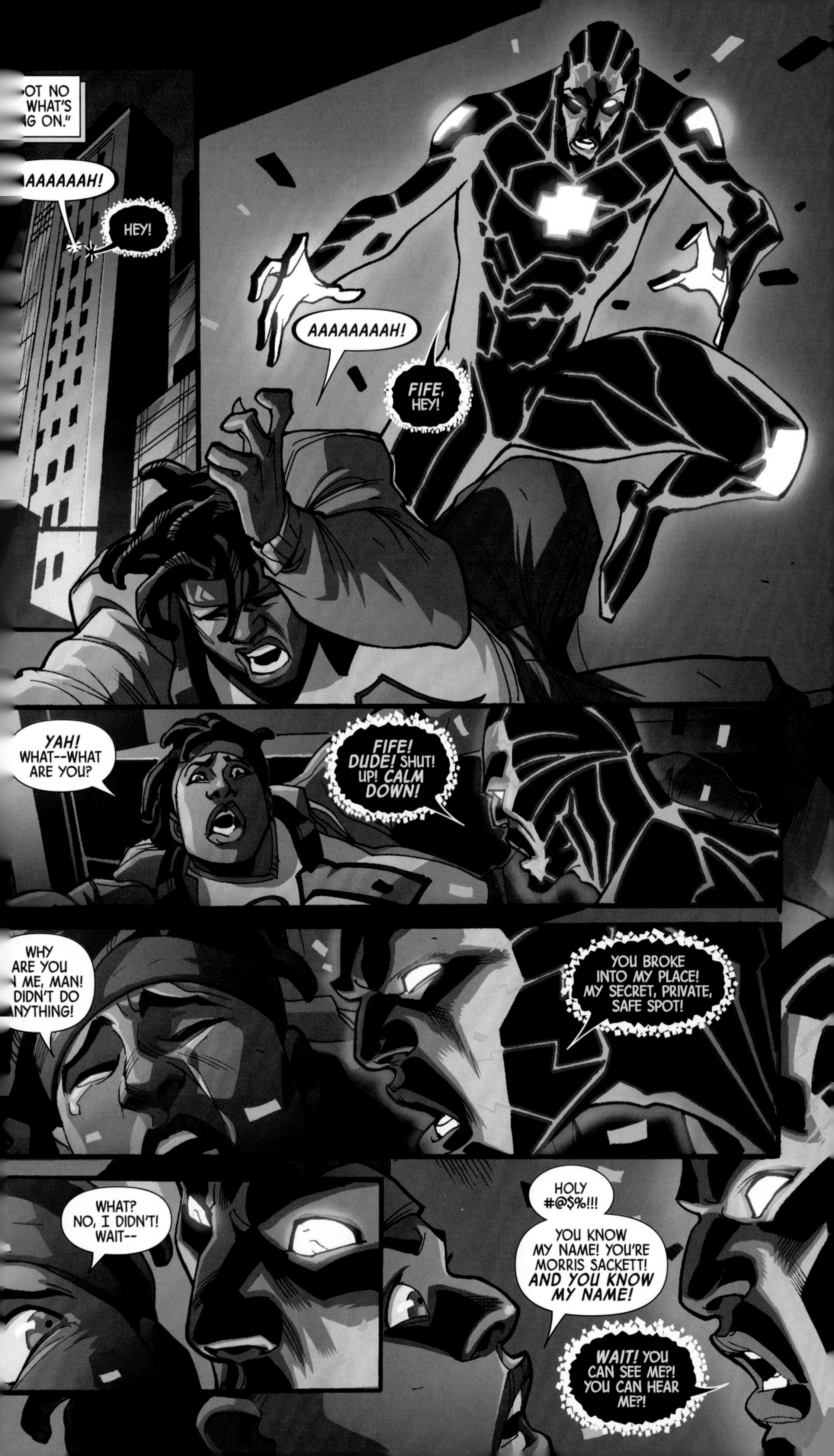

OT NO WHAT'S G ON."
AAAAAAAH!
HEY!
AAAAAAAAH!
FIFE, HEY!
YAH! WHAT--WHAT ARE YOU?
FIFE! DUDE! SHUT! UP! CALM DOWN!
WHY ARE YOU N ME, MAN! DIDN'T DO NYTHING!
YOU BROKE INTO MY PLACE! MY SECRET, PRIVATE, SAFE SPOT!
WHAT? NO, I DIDN'T! WAIT--
HOLY #@$%!!!
YOU KNOW MY NAME! YOU'RE MORRIS SACKETT! AND YOU KNOW MY NAME!
WAIT! YOU CAN SEE ME?! YOU CAN HEAR ME?!

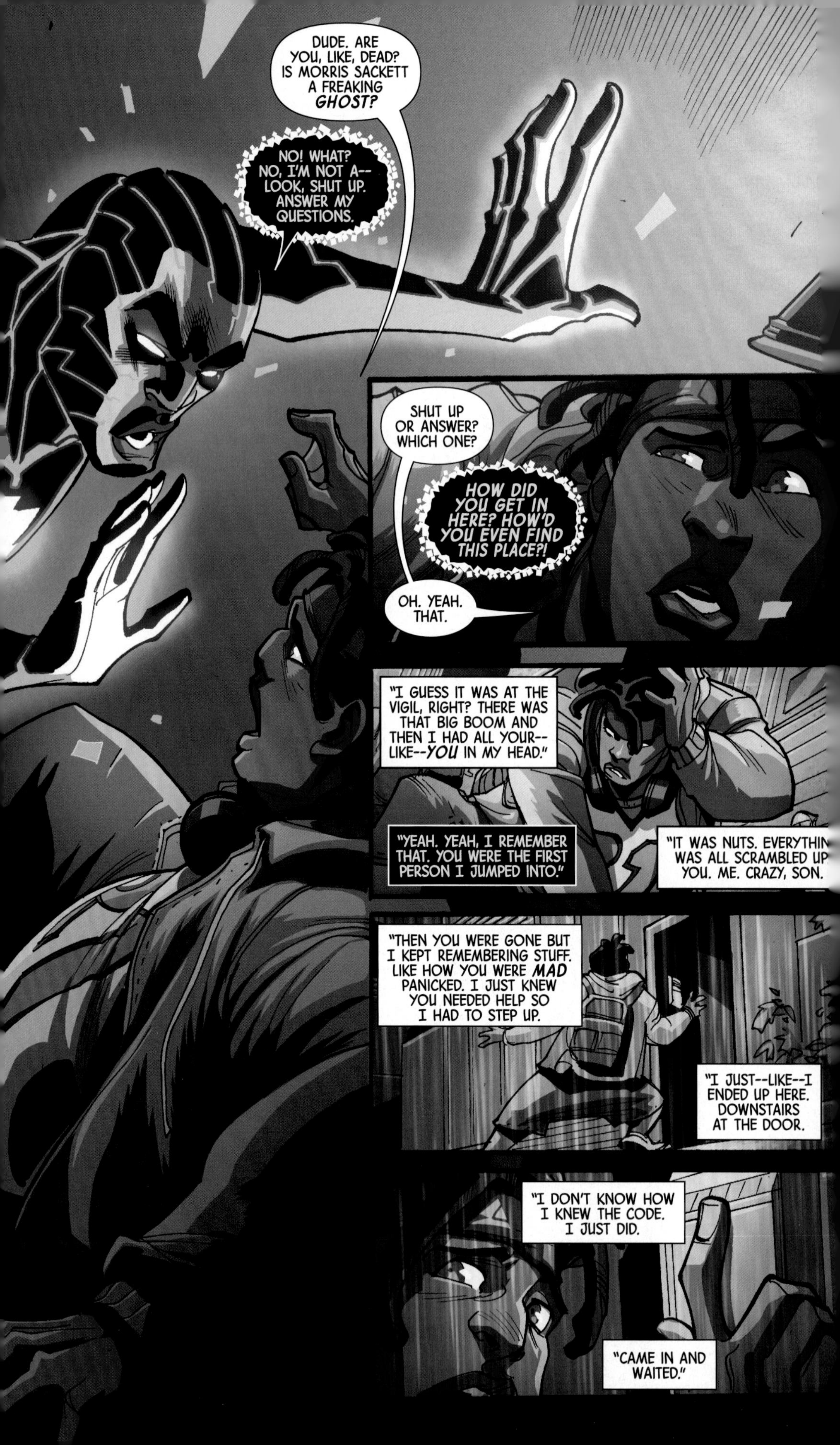
DUDE. ARE YOU, LIKE, DEAD? IS MORRIS SACKETT A FREAKING GHOST?
NO! WHAT? NO, I'M NOT A-- LOOK, SHUT UP. ANSWER MY QUESTIONS.
SHUT UP OR ANSWER? WHICH ONE?
HOW DID YOU GET IN HERE? HOW'D YOU EVEN FIND THIS PLACE?!
OH. YEAH. THAT.
"I GUESS IT WAS AT THE VIGIL, RIGHT? THERE WAS THAT BIG BOOM AND THEN I HAD ALL YOUR-- LIKE--YOU IN MY HEAD."
"YEAH. YEAH, I REMEMBER THAT. YOU WERE THE FIRST PERSON I JUMPED INTO."
"IT WAS NUTS. EVERYTHIN WAS ALL SCRAMBLED UP YOU. ME. CRAZY, SON.
"THEN YOU WERE GONE BUT I KEPT REMEMBERING STUFF. LIKE HOW YOU WERE MAD PANICKED. I JUST KNEW YOU NEEDED HELP SO I HAD TO STEP UP.
"I JUST--LIKE--I ENDED UP HERE. DOWNSTAIRS AT THE DOOR.
"I DON'T KNOW HOW I KNEW THE CODE. I JUST DID.
"CAME IN AND WAITED."

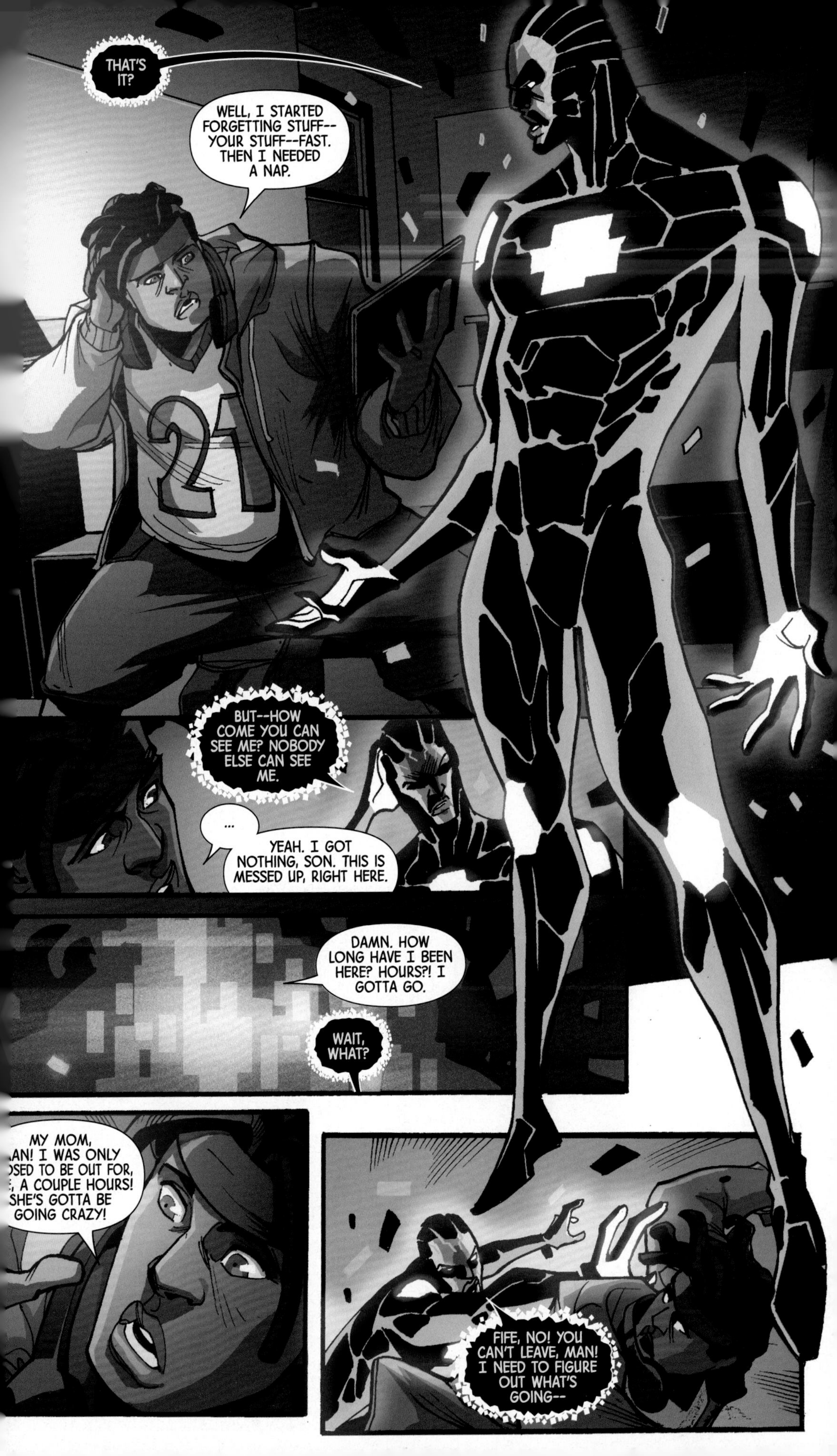
THAT'S IT?
WELL, I STARTED FORGETTING STUFF-- YOUR STUFF--FAST. THEN I NEEDED A NAP.
BUT--HOW COME YOU CAN SEE ME? NOBODY ELSE CAN SEE ME.
...
YEAH. I GOT NOTHING, SON. THIS IS MESSED UP, RIGHT HERE.
DAMN. HOW LONG HAVE I BEEN HERE? HOURS?! I GOTTA GO.
WAIT, WHAT?
MY MOM, AN! I WAS ONLY OSED TO BE OUT FOR, , A COUPLE HOURS! SHE'S GOTTA BE GOING CRAZY!
FIFE, NO! YOU CAN'T LEAVE, MAN! I NEED TO FIGURE OUT WHAT'S GOING--

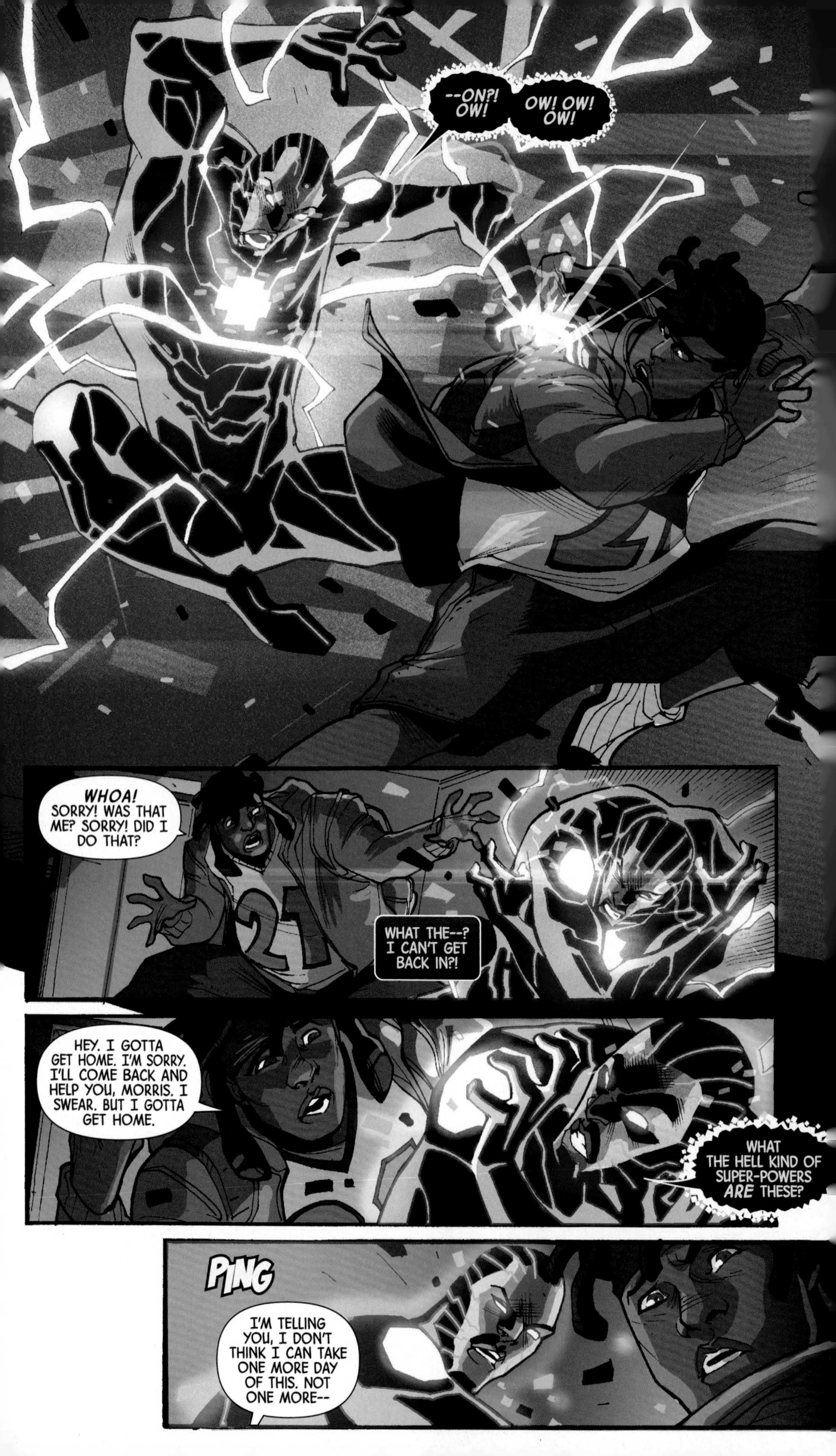
--ON?! OW!
OW! OW! OW!
WHOA! SORRY! WAS THAT ME? SORRY! DID I DO THAT?
WHAT THE--? I CAN'T GET BACK IN?!
HEY. I GOTTA GET HOME. I'M SORRY. I'LL COME BACK AND HELP YOU, MORRIS. I SWEAR. BUT I GOTTA GET HOME.
WHAT THE HELL KIND OF SUPER-POWERS ARE THESE?
PING
I'M TELLING YOU, I DON'T THINK I CAN TAKE ONE MORE DAY OF THIS. NOT ONE MORE--

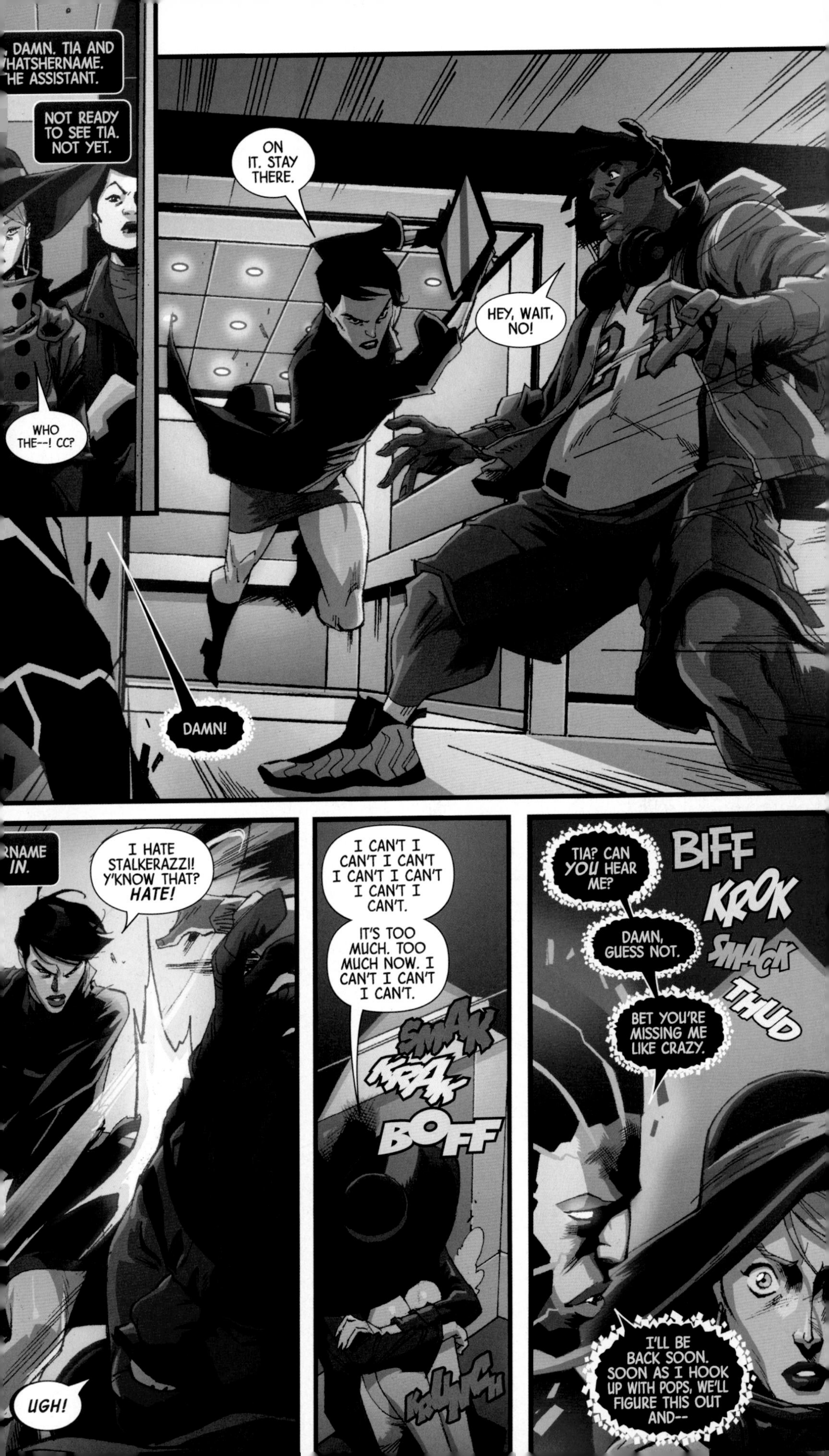

DAMN. TIA AND
HATSHERNAME.
HE ASSISTANT.
NOT READY TO SEE TIA. NOT YET.
WHO THE--! CC?
ON IT. STAY THERE.
HEY, WAIT, NO!
DAMN!
RNAME
IN.
I HATE STALKERAZZI! Y'KNOW THAT? HATE!
UGH!
I CAN'T I CAN'T I CAN'T I CAN'T I CAN'T I CAN'T I CAN'T.
IT'S TOO MUCH. TOO MUCH NOW. I CAN'T I CAN'T I CAN'T.
SMAK
KRAK
BOFF
KRUNCH
TIA? CAN YOU HEAR ME?
BIFF
KROK
SMACK
THUD
DAMN, GUESS NOT.
BET YOU'RE MISSING ME LIKE CRAZY.
I'LL BE BACK SOON. SOON AS I HOOK UP WITH POPS, WE'LL FIGURE THIS OUT AND--

WELL? COME ON. WE NEED TO TAPE HIM UP.

WOW. WHATSERNAME IS--

CC?

CC! YEAH! THAT'S IT! DAMN, I CAN NEVER REMEMBER THAT.

HOW DO THEY ALWAYS FIND ME? THIS WAS SUPPOSED TO BE MY SAFE PLACE!

YEAH. THIS ONE IS MY BAD.

TIA. *UGH.* FOCUS. TAPE? OVER THERE. MIDDLE SHELF.

IT WAS BAD BEFORE, BUT SINCE WHAT HAPPENED TO MORRIS...

LOOK, IT'S ONE GUY. WE JUST NEED TO CALL THE COPS AND--

NO! AR YOU CRAZ YOU CRAZ COPS? N NO WA

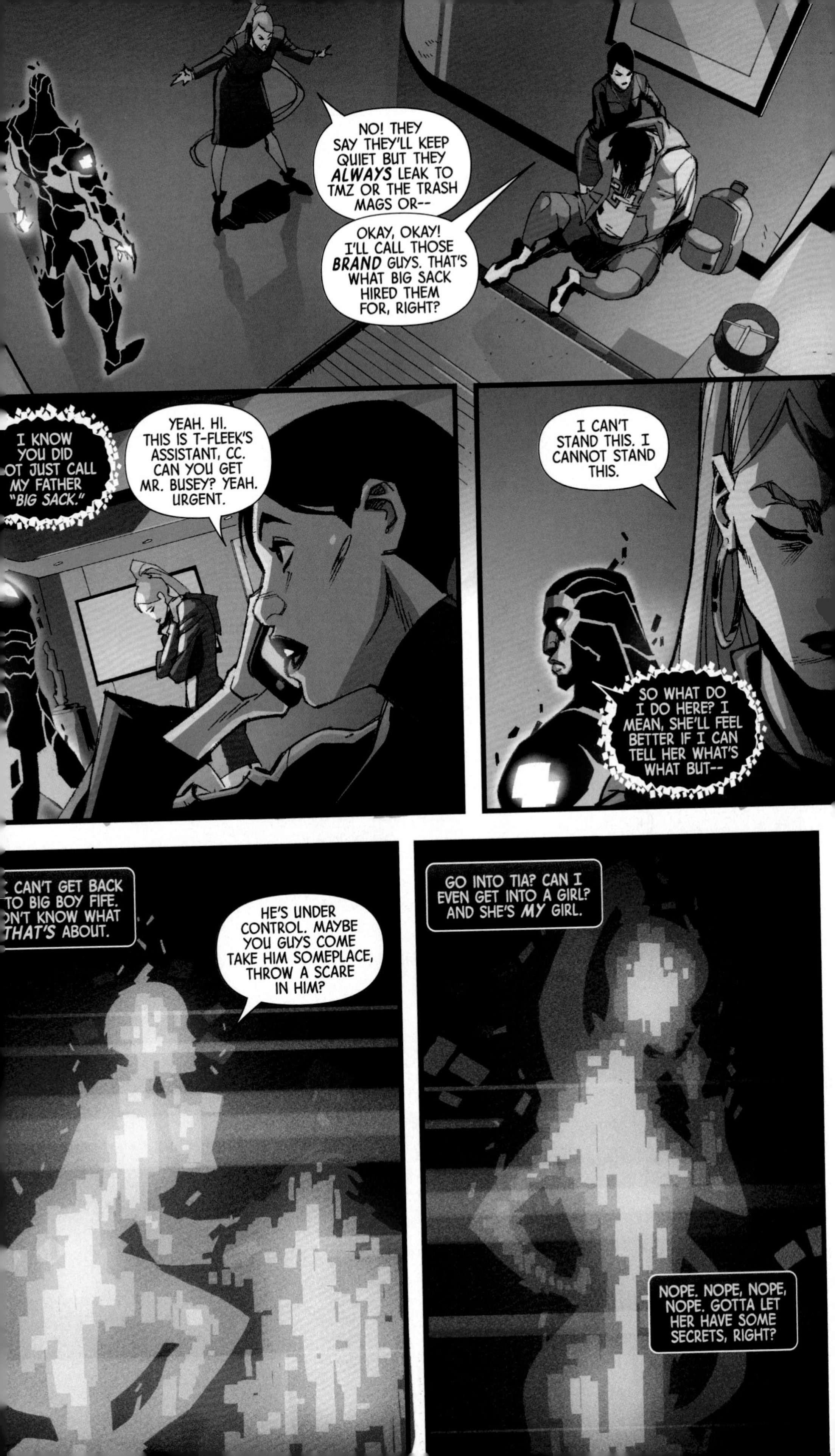
NO! THEY SAY THEY'LL KEEP QUIET BUT THEY ALWAYS LEAK TO TMZ OR THE TRASH MAGS OR--
OKAY, OKAY! I'LL CALL THOSE BRAND GUYS. THAT'S WHAT BIG SACK HIRED THEM FOR, RIGHT?
I KNOW YOU DID OT JUST CALL MY FATHER "BIG SACK."
YEAH. HI. THIS IS T-FLEEK'S ASSISTANT, CC. CAN YOU GET MR. BUSEY? YEAH. URGENT.
I CAN'T STAND THIS. I CANNOT STAND THIS.
SO WHAT DO I DO HERE? I MEAN, SHE'LL FEEL BETTER IF I CAN TELL HER WHAT'S WHAT BUT--
CAN'T GET BACK TO BIG BOY FIFE. ON'T KNOW WHAT THAT'S ABOUT.
HE'S UNDER CONTROL. MAYBE YOU GUYS COME TAKE HIM SOMEPLACE, THROW A SCARE IN HIM?
GO INTO TIA? CAN I EVEN GET INTO A GIRL? AND SHE'S MY GIRL.
NOPE. NOPE, NOPE, NOPE. GOTTA LET HER HAVE SOME SECRETS, RIGHT?

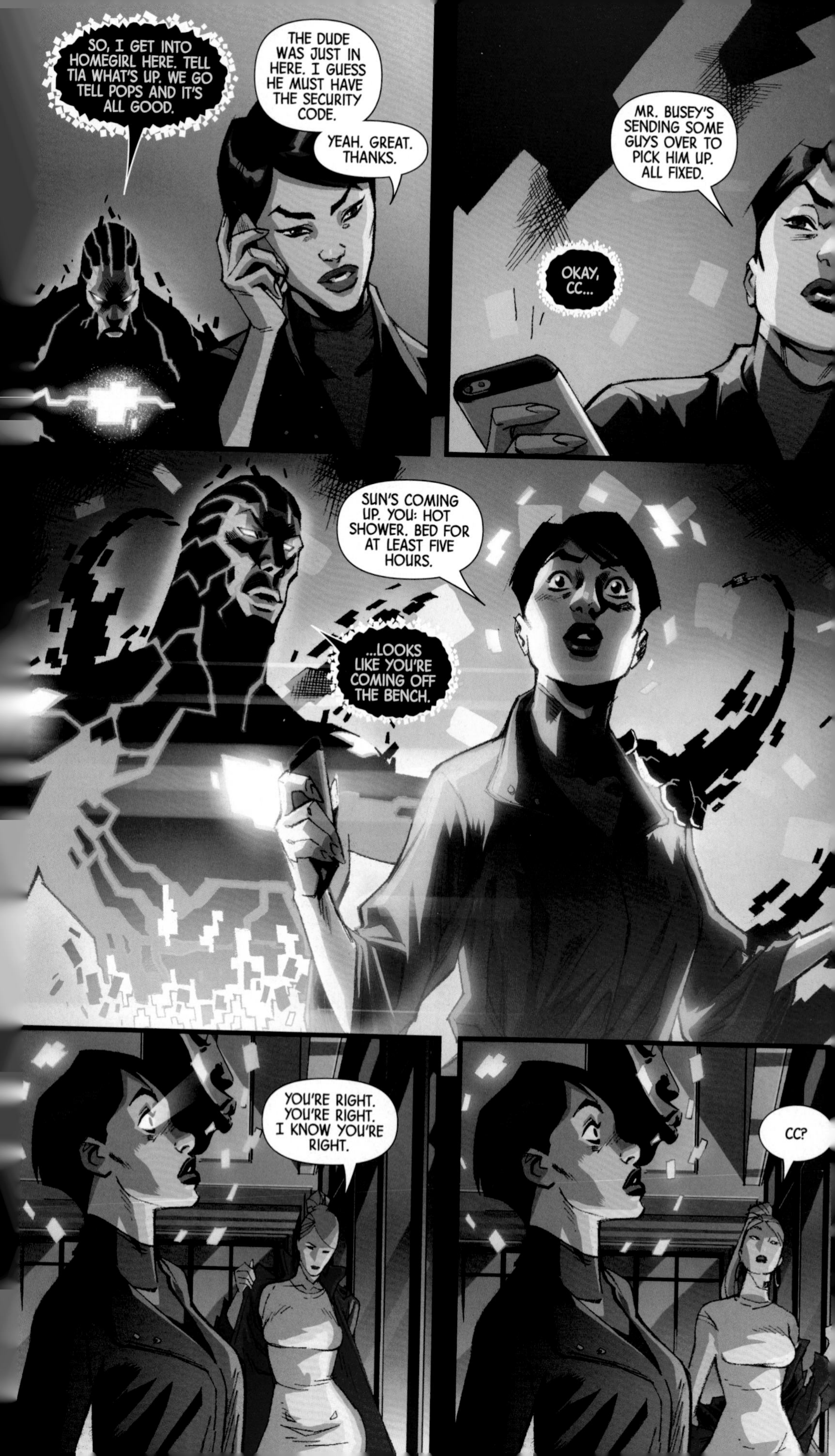
SO, I GET INTO HOMEGIRL HERE. TELL TIA WHAT'S UP. WE GO TELL POPS AND IT'S ALL GOOD.
THE DUDE WAS JUST IN HERE. I GUESS HE MUST HAVE THE SECURITY CODE.
YEAH. GREAT. THANKS.
MR. BUSEY'S SENDING SOME GUYS OVER TO PICK HIM UP. ALL FIXED.
OKAY, CC...
SUN'S COMING UP. YOU: HOT SHOWER. BED FOR AT LEAST FIVE HOURS.
...LOOKS LIKE YOU'RE COMING OFF THE BENCH.
YOU'RE RIGHT. YOU'RE RIGHT. I KNOW YOU'RE RIGHT.
CC?

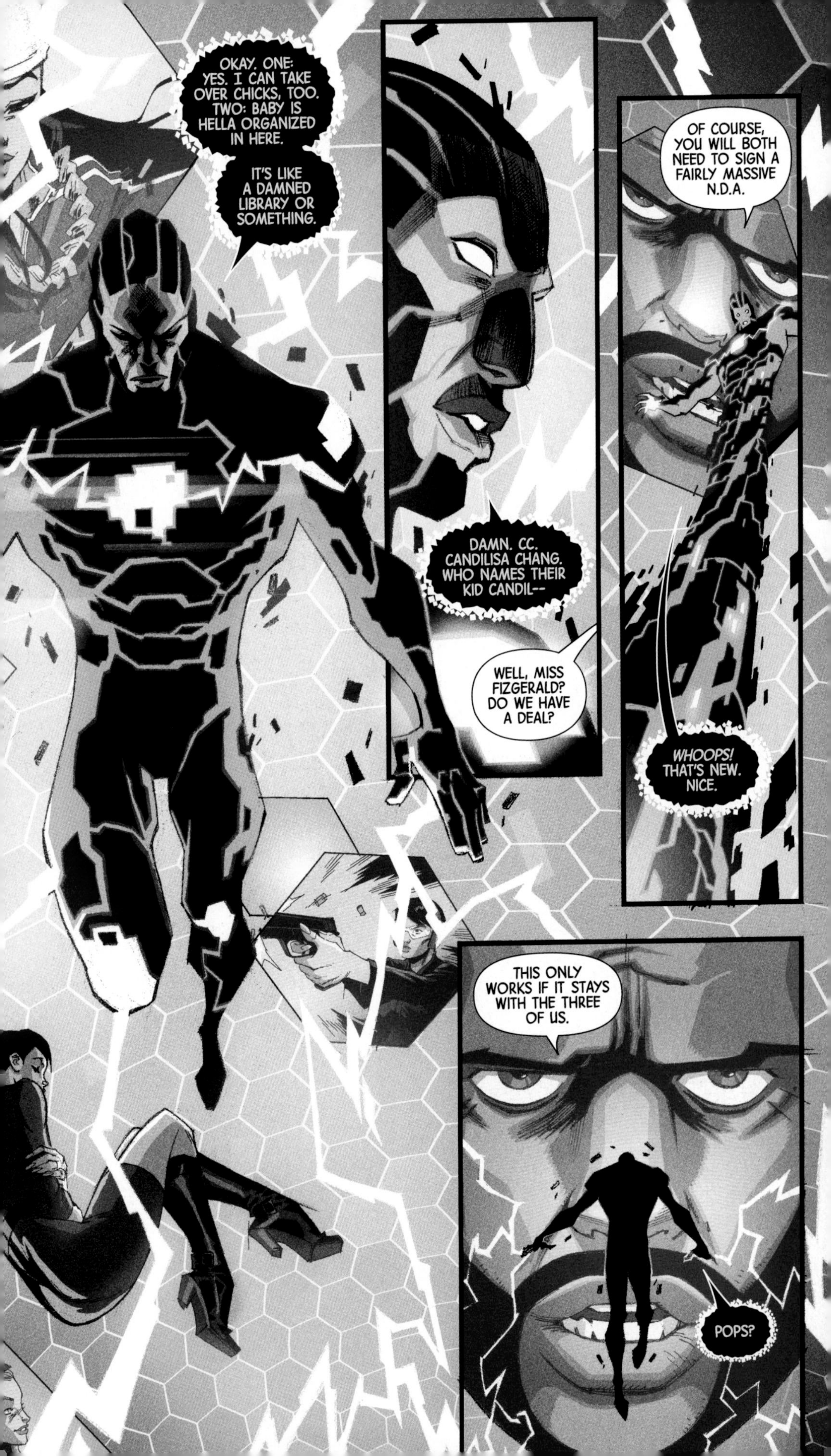
OKAY. ONE: YES. I CAN TAKE OVER CHICKS, TOO. TWO: BABY IS HELLA ORGANIZED IN HERE.
IT'S LIKE A DAMNED LIBRARY OR SOMETHING.
DAMN. CC. CANDILISA CHANG. WHO NAMES THEIR KID CANDIL--
WELL, MISS FIZGERALD? DO WE HAVE A DEAL?
OF COURSE, YOU WILL BOTH NEED TO SIGN A FAIRLY MASSIVE N.D.A.
WHOOPS! THAT'S NEW. NICE.
THIS ONLY WORKS IF IT STAYS WITH THE THREE OF US.
POPS?

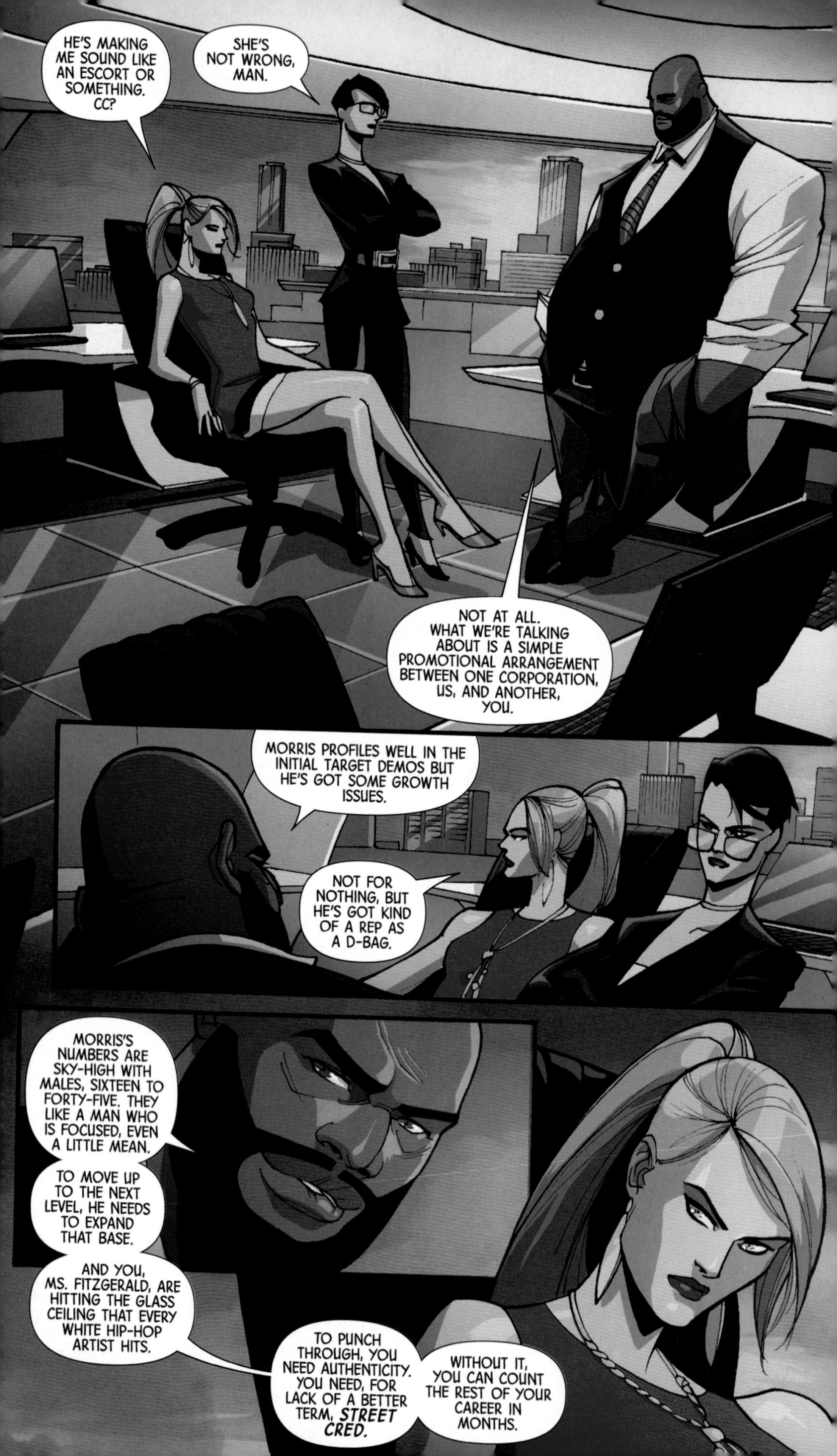
HE'S MAKING ME SOUND LIKE AN ESCORT OR SOMETHING. CC?
SHE'S NOT WRONG, MAN.
NOT AT ALL. WHAT WE'RE TALKING ABOUT IS A SIMPLE PROMOTIONAL ARRANGEMENT BETWEEN ONE CORPORATION, US, AND ANOTHER, YOU.
MORRIS PROFILES WELL IN THE INITIAL TARGET DEMOS BUT HE'S GOT SOME GROWTH ISSUES.
NOT FOR NOTHING, BUT HE'S GOT KIND OF A REP AS A D-BAG.
MORRIS'S NUMBERS ARE SKY-HIGH WITH MALES, SIXTEEN TO FORTY-FIVE. THEY LIKE A MAN WHO IS FOCUSED, EVEN A LITTLE MEAN.
TO MOVE UP TO THE NEXT LEVEL, HE NEEDS TO EXPAND THAT BASE.
AND YOU, MS. FITZGERALD, ARE HITTING THE GLASS CEILING THAT EVERY WHITE HIP-HOP ARTIST HITS.
TO PUNCH THROUGH, YOU NEED AUTHENTICITY. YOU NEED, FOR LACK OF A BETTER TERM, ***STREET CRED.***
WITHOUT IT, YOU CAN COUNT THE REST OF YOUR CAREER IN MONTHS.

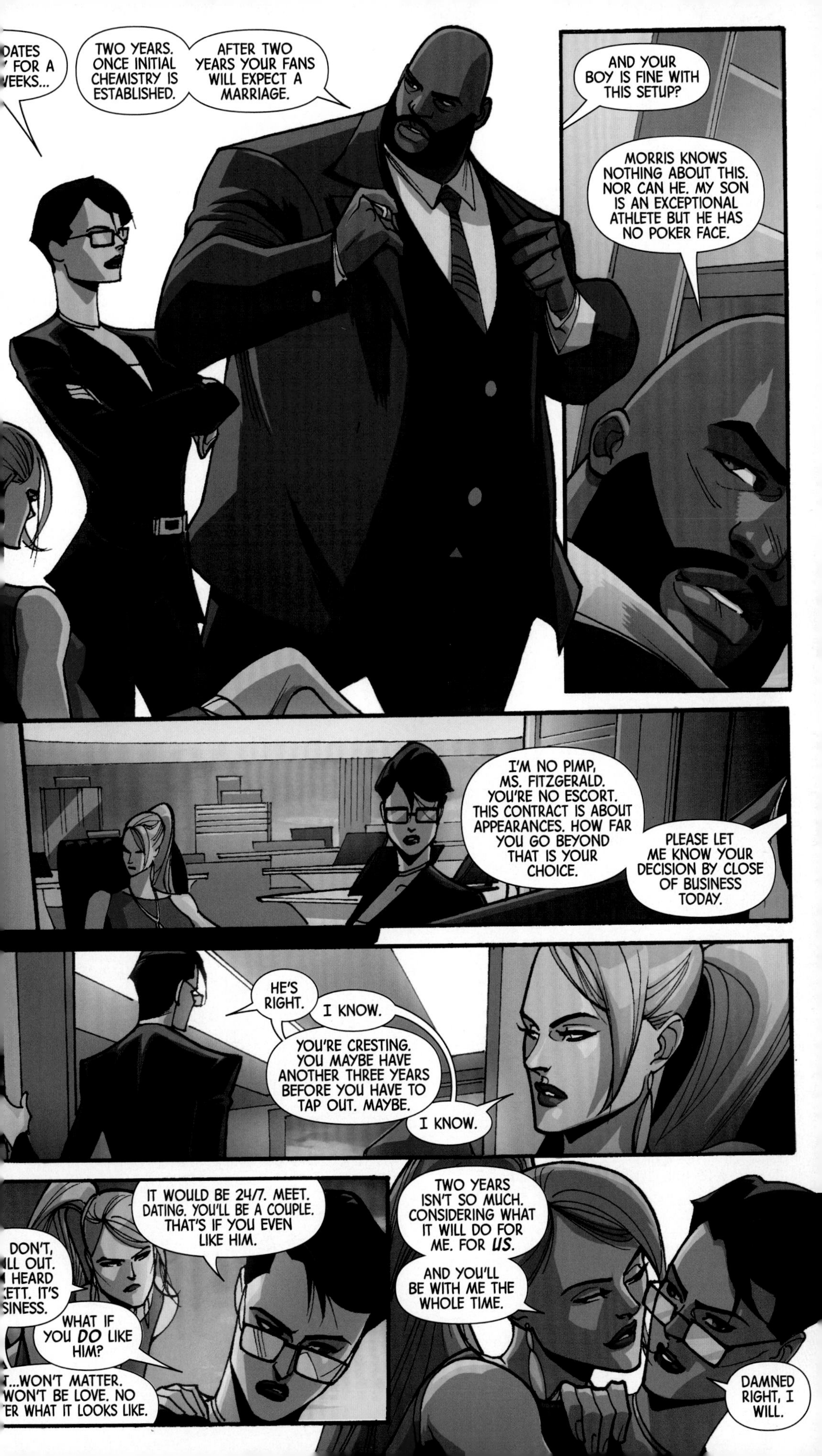

DATES FOR A
TWO YEARS. ONCE INITIAL CHEMISTRY IS ESTABLISHED.
AFTER TWO YEARS YOUR FANS WILL EXPECT A MARRIAGE.
AND YOUR BOY IS FINE WITH THIS SETUP?
MORRIS KNOWS NOTHING ABOUT THIS. NOR CAN HE. MY SON IS AN EXCEPTIONAL ATHLETE BUT HE HAS NO POKER FACE.
I'M NO PIMP, MS. FITZGERALD. YOU'RE NO ESCORT. THIS CONTRACT IS ABOUT APPEARANCES. HOW FAR YOU GO BEYOND THAT IS YOUR CHOICE.
PLEASE LET ME KNOW YOUR DECISION BY CLOSE OF BUSINESS TODAY.
HE'S RIGHT.
I KNOW.
YOU'RE CRESTING. YOU MAYBE HAVE ANOTHER THREE YEARS BEFORE YOU HAVE TO TAP OUT. MAYBE.
I KNOW.
IT WOULD BE 24/7. MEET. DATING. YOU'LL BE A COUPLE. THAT'S IF YOU EVEN LIKE HIM.
DON'T, HEARD IT'S
WHAT IF YOU ***DO*** LIKE HIM?
...WON'T MATTER. WON'T BE LOVE. NO WHAT IT LOOKS LIKE.
TWO YEARS ISN'T SO MUCH. CONSIDERING WHAT IT WILL DO FOR ME. FOR ***US***.
AND YOU'LL BE WITH ME THE WHOLE TIME.
DAMNED RIGHT, I WILL.

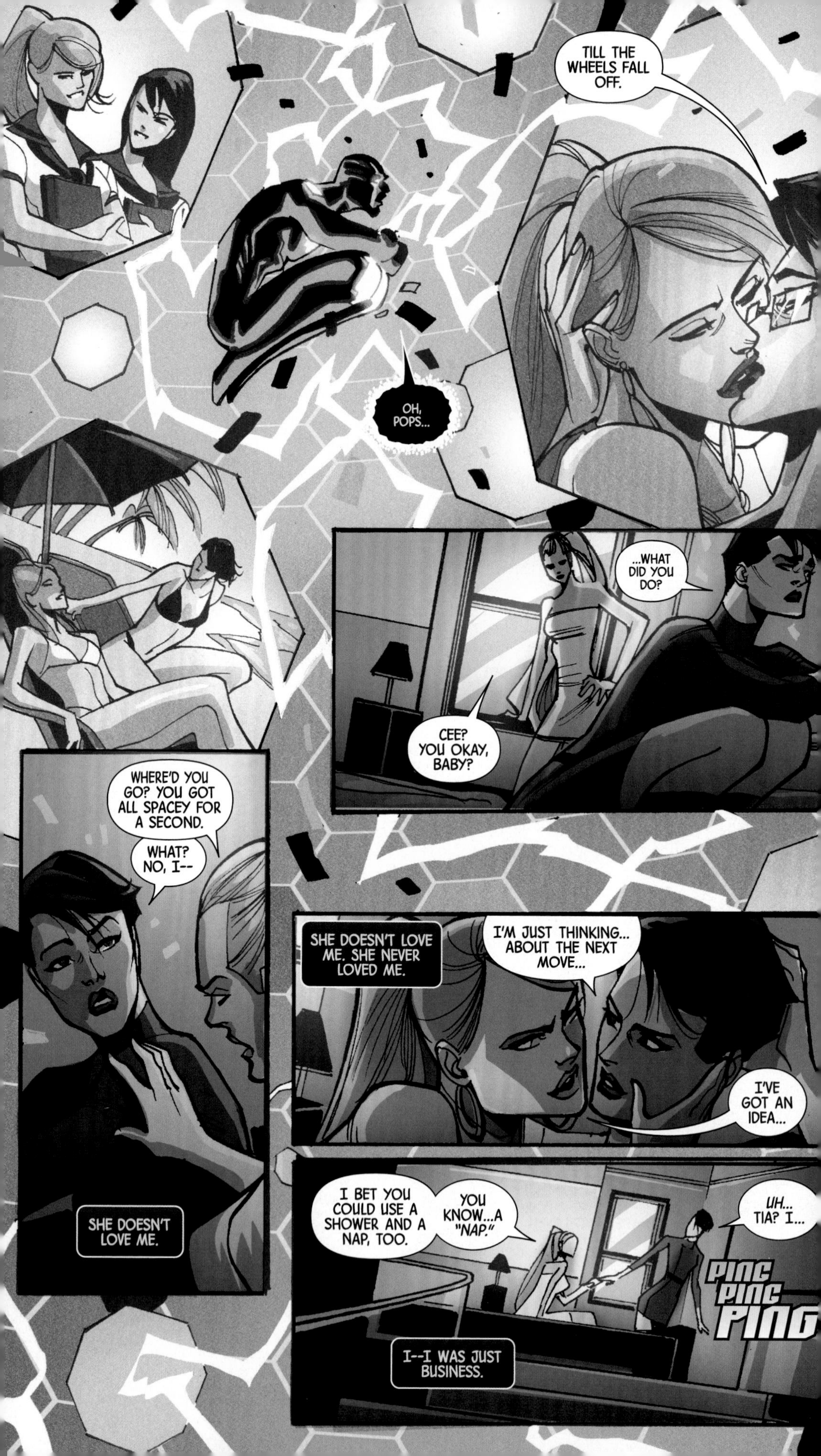
TILL THE WHEELS FALL OFF.
OH, POPS...
...WHAT DID YOU DO?
CEE? YOU OKAY, BABY?
WHERE'D YOU GO? YOU GOT ALL SPACEY FOR A SECOND.
WHAT? NO, I--
SHE DOESN'T LOVE ME.
SHE DOESN'T LOVE ME. SHE NEVER LOVED ME.
I'M JUST THINKING... ABOUT THE NEXT MOVE...
I'VE GOT AN IDEA...
I BET YOU COULD USE A SHOWER AND A NAP, TOO.
YOU KNOW...A "NAP."
UH... TIA? I...
PING PING PING
I--I WAS JUST BUSINESS.

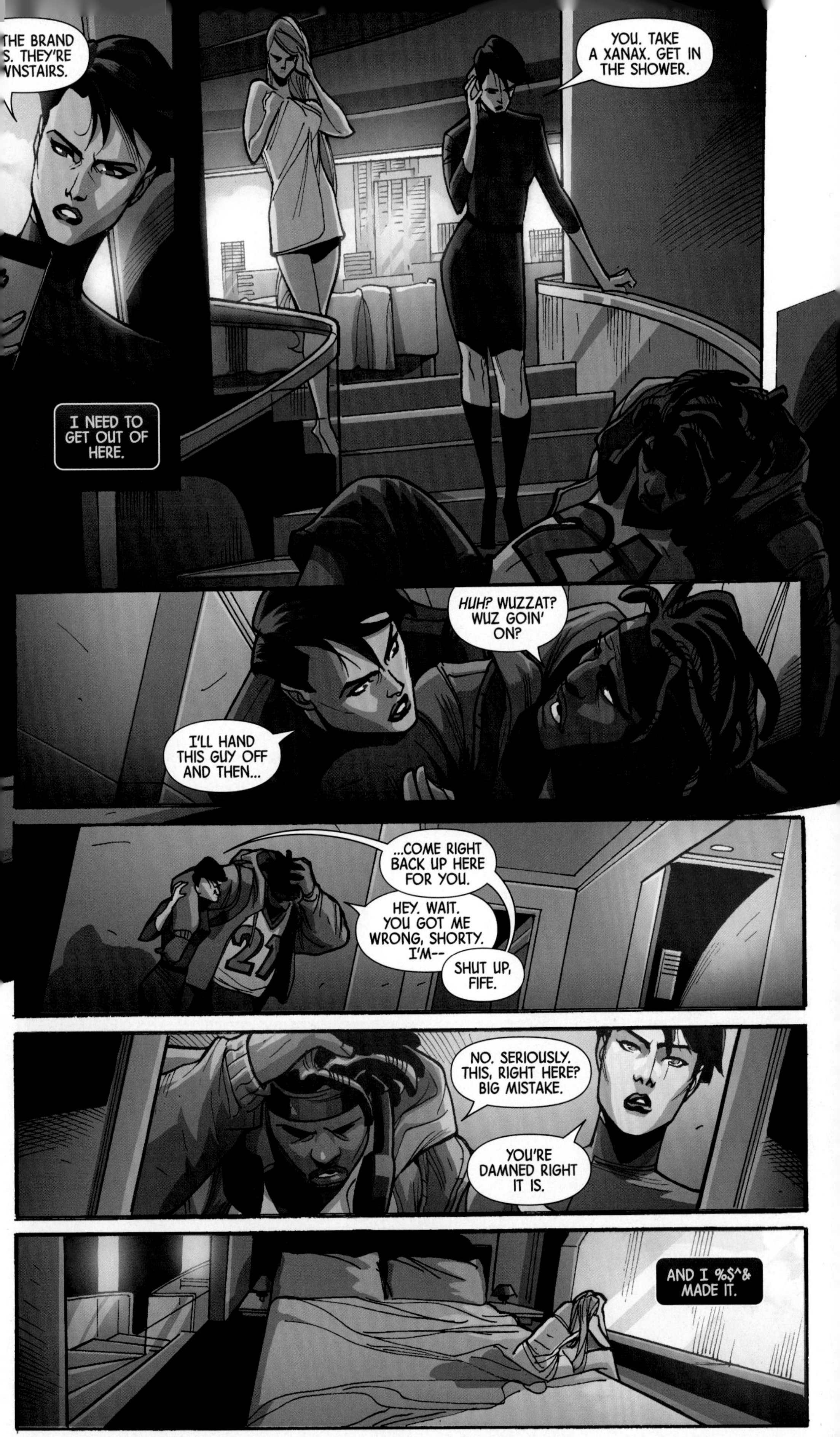
THE BRAND
S. THEY'RE
WNSTAIRS.
YOU. TAKE A XANAX. GET IN THE SHOWER.
I NEED TO GET OUT OF HERE.
HUH? WUZZAT? WUZ GOIN' ON?
I'LL HAND THIS GUY OFF AND THEN...
...COME RIGHT BACK UP HERE FOR YOU.
HEY. WAIT. YOU GOT ME WRONG, SHORTY. I'M--
SHUT UP, FIFE.
NO. SERIOUSLY. THIS, RIGHT HERE? BIG MISTAKE.
YOU'RE DAMNED RIGHT IT IS.
AND I %$^& MADE IT.

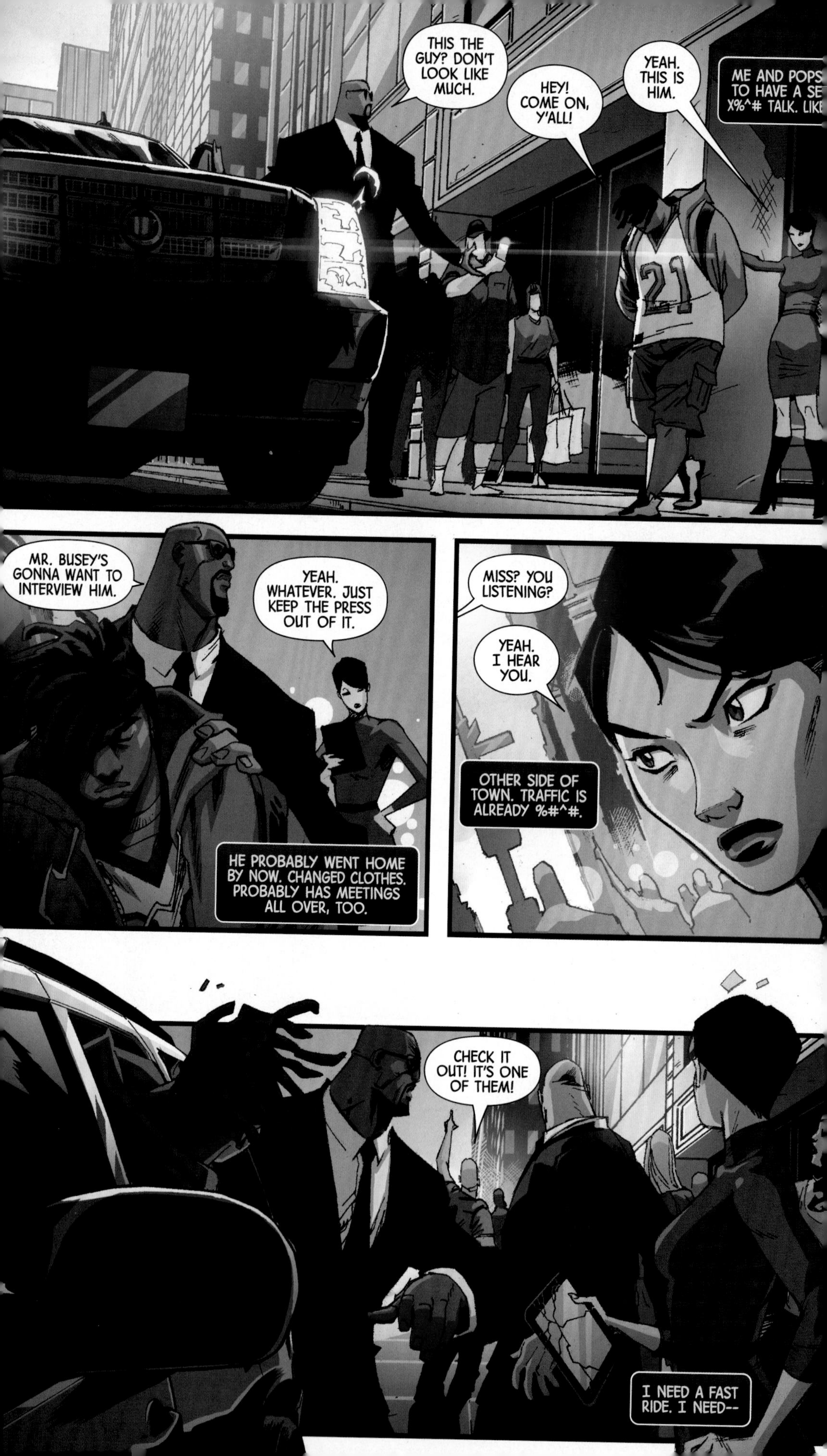
THIS THE GUY? DON'T LOOK LIKE MUCH.
HEY! COME ON, Y'ALL!
YEAH. THIS IS HIM.
ME AND POPS TO HAVE A SE X%^# TALK. LIK
MR. BUSEY'S GONNA WANT TO INTERVIEW HIM.
YEAH. WHATEVER. JUST KEEP THE PRESS OUT OF IT.
HE PROBABLY WENT HOME BY NOW. CHANGED CLOTHES. PROBABLY HAS MEETINGS ALL OVER, TOO.
MISS? YOU LISTENING?
YEAH. I HEAR YOU.
OTHER SIDE OF TOWN. TRAFFIC IS ALREADY %#^#.
CHECK IT OUT! IT'S ONE OF THEM!
I NEED A FAST RIDE. I NEED--

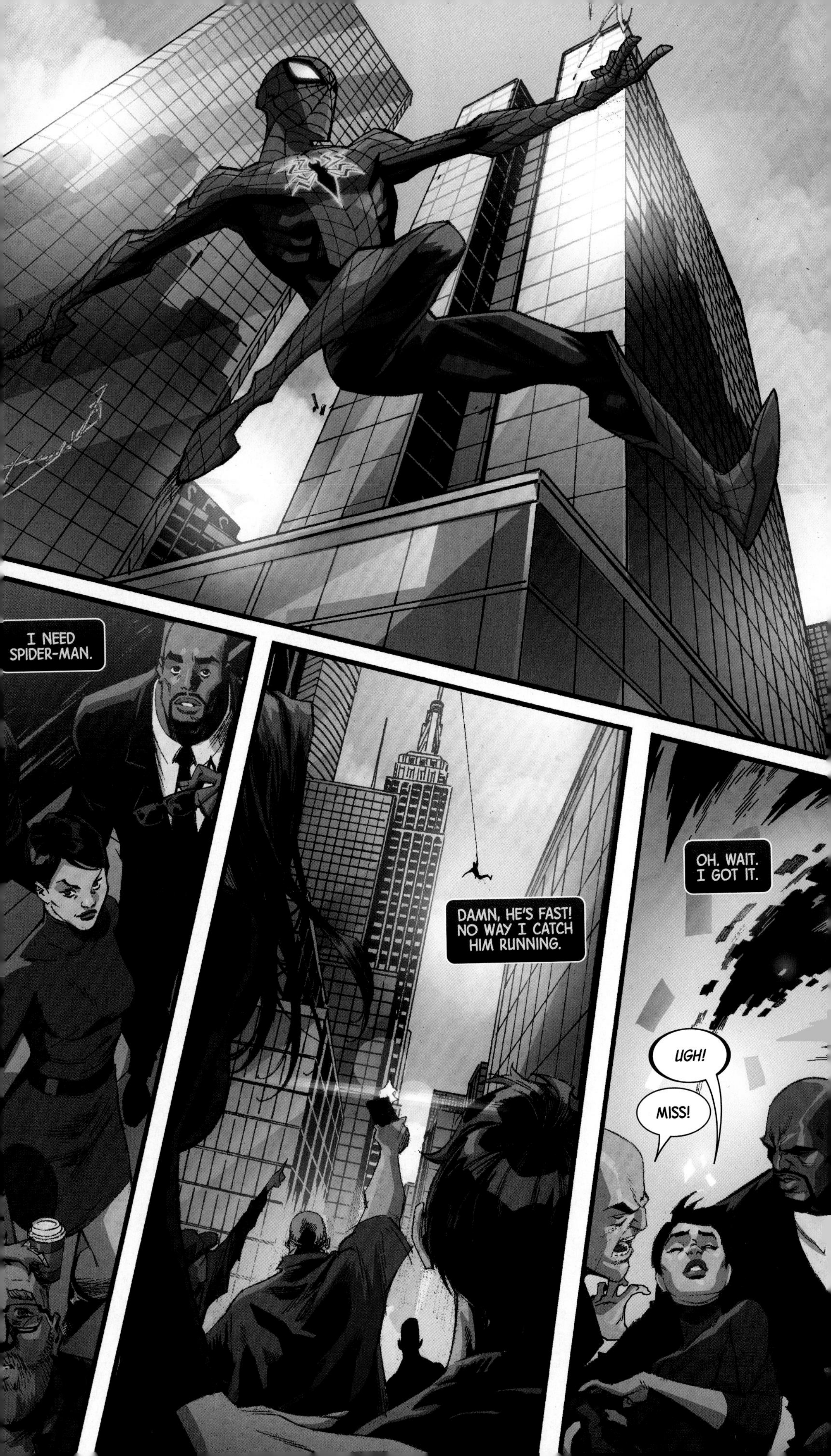
I NEED SPIDER-MAN.
DAMN, HE'S FAST! NO WAY I CATCH HIM RUNNING.
OH. WAIT. I GOT IT.
UGH!
MISS!

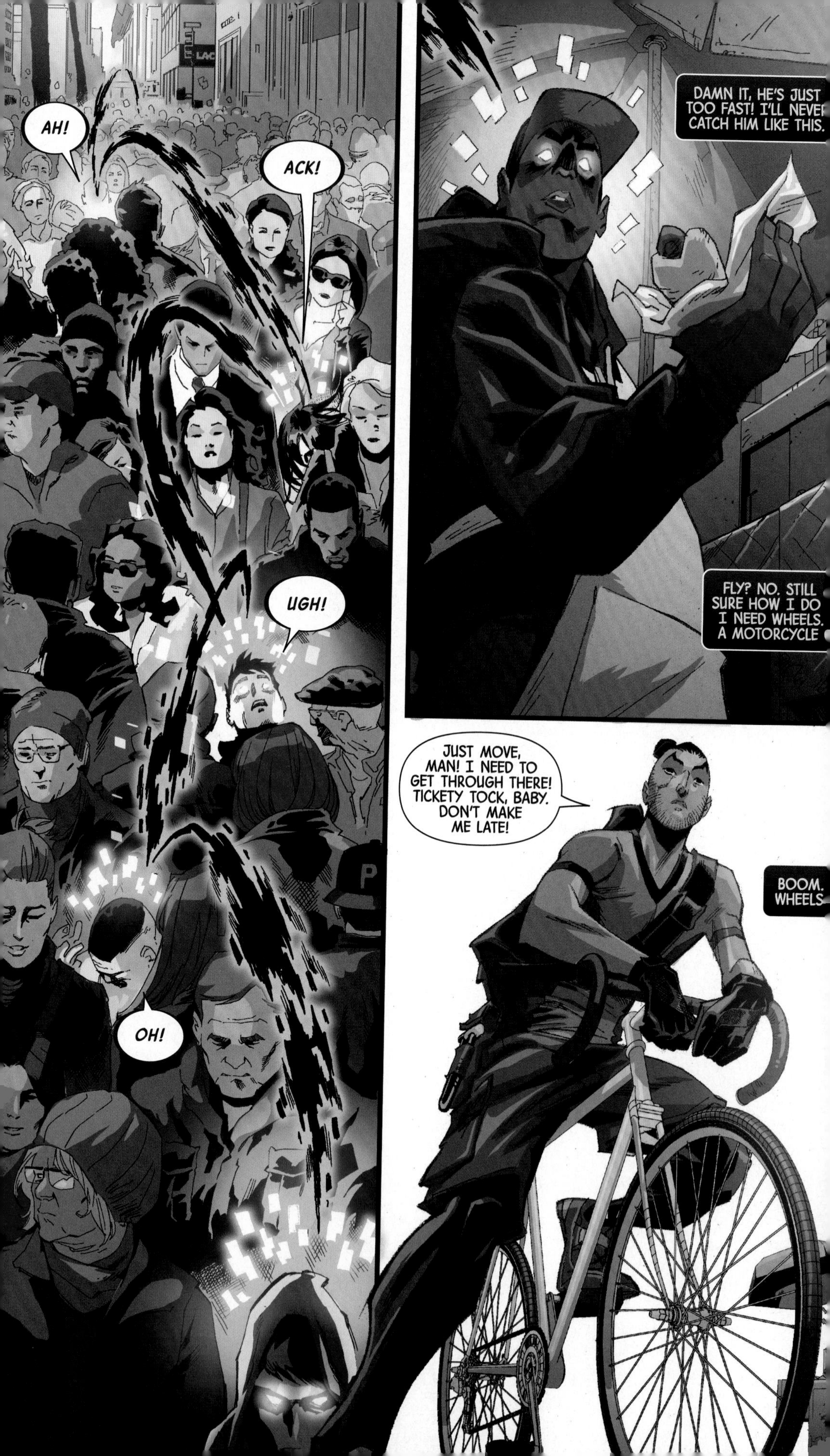
AH!
ACK!
UGH!
OH!
DAMN IT, HE'S JUST TOO FAST! I'LL NEVER CATCH HIM LIKE THIS.
FLY? NO. STILL SURE HOW I DO I NEED WHEELS. A MOTORCYCLE
JUST MOVE, MAN! I NEED TO GET THROUGH THERE! TICKETY TOCK, BABY. DON'T MAKE ME LATE!
BOOM. WHEELS

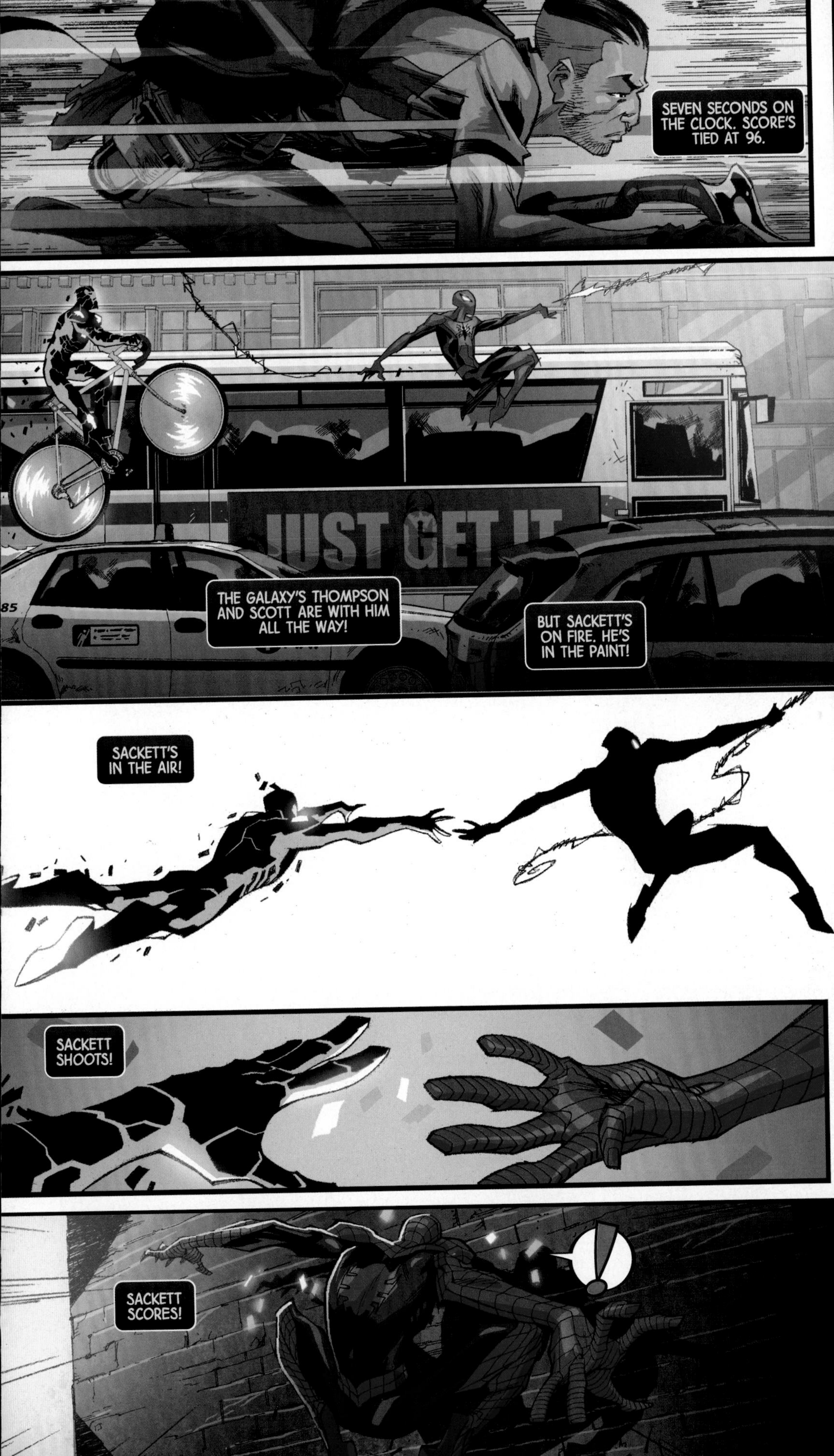
SEVEN SECONDS ON THE CLOCK. SCORE'S TIED AT 96.
JUST GET IT
THE GALAXY'S THOMPSON AND SCOTT ARE WITH HIM ALL THE WAY!
BUT SACKETT'S ON FIRE. HE'S IN THE PAINT!
SACKETT'S IN THE AIR!
SACKETT SHOOTS!
!
SACKETT SCORES!

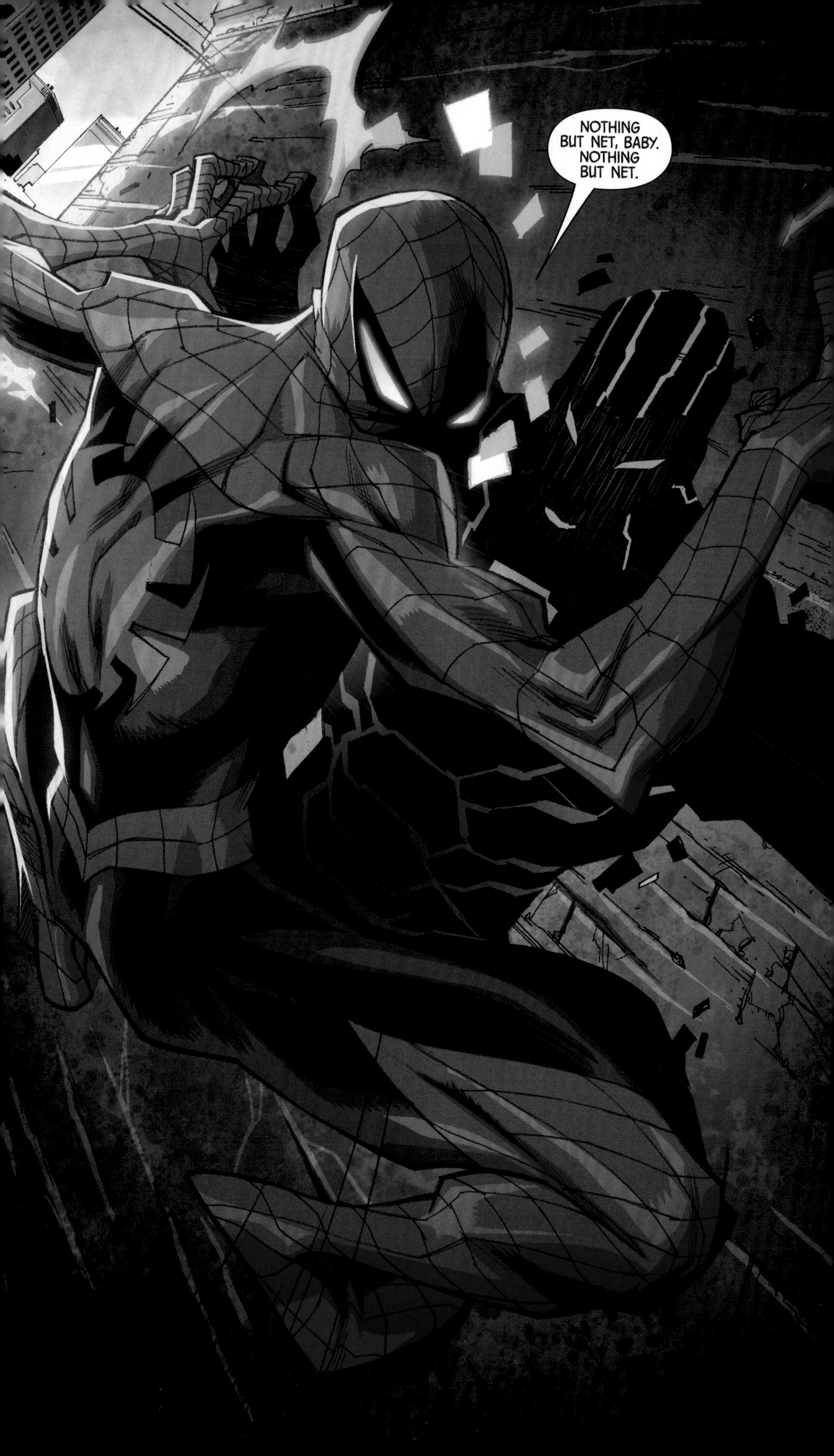
NOTHING BUT NET, BABY. NOTHING BUT NET.

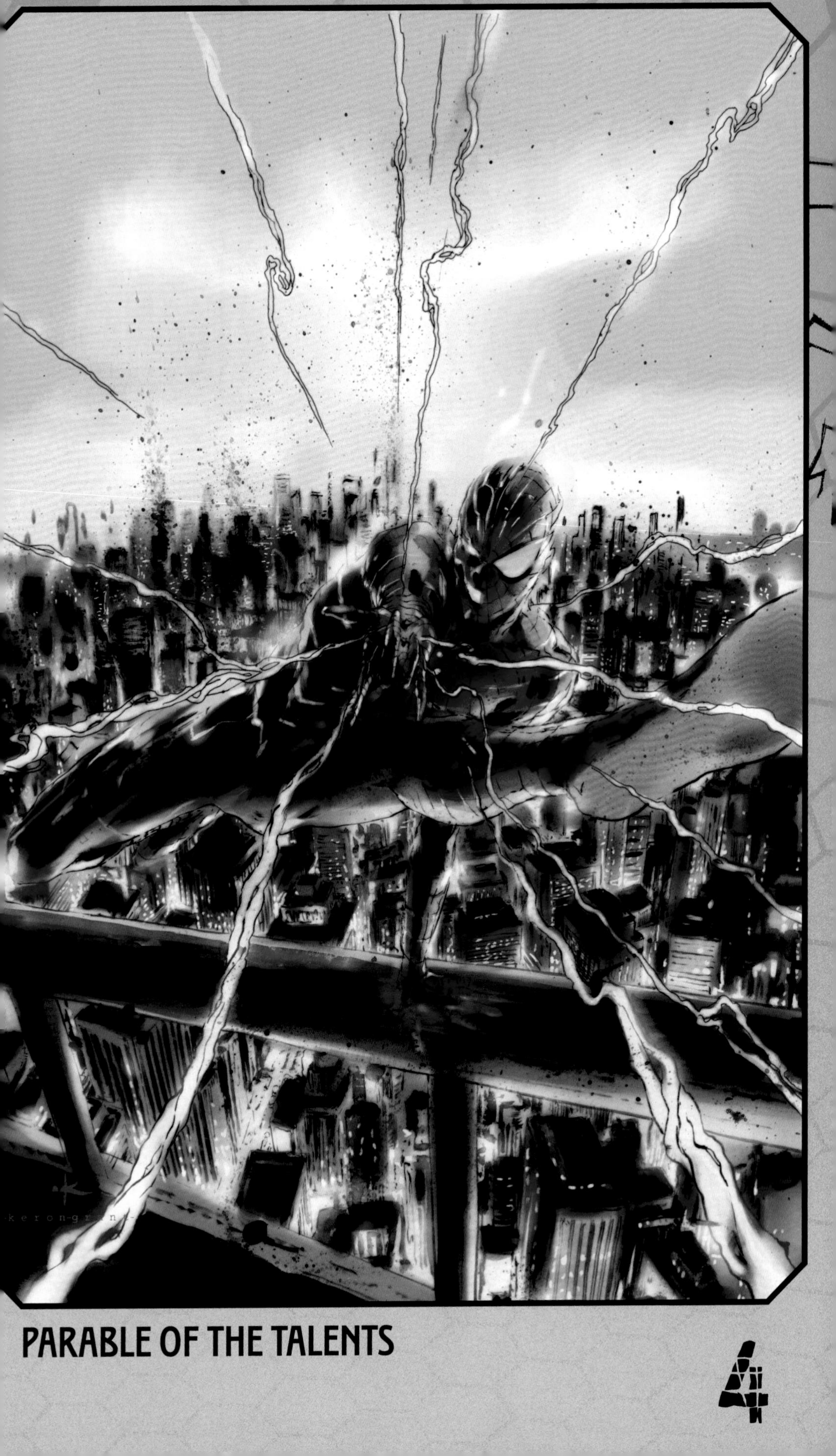

PARABLE OF THE TALENTS

4

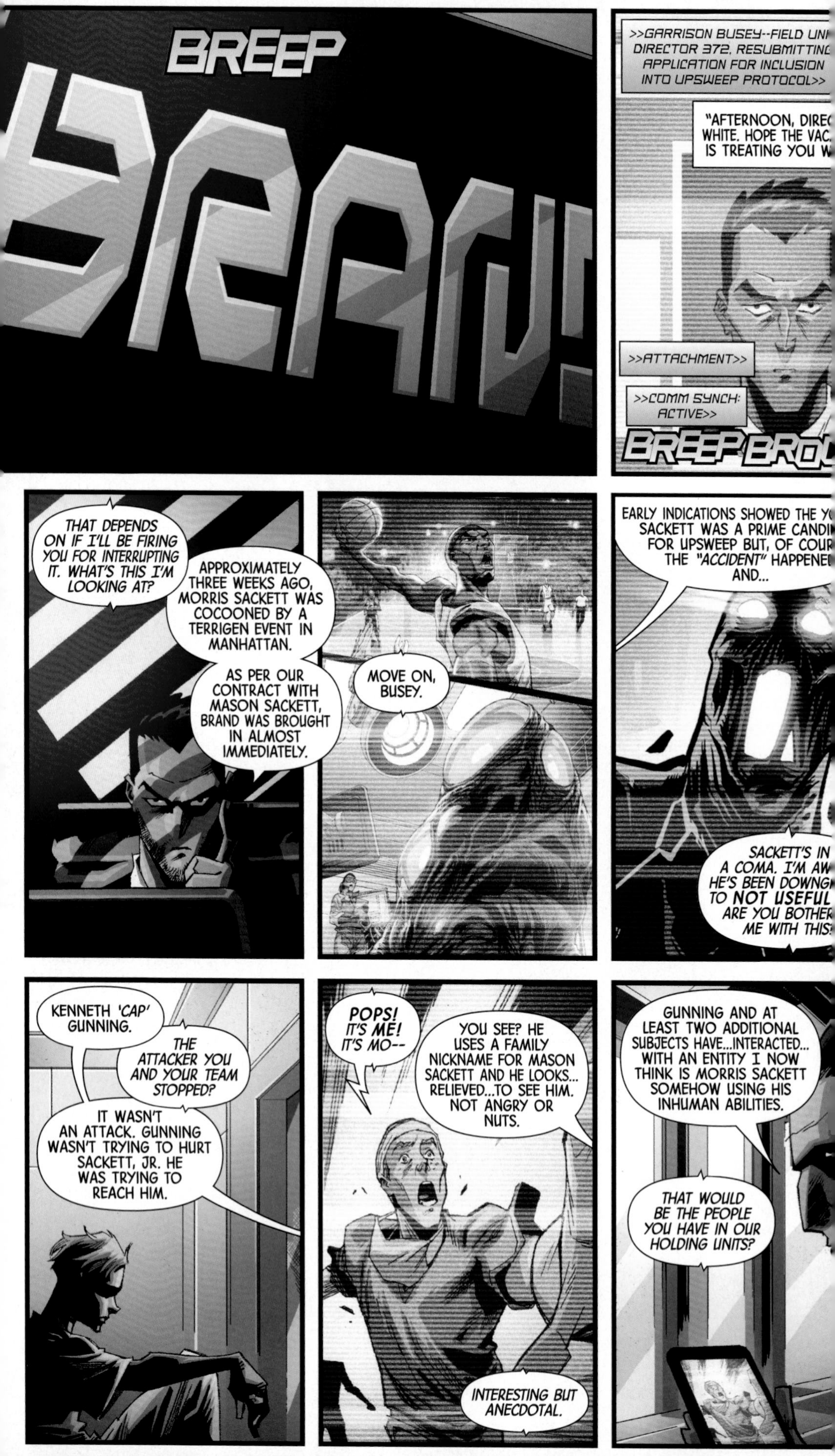
BREEP
>>GARRISON BUSEY--FIELD UNI
DIRECTOR 372, RESUBMITTING
APPLICATION FOR INCLUSION
INTO UPSWEEP PROTOCOL>>
"AFTERNOON, DIREC
WHITE. HOPE THE VAC.
IS TREATING YOU W
>>ATTACHMENT>>
>>COMM SYNCH: ACTIVE>>
BREEP BRO
THAT DEPENDS ON IF I'LL BE FIRING YOU FOR INTERRUPTING IT. WHAT'S THIS I'M LOOKING AT?
APPROXIMATELY THREE WEEKS AGO, MORRIS SACKETT WAS COCOONED BY A TERRIGEN EVENT IN MANHATTAN.
AS PER OUR CONTRACT WITH MASON SACKETT, BRAND WAS BROUGHT IN ALMOST IMMEDIATELY.
MOVE ON, BUSEY.
EARLY INDICATIONS SHOWED THE Y
SACKETT WAS A PRIME CANDI
FOR UPSWEEP BUT, OF COUR
THE "ACCIDENT" HAPPENE
AND...
SACKETT'S IN
A COMA. I'M AW
HE'S BEEN DOWNG
TO NOT USEFUL
ARE YOU BOTHER
ME WITH THIS
KENNETH 'CAP' GUNNING.
THE ATTACKER YOU AND YOUR TEAM STOPPED?
IT WASN'T AN ATTACK. GUNNING WASN'T TRYING TO HURT SACKETT, JR. HE WAS TRYING TO REACH HIM.
POPS! IT'S ME! IT'S MO--
YOU SEE? HE USES A FAMILY NICKNAME FOR MASON SACKETT AND HE LOOKS... RELIEVED...TO SEE HIM. NOT ANGRY OR NUTS.
INTERESTING BUT ANECDOTAL.
GUNNING AND AT LEAST TWO ADDITIONAL SUBJECTS HAVE...INTERACTED... WITH AN ENTITY I NOW THINK IS MORRIS SACKETT SOMEHOW USING HIS INHUMAN ABILITIES.
THAT WOULD BE THE PEOPLE YOU HAVE IN OUR HOLDING UNITS?

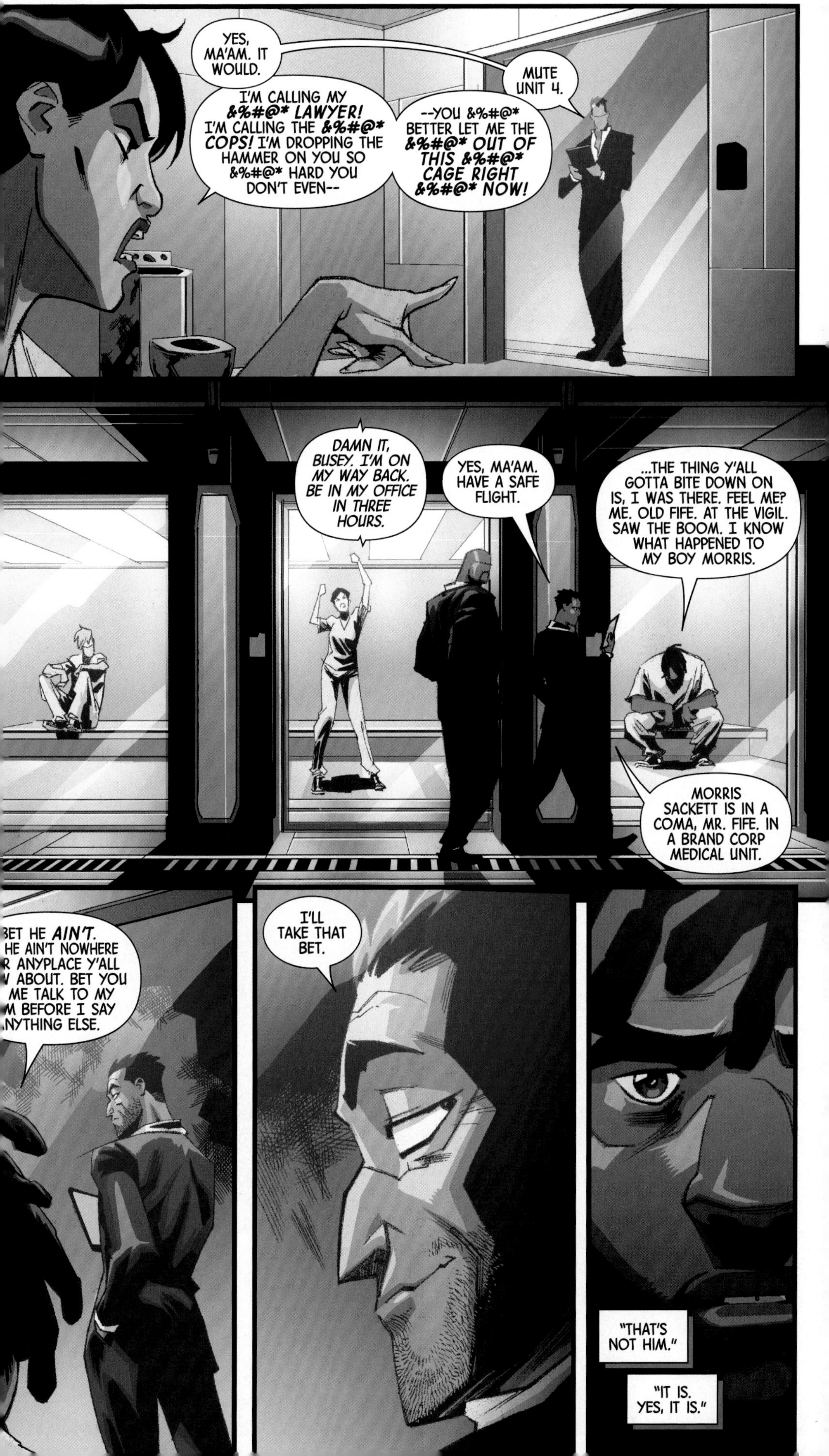

YES, MA'AM. IT WOULD.
MUTE UNIT 4.
I'M CALLING MY &%#@* LAWYER! I'M CALLING THE &%#@* COPS! I'M DROPPING THE HAMMER ON YOU SO &%#@* HARD YOU DON'T EVEN--
--YOU &%#@* BETTER LET ME THE &%#@* OUT OF THIS &%#@* CAGE RIGHT &%#@* NOW!
DAMN IT, BUSEY. I'M ON MY WAY BACK. BE IN MY OFFICE IN THREE HOURS.
YES, MA'AM. HAVE A SAFE FLIGHT.
...THE THING Y'ALL GOTTA BITE DOWN ON IS, I WAS THERE. FEEL ME? ME. OLD FIFE. AT THE VIGIL. SAW THE BOOM. I KNOW WHAT HAPPENED TO MY BOY MORRIS.
MORRIS SACKETT IS IN A COMA, MR. FIFE. IN A BRAND CORP MEDICAL UNIT.
BET HE AIN'T. HE AIN'T NOWHERE ANYPLACE Y'ALL ABOUT. BET YOU ME TALK TO MY M BEFORE I SAY ANYTHING ELSE.
I'LL TAKE THAT BET.
"THAT'S NOT HIM."
"IT IS. YES, IT IS."

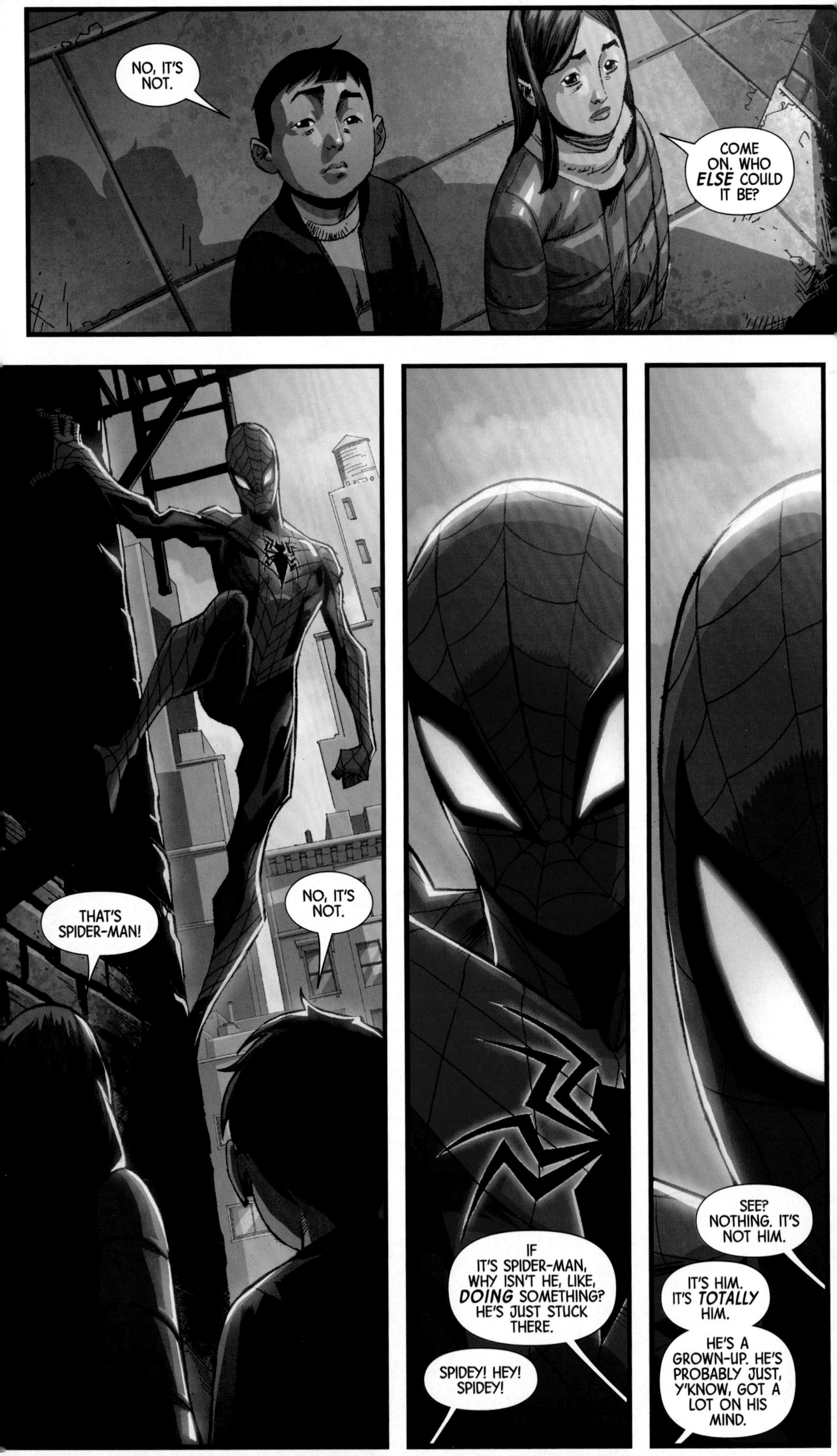
NO, IT'S NOT.
COME ON. WHO ELSE COULD IT BE?
THAT'S SPIDER-MAN!
NO, IT'S NOT.
IF IT'S SPIDER-MAN, WHY ISN'T HE, LIKE, DOING SOMETHING? HE'S JUST STUCK THERE.
SPIDEY! HEY! SPIDEY!
SEE? NOTHING. IT'S NOT HIM.
IT'S HIM. IT'S TOTALLY HIM.
HE'S A GROWN-UP. HE'S PROBABLY JUST, Y'KNOW, GOT A LOT ON HIS MIND.

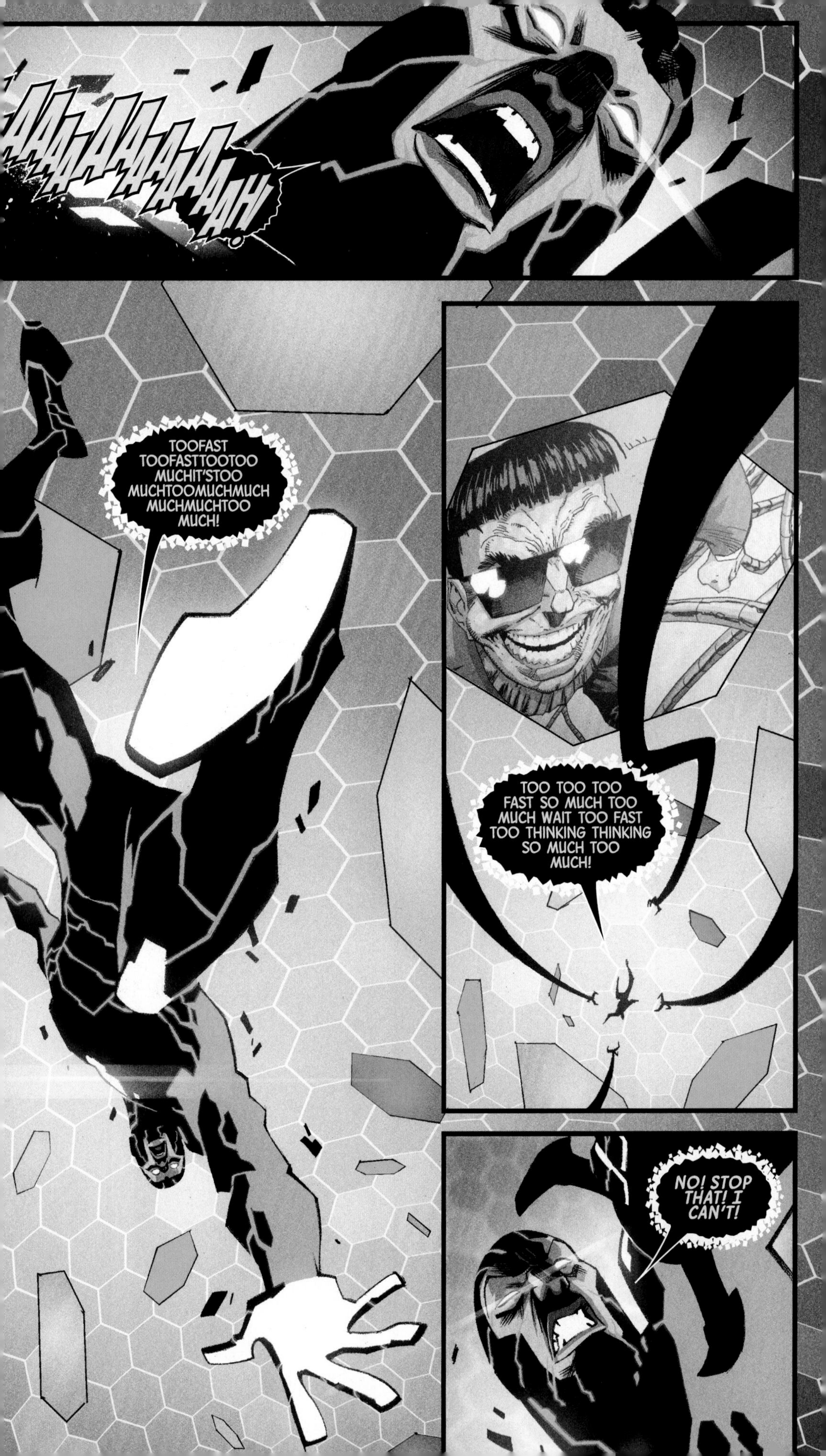
AAAAAAAAAAAAAAAH!
TOOFAST TOOFASTTOOTOO MUCHIT'STOO MUCHTOOMUCHMUCH MUCHMUCHTOO MUCH!
TOO TOO TOO FAST SO MUCH TOO MUCH WAIT TOO FAST TOO THINKING THINKING SO MUCH TOO MUCH!
NO! STOP THAT! I CAN'T!

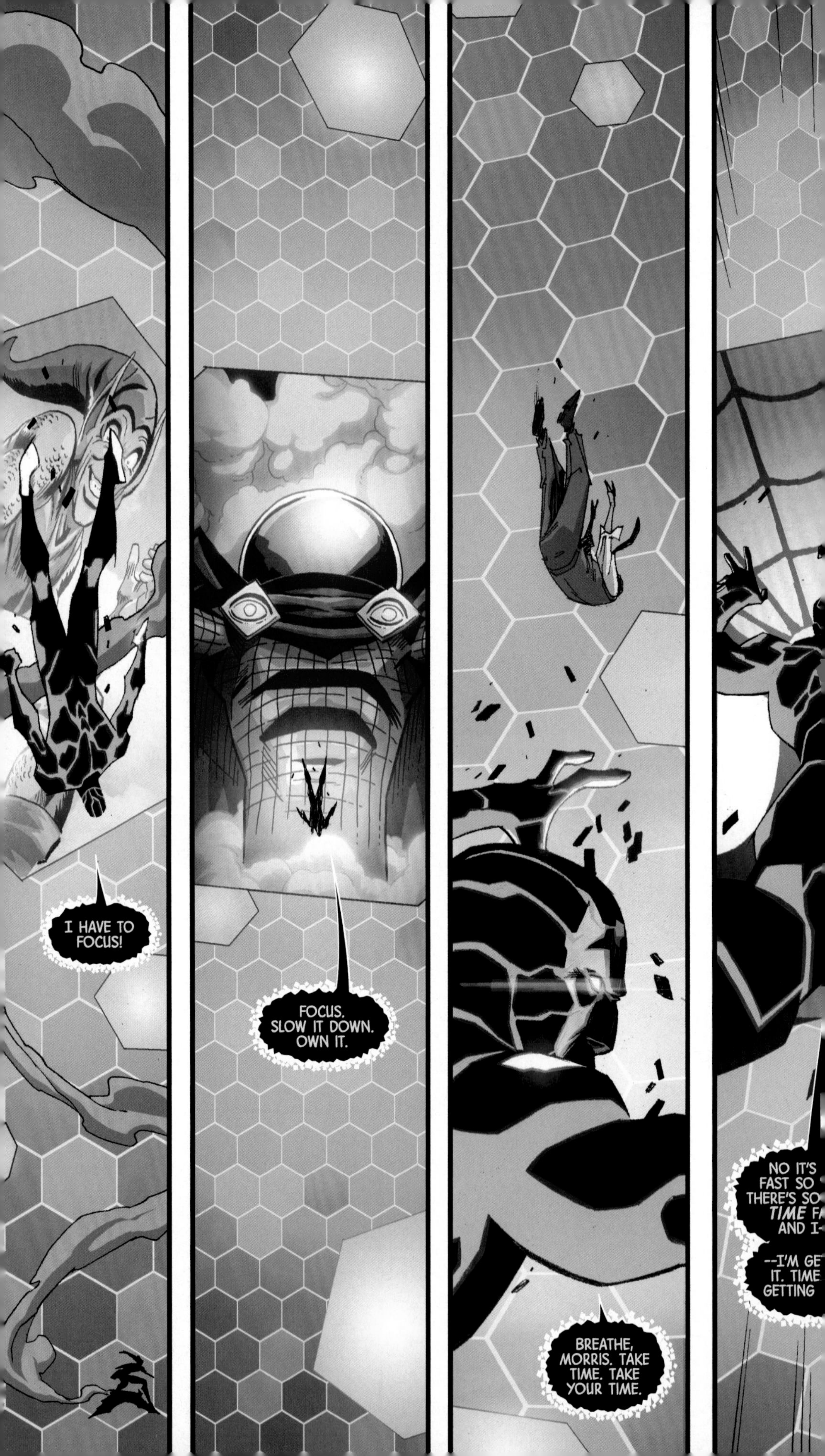
I HAVE TO FOCUS!
FOCUS. SLOW IT DOWN. OWN IT.
BREATHE, MORRIS. TAKE TIME. TAKE YOUR TIME.
NO IT'S
FAST SO
THERE'S SO
TIME
AND I
--I'M GE
IT. TIME
GETTING

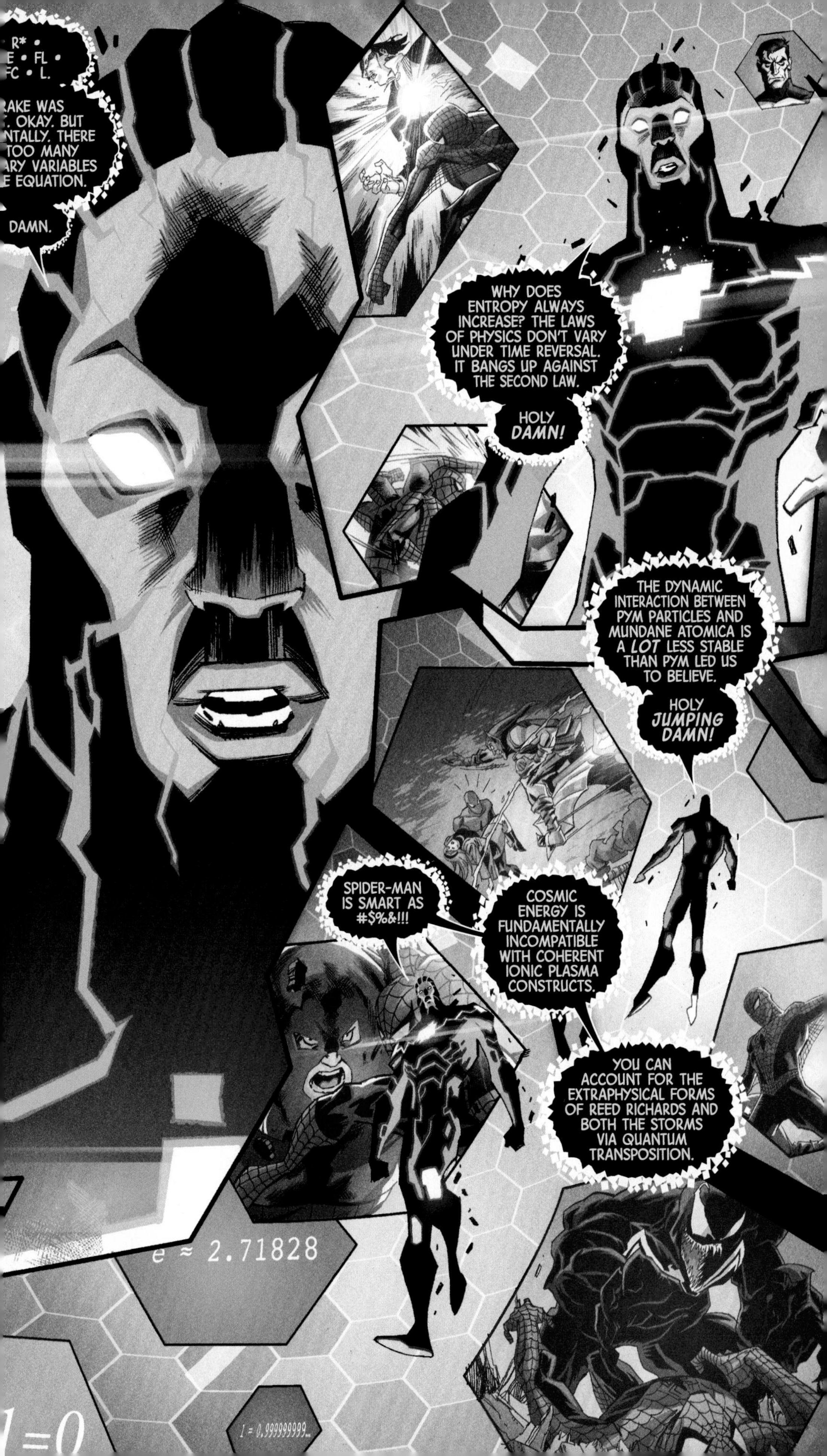

R* • E • FL • FC • L.
RAKE WAS . OKAY. BUT NTALLY. THERE TOO MANY ARY VARIABLES E EQUATION.
DAMN.
WHY DOES ENTROPY ALWAYS INCREASE? THE LAWS OF PHYSICS DON'T VARY UNDER TIME REVERSAL. IT BANGS UP AGAINST THE SECOND LAW.
HOLY *DAMN!*
THE DYNAMIC INTERACTION BETWEEN PYM PARTICLES AND MUNDANE ATOMICA IS A *LOT* LESS STABLE THAN PYM LED US TO BELIEVE.
HOLY *JUMPING DAMN!*
SPIDER-MAN IS SMART AS #$%&!!!
COSMIC ENERGY IS FUNDAMENTALLY INCOMPATIBLE WITH COHERENT IONIC PLASMA CONSTRUCTS.
YOU CAN ACCOUNT FOR THE EXTRAPHYSICAL FORMS OF REED RICHARDS AND BOTH THE STORMS VIA QUANTUM TRANSPOSITION.
e ≈ 2.71828
1=0
1 = 0.999999999...

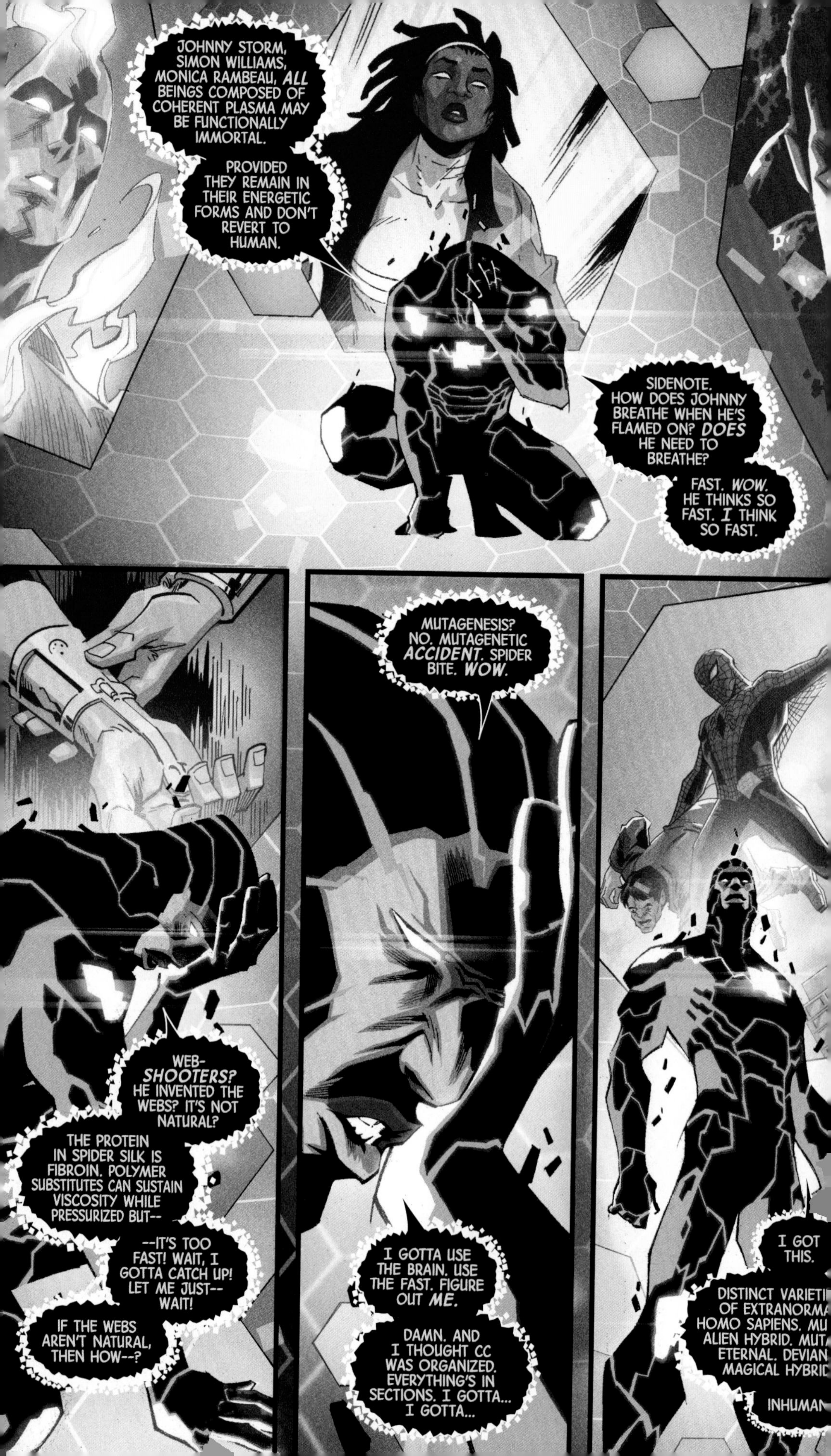
JOHNNY STORM, SIMON WILLIAMS, MONICA RAMBEAU, ALL BEINGS COMPOSED OF COHERENT PLASMA MAY BE FUNCTIONALLY IMMORTAL.
PROVIDED THEY REMAIN IN THEIR ENERGETIC FORMS AND DON'T REVERT TO HUMAN.
SIDENOTE. HOW DOES JOHNNY BREATHE WHEN HE'S FLAMED ON? DOES HE NEED TO BREATHE?
FAST. WOW. HE THINKS SO FAST. I THINK SO FAST.
WEB-SHOOTERS? HE INVENTED THE WEBS? IT'S NOT NATURAL?
THE PROTEIN IN SPIDER SILK IS FIBROIN. POLYMER SUBSTITUTES CAN SUSTAIN VISCOSITY WHILE PRESSURIZED BUT--
--IT'S TOO FAST! WAIT, I GOTTA CATCH UP! LET ME JUST-- WAIT!
IF THE WEBS AREN'T NATURAL, THEN HOW--?
MUTAGENESIS? NO. MUTAGENETIC ACCIDENT. SPIDER BITE. WOW.
I GOTTA USE THE BRAIN. USE THE FAST. FIGURE OUT ME.
DAMN. AND I THOUGHT CC WAS ORGANIZED. EVERYTHING'S IN SECTIONS. I GOTTA... I GOTTA...
I GOT THIS.
DISTINCT VARIETI OF EXTRANORMA HOMO SAPIENS. MU ALIEN HYBRID. MUT ETERNAL. DEVIAN MAGICAL HYBRI
INHUMAN

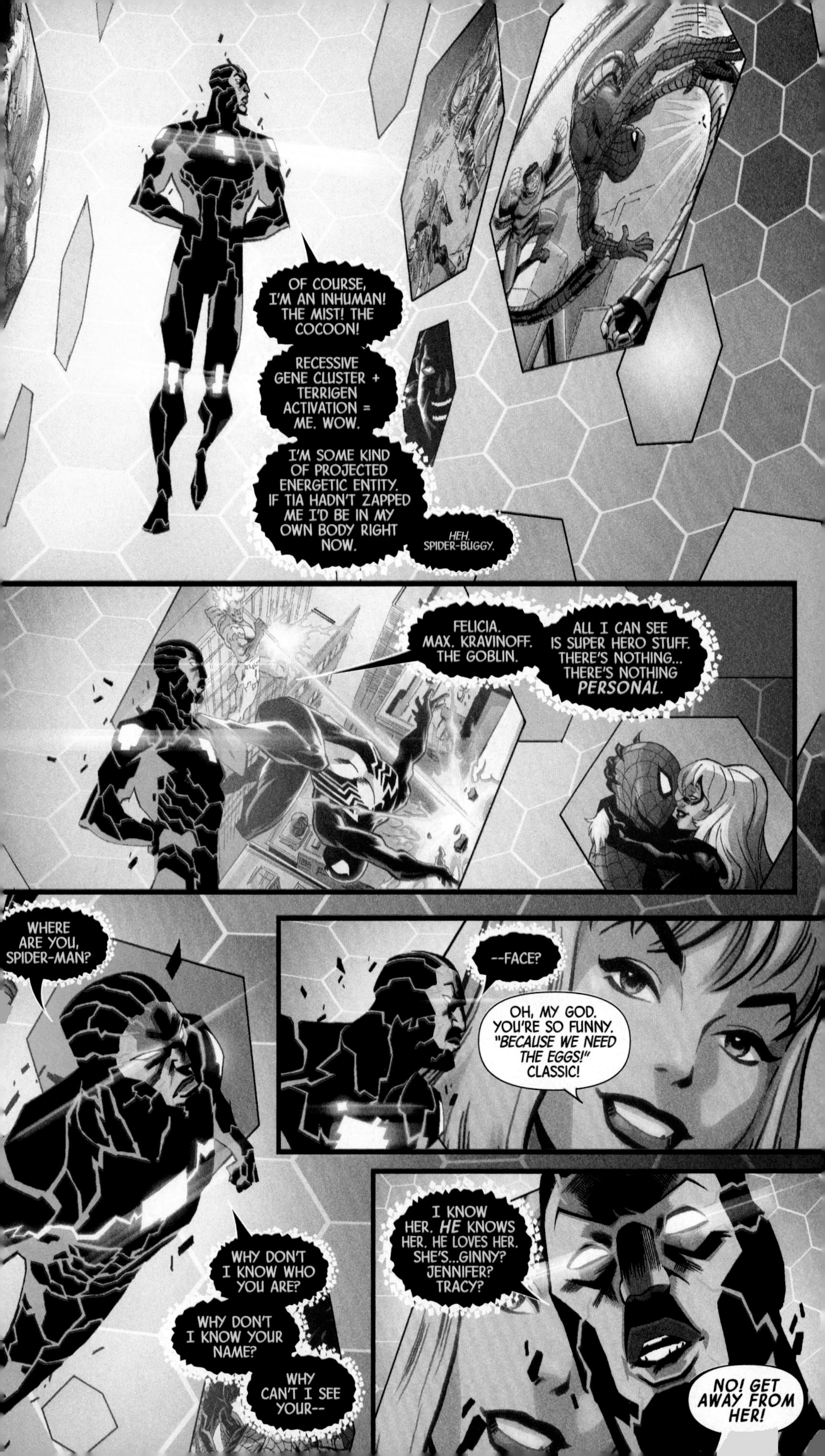

OF COURSE, I'M AN INHUMAN! THE MIST! THE COCOON!
RECESSIVE GENE CLUSTER + TERRIGEN ACTIVATION = ME. WOW.
I'M SOME KIND OF PROJECTED ENERGETIC ENTITY. IF TIA HADN'T ZAPPED ME I'D BE IN MY OWN BODY RIGHT NOW.
HEH. SPIDER-BUGGY.
FELICIA. MAX. KRAVINOFF. THE GOBLIN.
ALL I CAN SEE IS SUPER HERO STUFF. THERE'S NOTHING... THERE'S NOTHING *PERSONAL*.
WHERE ARE YOU, SPIDER-MAN?
WHY DON'T I KNOW WHO YOU ARE?
WHY DON'T I KNOW YOUR NAME?
WHY CAN'T I SEE YOUR--
--FACE?
OH, MY GOD. YOU'RE SO FUNNY. *"BECAUSE WE NEED THE EGGS!"* CLASSIC!
I KNOW HER. *HE* KNOWS HER. HE LOVES HER. SHE'S...GINNY? JENNIFER? TRACY?
NO! GET AWAY FROM HER!

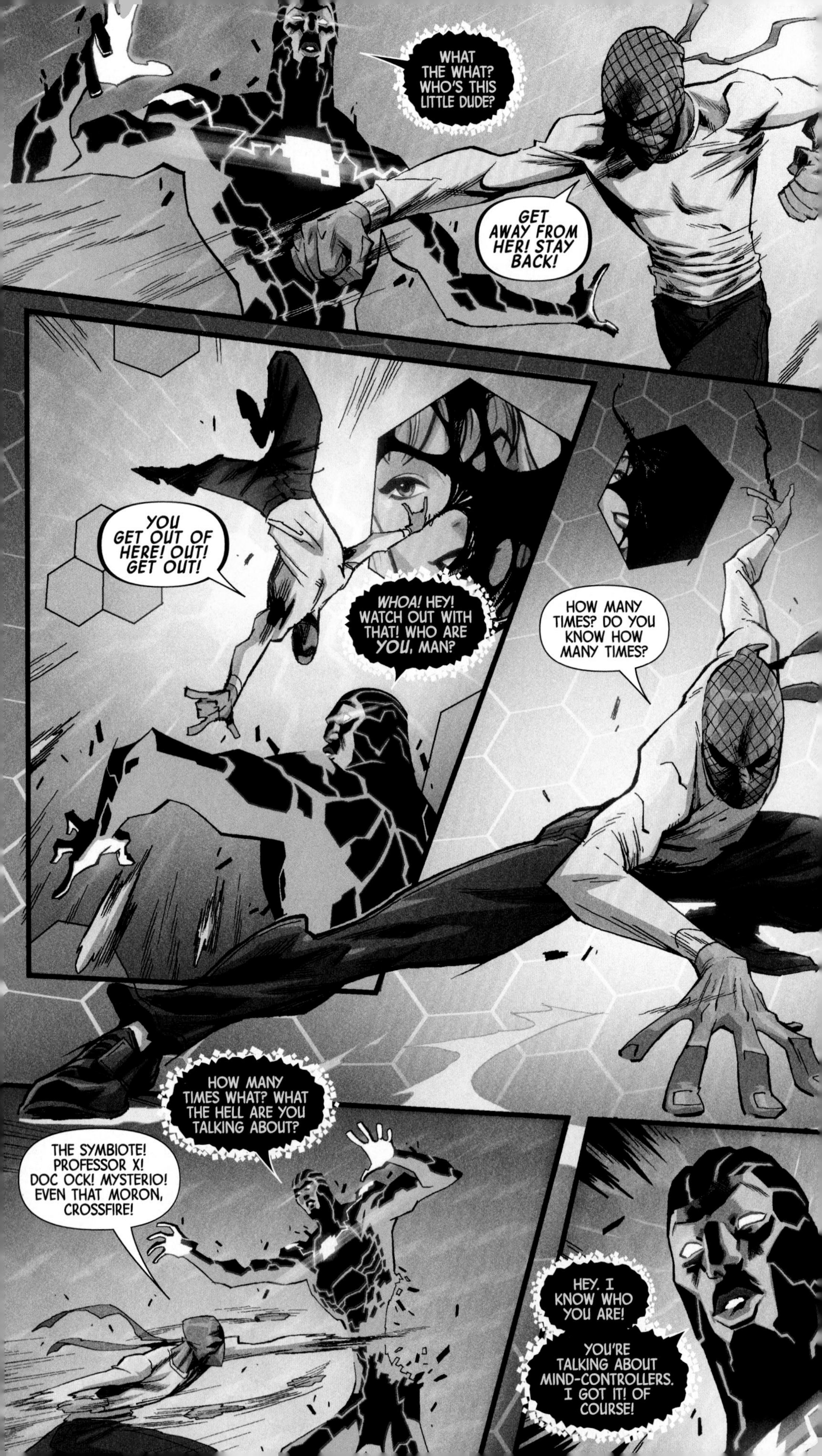

WHAT THE WHAT? WHO'S THIS LITTLE DUDE?
GET AWAY FROM HER! STAY BACK!
YOU GET OUT OF HERE! OUT! GET OUT!
WHOA! HEY! WATCH OUT WITH THAT! WHO ARE YOU, MAN?
HOW MANY TIMES? DO YOU KNOW HOW MANY TIMES?
HOW MANY TIMES WHAT? WHAT THE HELL ARE YOU TALKING ABOUT?
THE SYMBIOTE! PROFESSOR X! DOC OCK! MYSTERIO! EVEN THAT MORON, CROSSFIRE!
HEY. I KNOW WHO YOU ARE!
YOU'RE TALKING ABOUT MIND-CONTROLLERS. I GOT IT! OF COURSE!

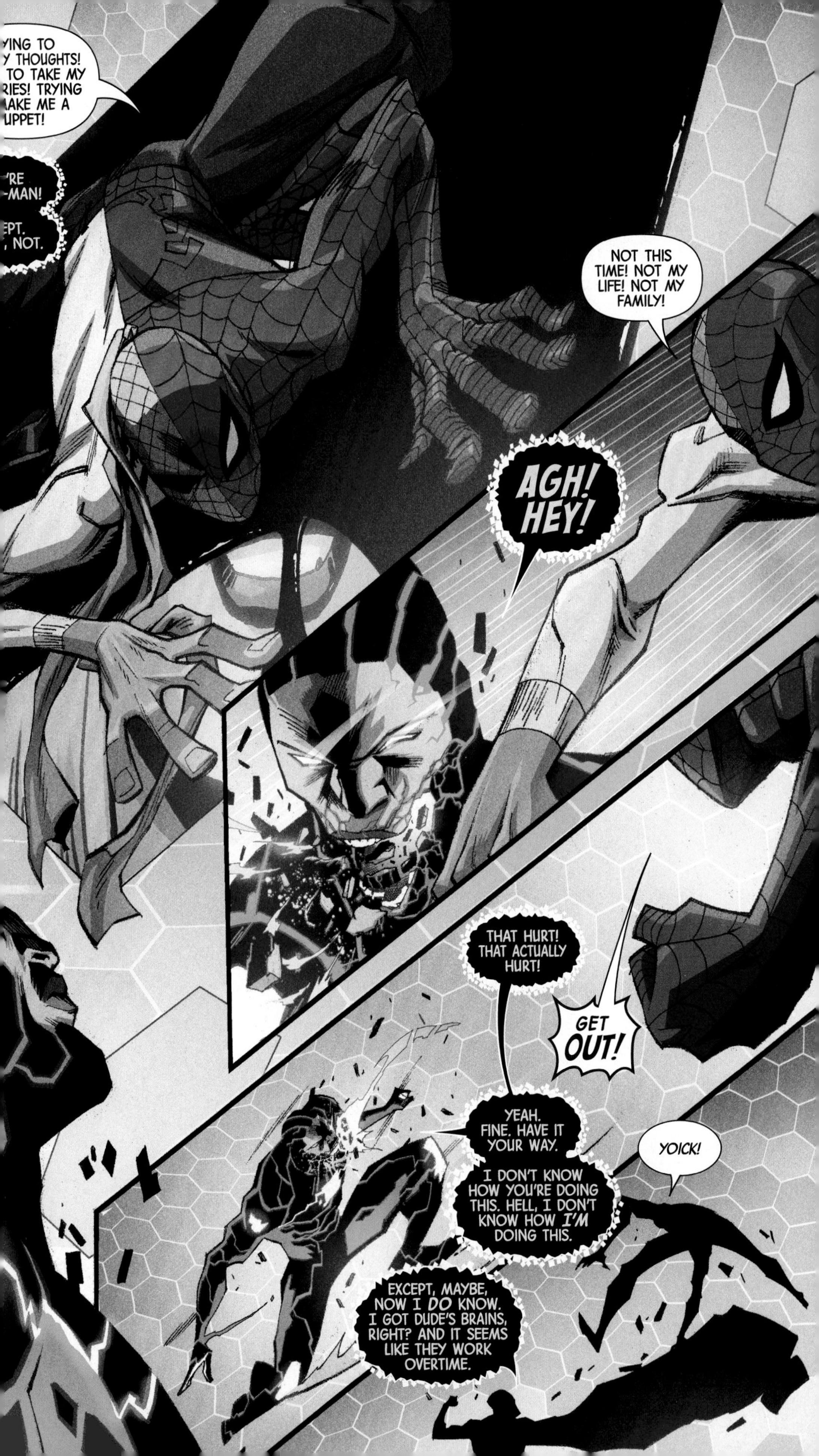

YING TO Y THOUGHTS! TO TAKE MY RIES! TRYING AKE ME A UPPET!
'RE -MAN!
EPT. , NOT.
NOT THIS TIME! NOT MY LIFE! NOT MY FAMILY!
AGH! HEY!
THAT HURT! THAT ACTUALLY HURT!
GET OUT!
YEAH. FINE. HAVE IT YOUR WAY.
I DON'T KNOW HOW YOU'RE DOING THIS. HELL, I DON'T KNOW HOW *I'M* DOING THIS.
YOICK!
EXCEPT, MAYBE, NOW I *DO* KNOW. I GOT DUDE'S BRAINS, RIGHT? AND IT SEEMS LIKE THEY WORK OVERTIME.

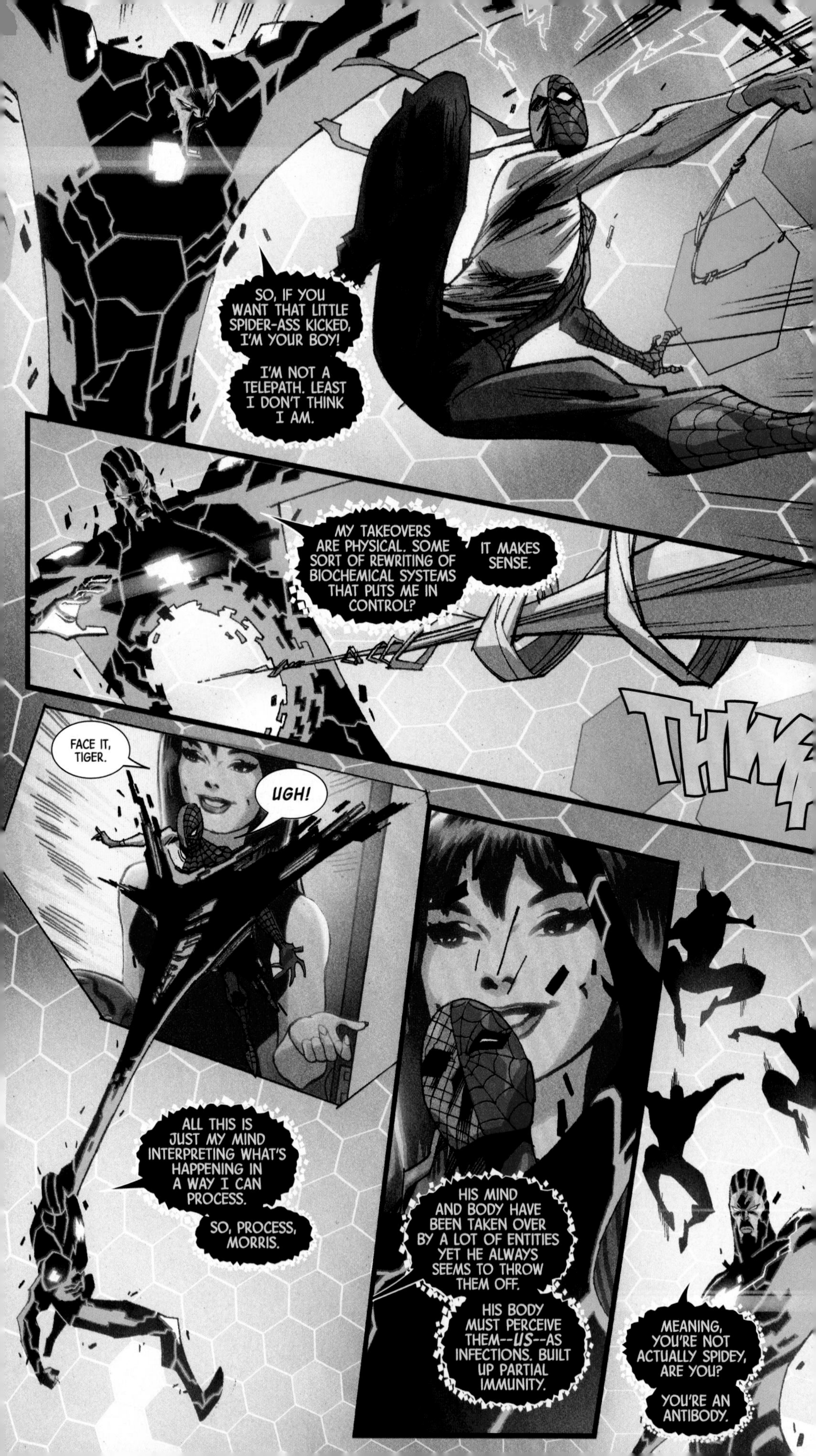
SO, IF YOU WANT THAT LITTLE SPIDER-ASS KICKED, I'M YOUR BOY!
I'M NOT A TELEPATH. LEAST I DON'T THINK I AM.
MY TAKEOVERS ARE PHYSICAL. SOME SORT OF REWRITING OF BIOCHEMICAL SYSTEMS THAT PUTS ME IN CONTROL?
IT MAKES SENSE.
THWK
FACE IT, TIGER.
UGH!
ALL THIS IS JUST MY MIND INTERPRETING WHAT'S HAPPENING IN A WAY I CAN PROCESS.
SO, PROCESS, MORRIS.
HIS MIND AND BODY HAVE BEEN TAKEN OVER BY A LOT OF ENTITIES YET HE ALWAYS SEEMS TO THROW THEM OFF.
HIS BODY MUST PERCEIVE THEM--US--AS INFECTIONS. BUILT UP PARTIAL IMMUNITY.
MEANING, YOU'RE NOT ACTUALLY SPIDEY, ARE YOU?
YOU'RE AN ANTIBODY.

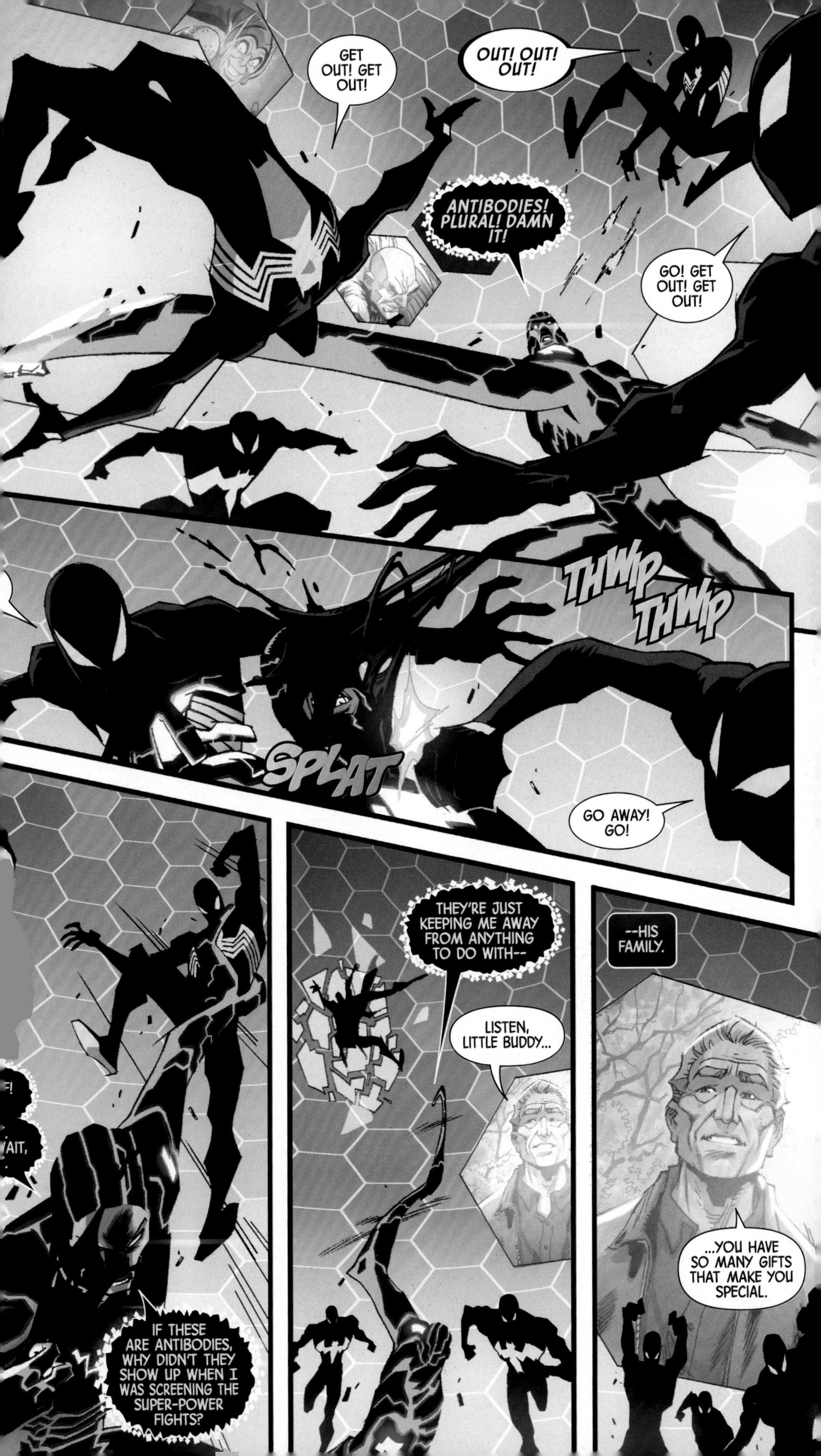
GET OUT! GET OUT!
OUT! OUT! OUT!
ANTIBODIES! PLURAL! DAMN IT!
GO! GET OUT! GET OUT!
THWIP THWIP
SPLAT
GO AWAY! GO!
IF THESE ARE ANTIBODIES, WHY DIDN'T THEY SHOW UP WHEN I WAS SCREENING THE SUPER-POWER FIGHTS?
THEY'RE JUST KEEPING ME AWAY FROM ANYTHING TO DO WITH--
LISTEN, LITTLE BUDDY...
--HIS FAMILY.
...YOU HAVE SO MANY GIFTS THAT MAKE YOU SPECIAL.

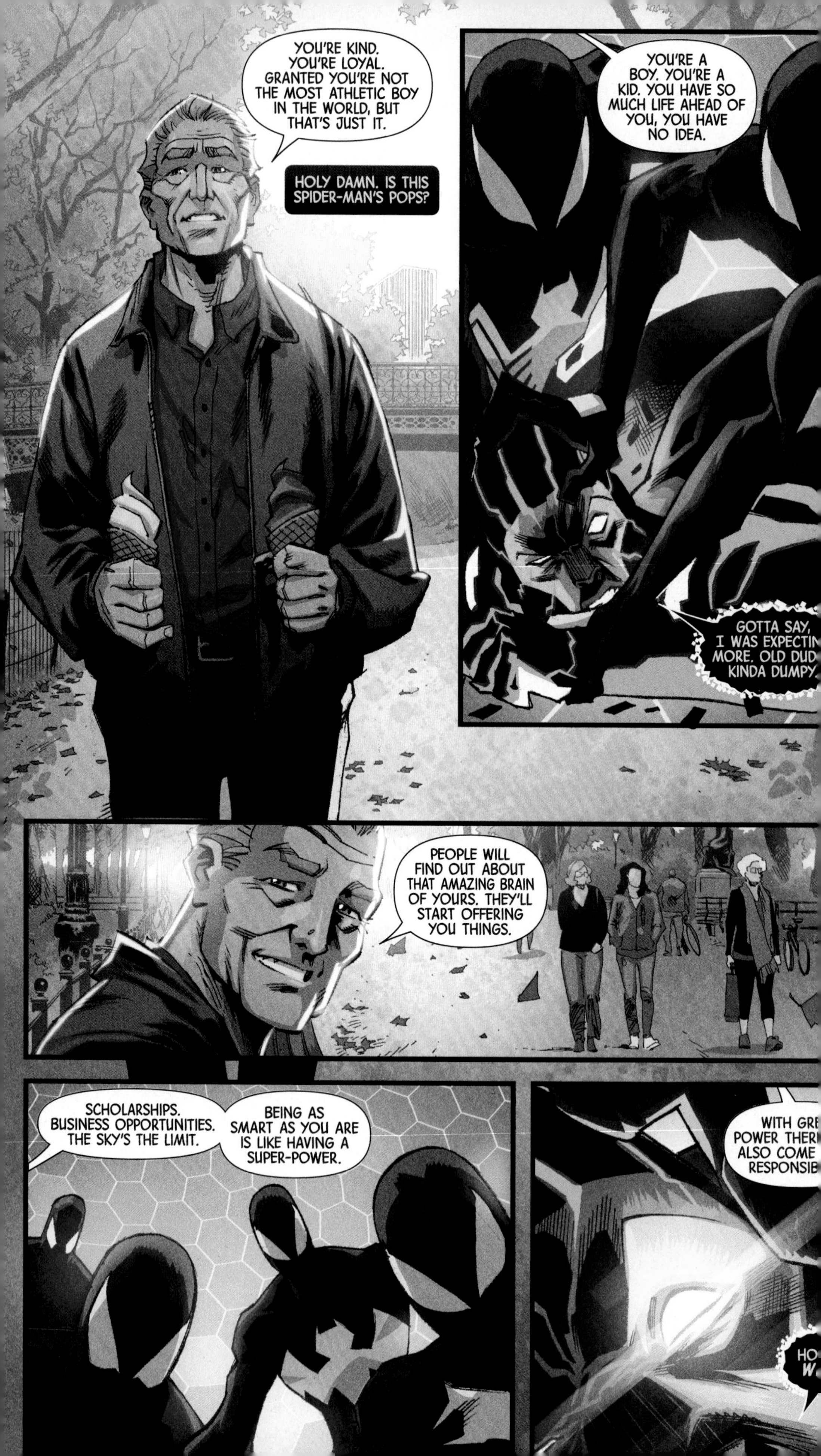
YOU'RE KIND. YOU'RE LOYAL. GRANTED YOU'RE NOT THE MOST ATHLETIC BOY IN THE WORLD, BUT THAT'S JUST IT.
HOLY DAMN. IS THIS SPIDER-MAN'S POPS?
YOU'RE A BOY. YOU'RE A KID. YOU HAVE SO MUCH LIFE AHEAD OF YOU, YOU HAVE NO IDEA.
GOTTA SAY, I WAS EXPECTIN MORE. OLD DUD KINDA DUMPY.
PEOPLE WILL FIND OUT ABOUT THAT AMAZING BRAIN OF YOURS. THEY'LL START OFFERING YOU THINGS.
SCHOLARSHIPS. BUSINESS OPPORTUNITIES. THE SKY'S THE LIMIT.
BEING AS SMART AS YOU ARE IS LIKE HAVING A SUPER-POWER.
WITH GR POWER THER ALSO COME RESPONSIB

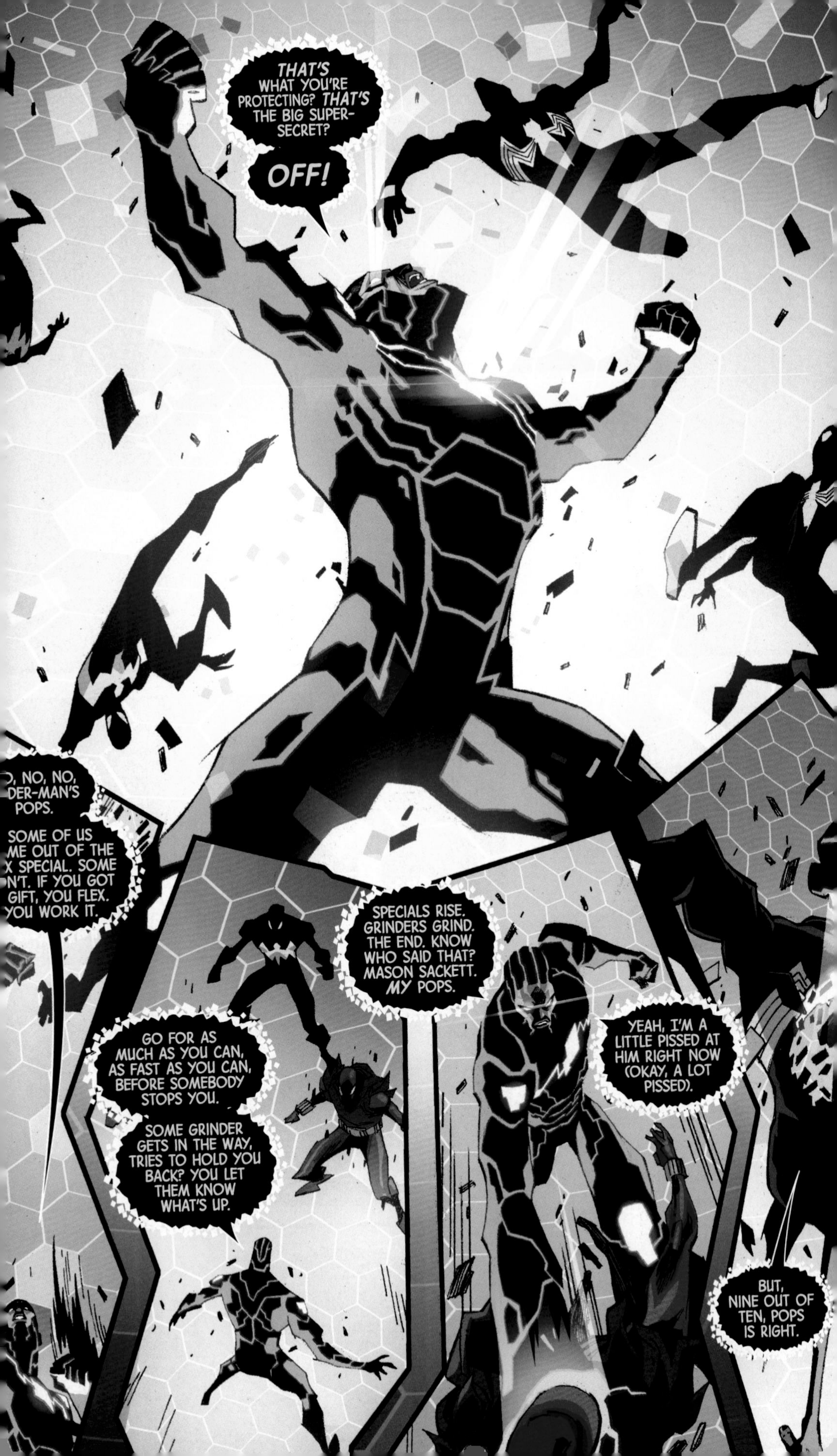
THAT'S WHAT YOU'RE PROTECTING? THAT'S THE BIG SUPER-SECRET?
OFF!
O, NO, NO, DER-MAN'S POPS.
SOME OF US ME OUT OF THE X SPECIAL. SOME N'T. IF YOU GOT GIFT, YOU FLEX. YOU WORK IT.
SPECIALS RISE. GRINDERS GRIND. THE END. KNOW WHO SAID THAT? MASON SACKETT. MY POPS.
GO FOR AS MUCH AS YOU CAN, AS FAST AS YOU CAN, BEFORE SOMEBODY STOPS YOU.
SOME GRINDER GETS IN THE WAY, TRIES TO HOLD YOU BACK? YOU LET THEM KNOW WHAT'S UP.
YEAH, I'M A LITTLE PISSED AT HIM RIGHT NOW (OKAY, A LOT PISSED).
BUT, NINE OUT OF TEN, POPS IS RIGHT.

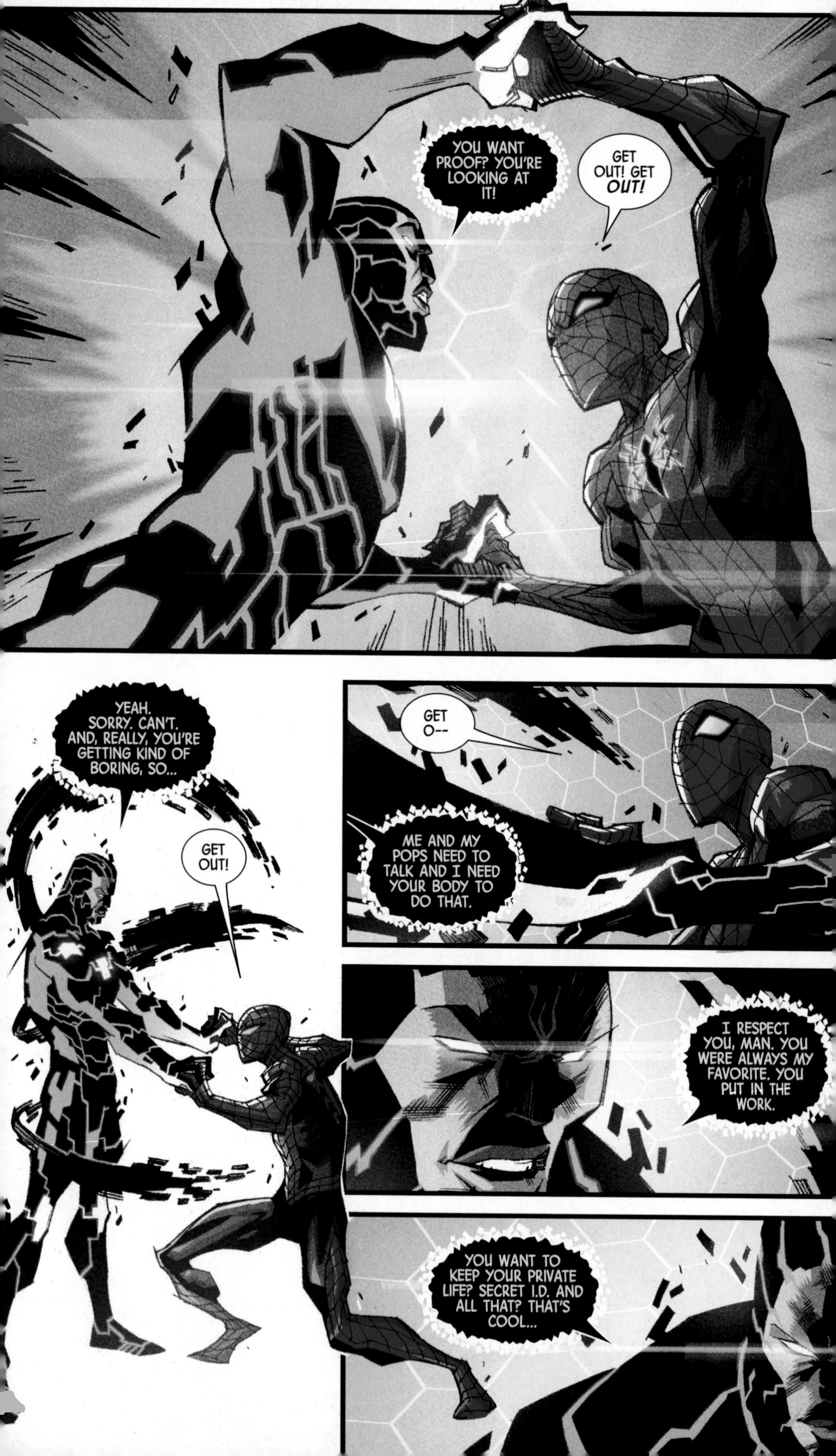

YOU WANT PROOF? YOU'RE LOOKING AT IT!
GET OUT! GET OUT!
YEAH. SORRY. CAN'T. AND, REALLY, YOU'RE GETTING KIND OF BORING, SO...
GET OUT!
GET O--
ME AND MY POPS NEED TO TALK AND I NEED YOUR BODY TO DO THAT.
I RESPECT YOU, MAN. YOU WERE ALWAYS MY FAVORITE. YOU PUT IN THE WORK.
YOU WANT TO KEEP YOUR PRIVATE LIFE? SECRET I.D. AND ALL THAT? THAT'S COOL...

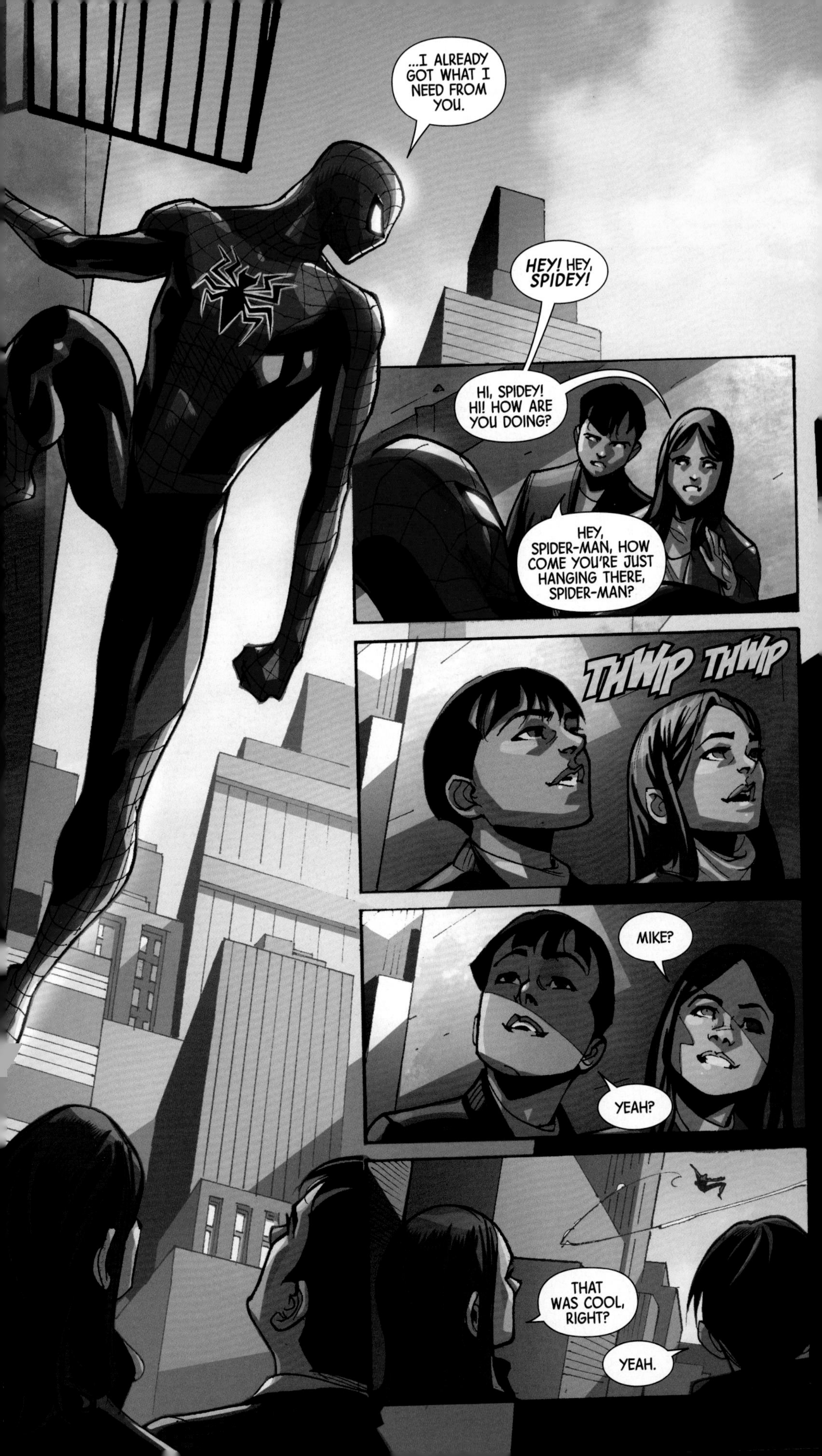
...I ALREADY GOT WHAT I NEED FROM YOU.
HEY! HEY, SPIDEY!
HI, SPIDEY! HI! HOW ARE YOU DOING?
HEY, SPIDER-MAN, HOW COME YOU'RE JUST HANGING THERE, SPIDER-MAN?
THWIP THWIP
MIKE?
YEAH?
THAT WAS COOL, RIGHT?
YEAH.

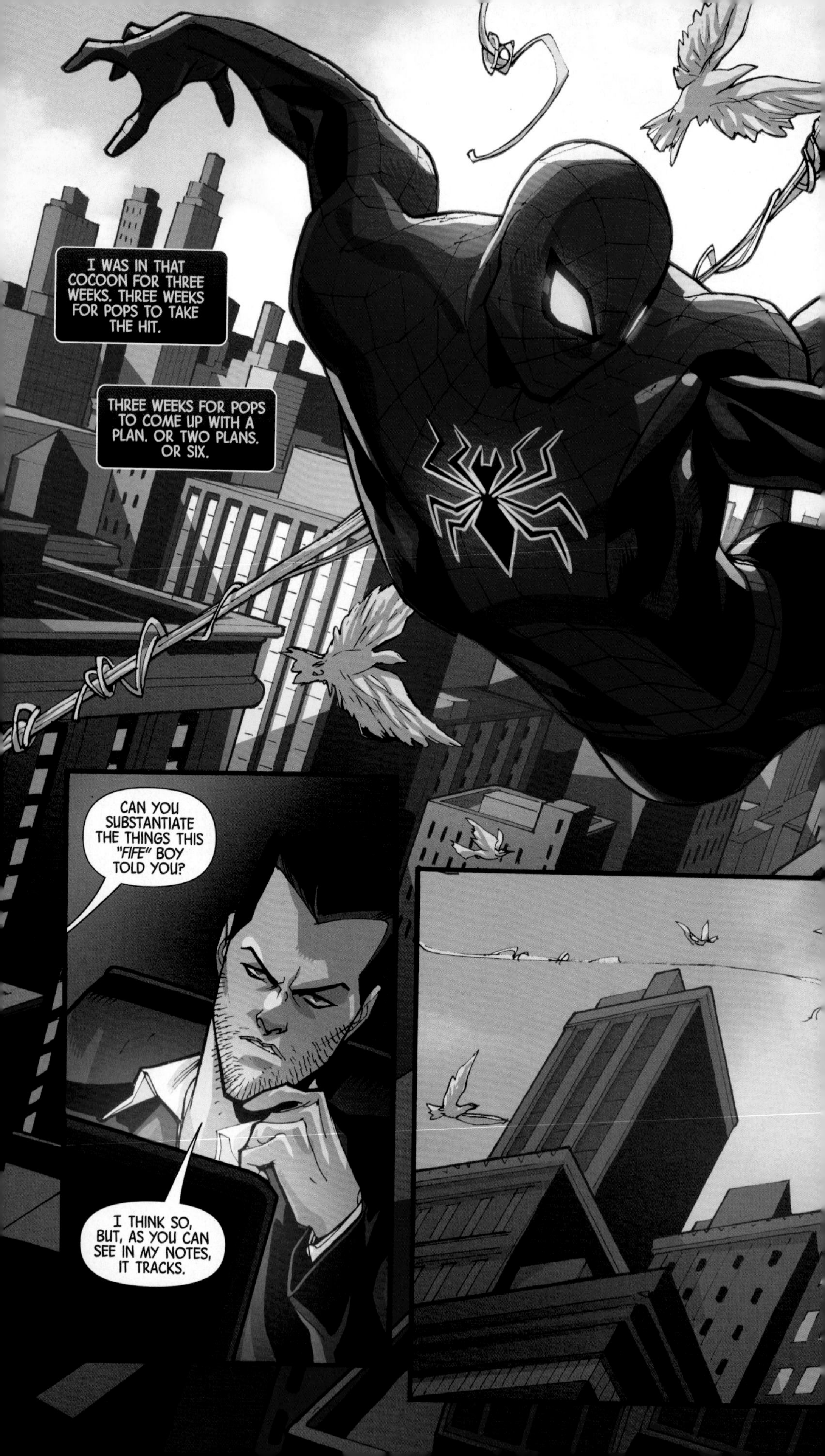
I WAS IN THAT COCOON FOR THREE WEEKS. THREE WEEKS FOR POPS TO TAKE THE HIT.
THREE WEEKS FOR POPS TO COME UP WITH A PLAN. OR TWO PLANS. OR SIX.
CAN YOU SUBSTANTIATE THE THINGS THIS "FIFE" BOY TOLD YOU?
I THINK SO, BUT, AS YOU CAN SEE IN MY NOTES, IT TRACKS.

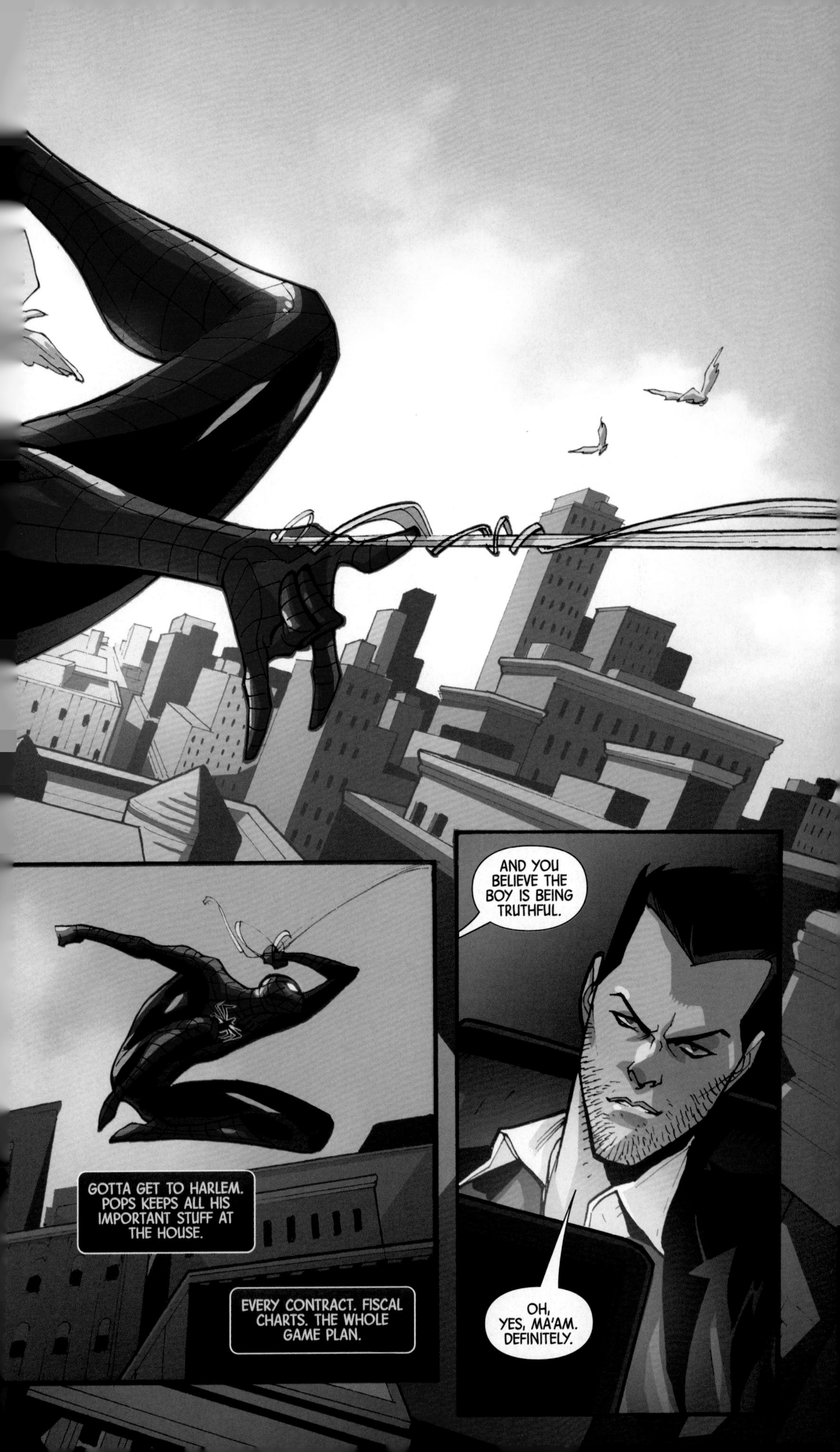
GOTTA GET TO HARLEM. POPS KEEPS ALL HIS IMPORTANT STUFF AT THE HOUSE.
EVERY CONTRACT. FISCAL CHARTS. THE WHOLE GAME PLAN.
AND YOU BELIEVE THE BOY IS BEING TRUTHFUL.
OH, YES, MA'AM. DEFINITELY.

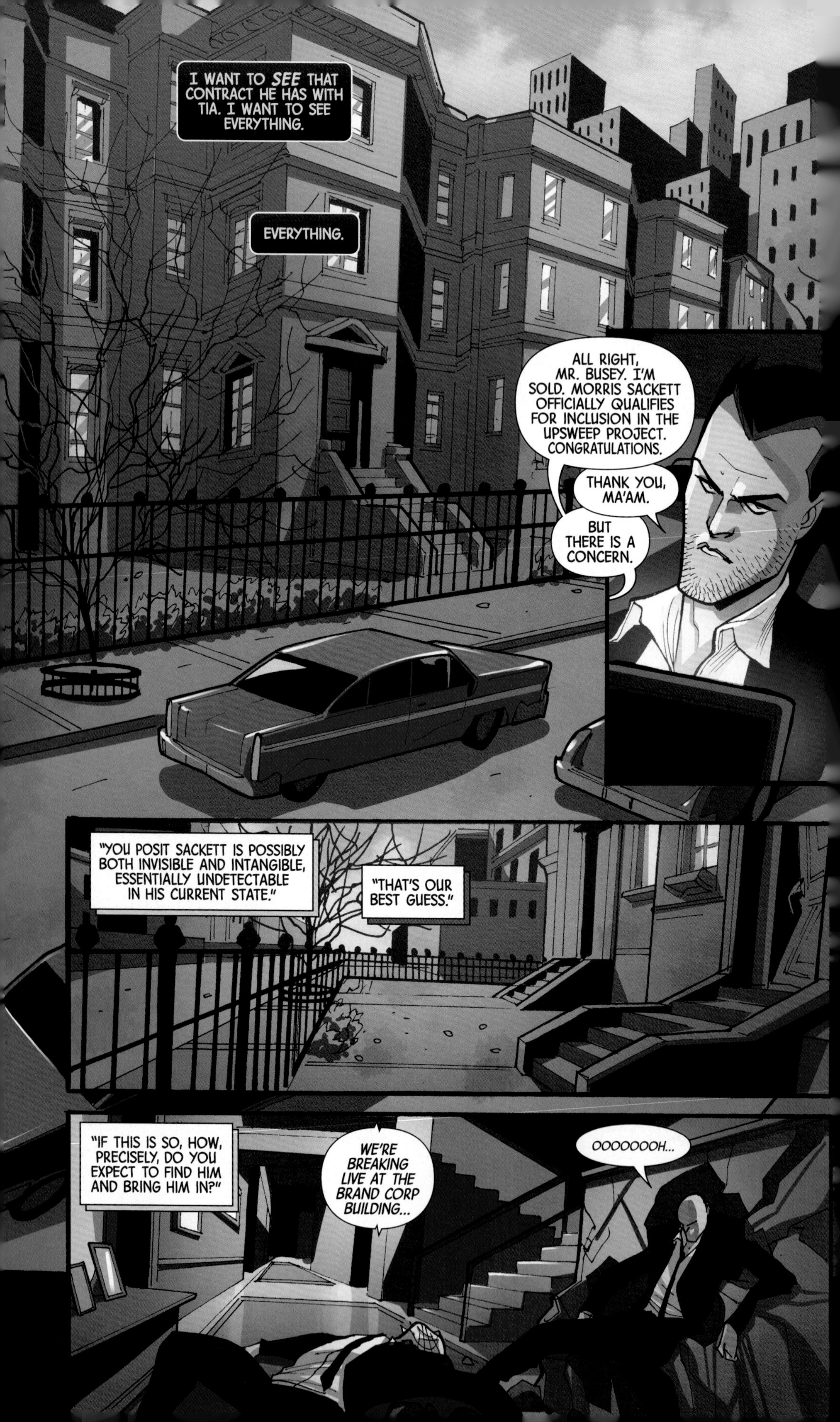
I WANT TO SEE THAT CONTRACT HE HAS WITH TIA. I WANT TO SEE EVERYTHING.
EVERYTHING.
ALL RIGHT, MR. BUSEY. I'M SOLD. MORRIS SACKETT OFFICIALLY QUALIFIES FOR INCLUSION IN THE UPSWEEP PROJECT. CONGRATULATIONS.
THANK YOU, MA'AM.
BUT THERE IS A CONCERN.
"YOU POSIT SACKETT IS POSSIBLY BOTH INVISIBLE AND INTANGIBLE, ESSENTIALLY UNDETECTABLE IN HIS CURRENT STATE."
"THAT'S OUR BEST GUESS."
"IF THIS IS SO, HOW, PRECISELY, DO YOU EXPECT TO FIND HIM AND BRING HIM IN?"
WE'RE BREAKING LIVE AT THE BRAND CORP BUILDING...
OOOOOOOH...

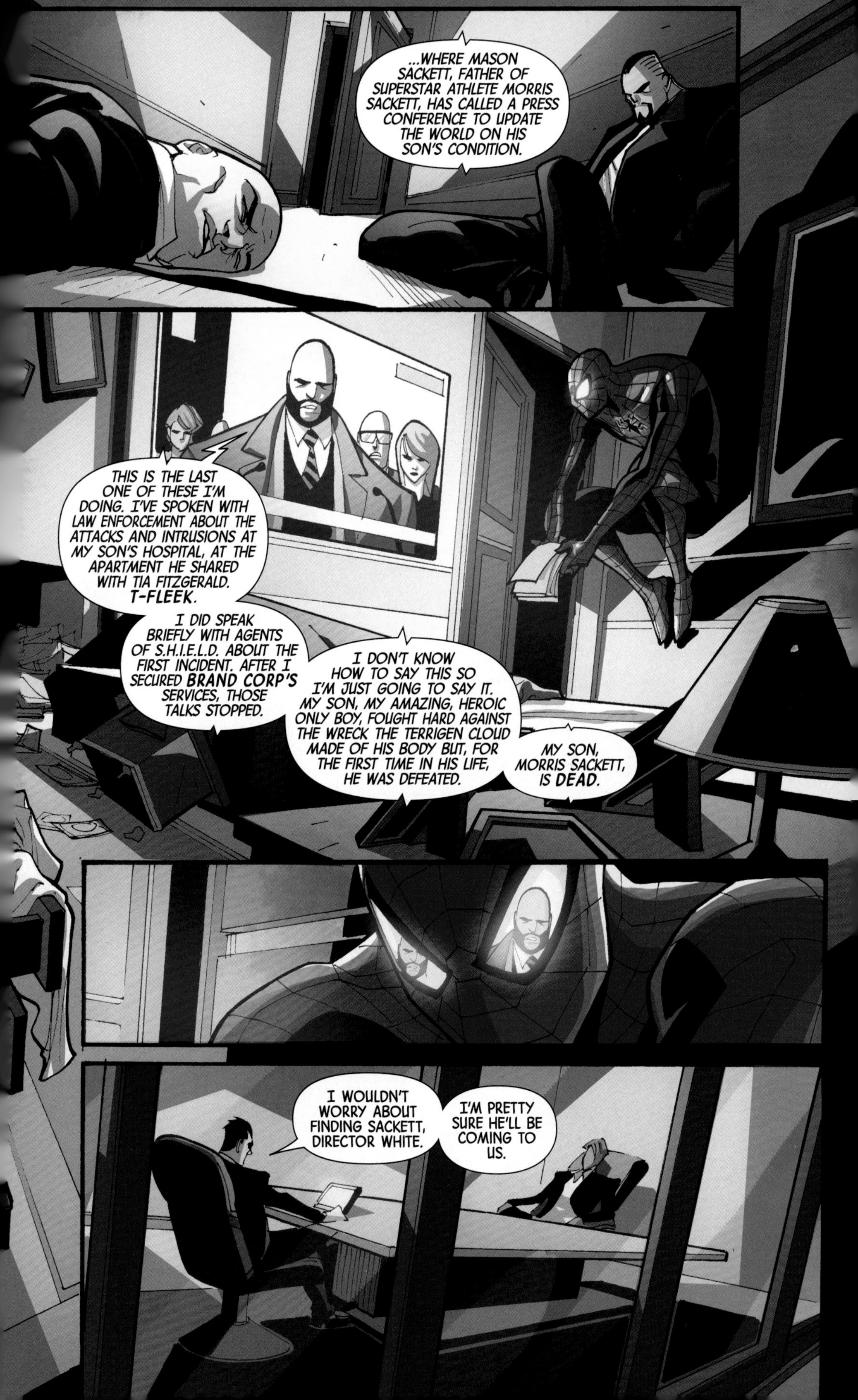
...WHERE MASON SACKETT, FATHER OF SUPERSTAR ATHLETE MORRIS SACKETT, HAS CALLED A PRESS CONFERENCE TO UPDATE THE WORLD ON HIS SON'S CONDITION.
THIS IS THE LAST ONE OF THESE I'M DOING. I'VE SPOKEN WITH LAW ENFORCEMENT ABOUT THE ATTACKS AND INTRUSIONS AT MY SON'S HOSPITAL, AT THE APARTMENT HE SHARED WITH TIA FITZGERALD. T-FLEEK.
I DID SPEAK BRIEFLY WITH AGENTS OF S.H.I.E.L.D. ABOUT THE FIRST INCIDENT. AFTER I SECURED BRAND CORP'S SERVICES, THOSE TALKS STOPPED.
I DON'T KNOW HOW TO SAY THIS SO I'M JUST GOING TO SAY IT. MY SON, MY AMAZING, HEROIC ONLY BOY, FOUGHT HARD AGAINST THE WRECK THE TERRIGEN CLOUD MADE OF HIS BODY BUT, FOR THE FIRST TIME IN HIS LIFE, HE WAS DEFEATED.
MY SON, MORRIS SACKETT, IS DEAD.
I WOULDN'T WORRY ABOUT FINDING SACKETT, DIRECTOR WHITE.
I'M PRETTY SURE HE'LL BE COMING TO US.

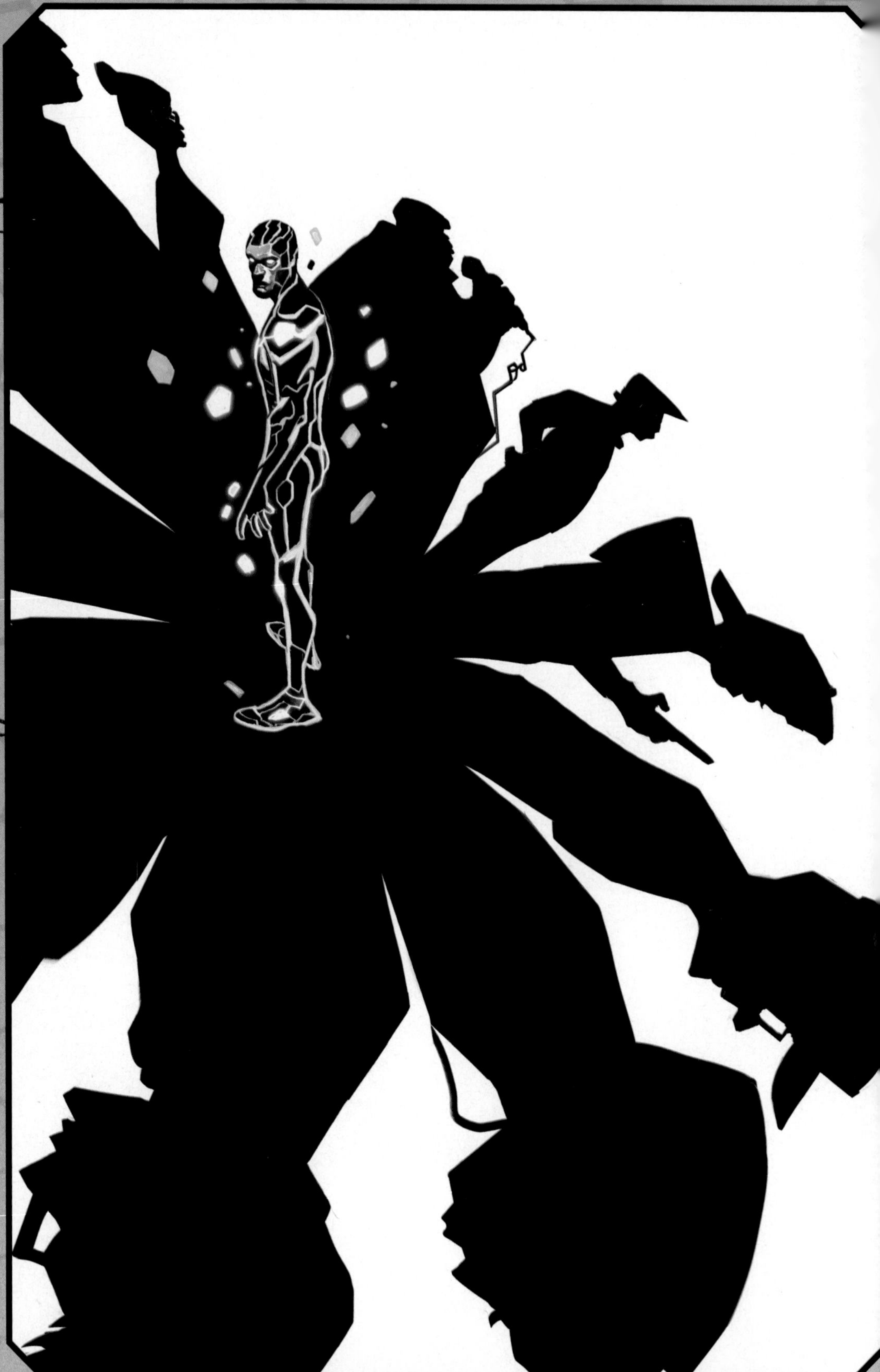

5

INVISIBLE MAN

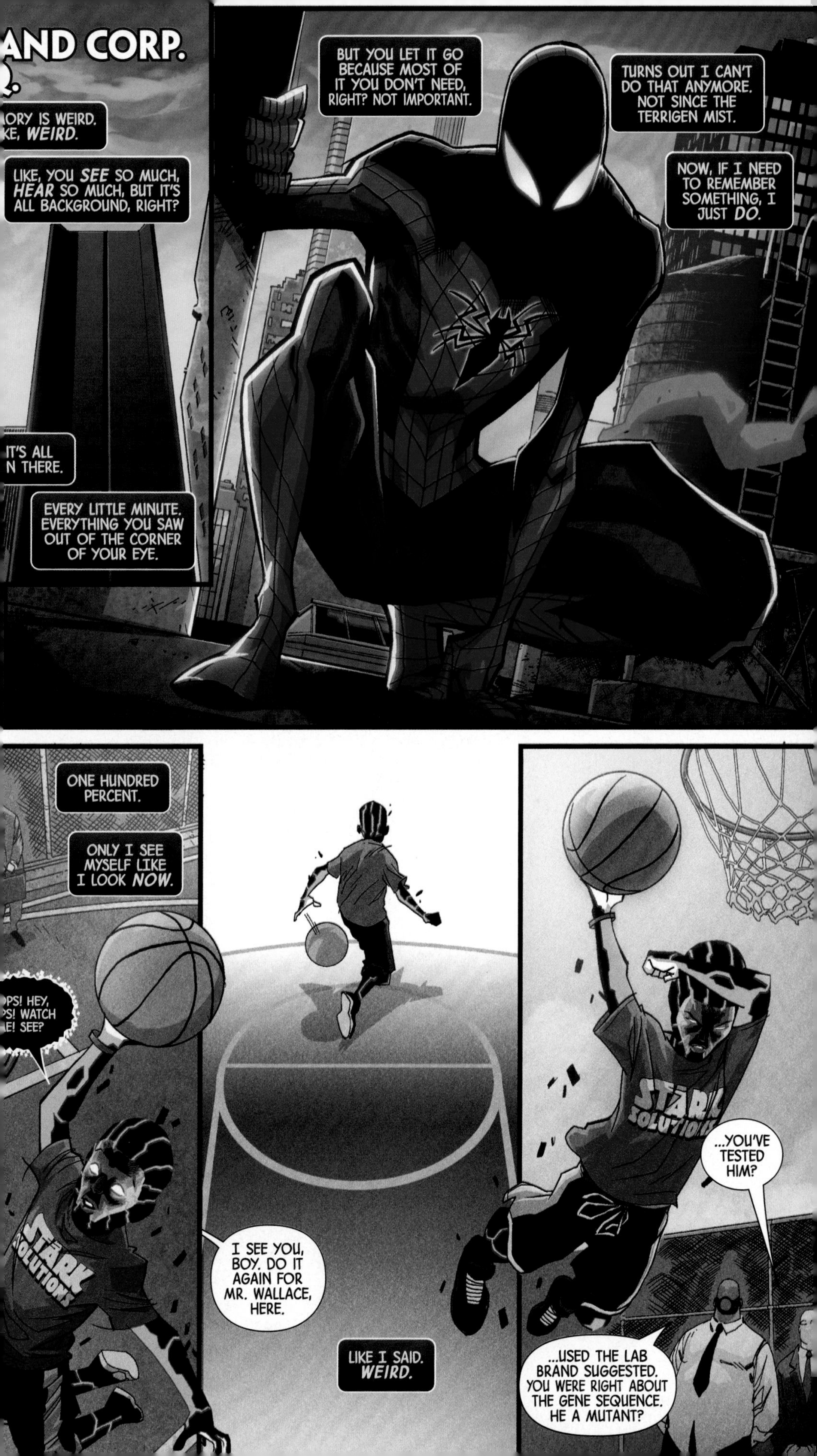

AND CORP.
ORY IS WEIRD.
KE, WEIRD.
LIKE, YOU SEE SO MUCH, HEAR SO MUCH, BUT IT'S ALL BACKGROUND, RIGHT?
IT'S ALL
N THERE.
EVERY LITTLE MINUTE. EVERYTHING YOU SAW OUT OF THE CORNER OF YOUR EYE.
BUT YOU LET IT GO BECAUSE MOST OF IT YOU DON'T NEED, RIGHT? NOT IMPORTANT.
TURNS OUT I CAN'T DO THAT ANYMORE. NOT SINCE THE TERRIGEN MIST.
NOW, IF I NEED TO REMEMBER SOMETHING, I JUST DO.
ONE HUNDRED PERCENT.
ONLY I SEE MYSELF LIKE I LOOK NOW.
PS! HEY,
PS! WATCH
E! SEE?
STARK SOLUTIONS
I SEE YOU, BOY. DO IT AGAIN FOR MR. WALLACE, HERE.
LIKE I SAID. WEIRD.
STARK SOLUTIONS
...YOU'VE TESTED HIM?
...USED THE LAB BRAND SUGGESTED. YOU WERE RIGHT ABOUT THE GENE SEQUENCE. HE A MUTANT?

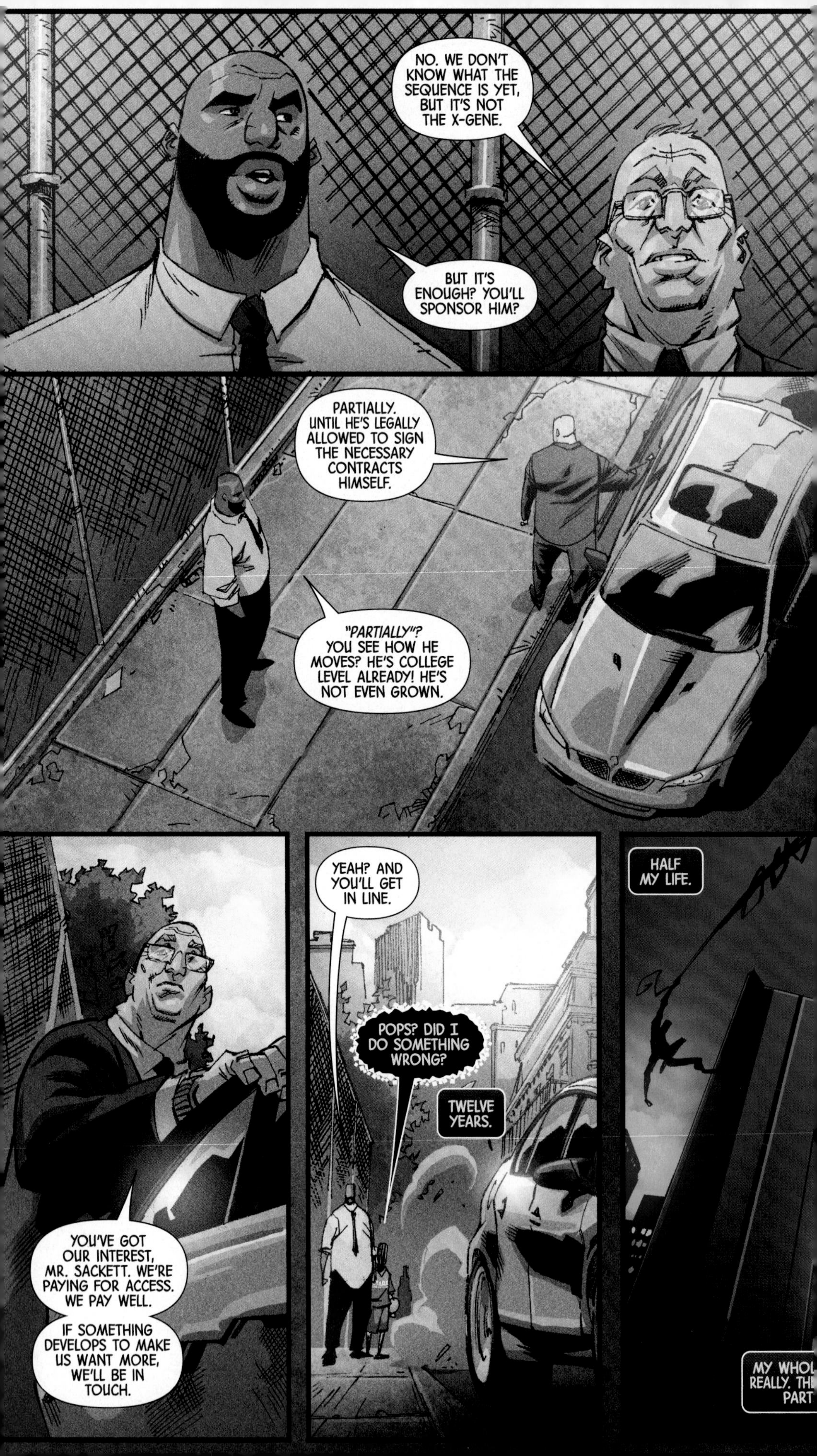

NO. WE DON'T KNOW WHAT THE SEQUENCE IS YET, BUT IT'S NOT THE X-GENE.
BUT IT'S ENOUGH? YOU'LL SPONSOR HIM?
PARTIALLY. UNTIL HE'S LEGALLY ALLOWED TO SIGN THE NECESSARY CONTRACTS HIMSELF.
"PARTIALLY"? YOU SEE HOW HE MOVES? HE'S COLLEGE LEVEL ALREADY! HE'S NOT EVEN GROWN.
YOU'VE GOT OUR INTEREST, MR. SACKETT. WE'RE PAYING FOR ACCESS. WE PAY WELL.
IF SOMETHING DEVELOPS TO MAKE US WANT MORE, WE'LL BE IN TOUCH.
YEAH? AND YOU'LL GET IN LINE.
POPS? DID I DO SOMETHING WRONG?
TWELVE YEARS.
HALF MY LIFE.

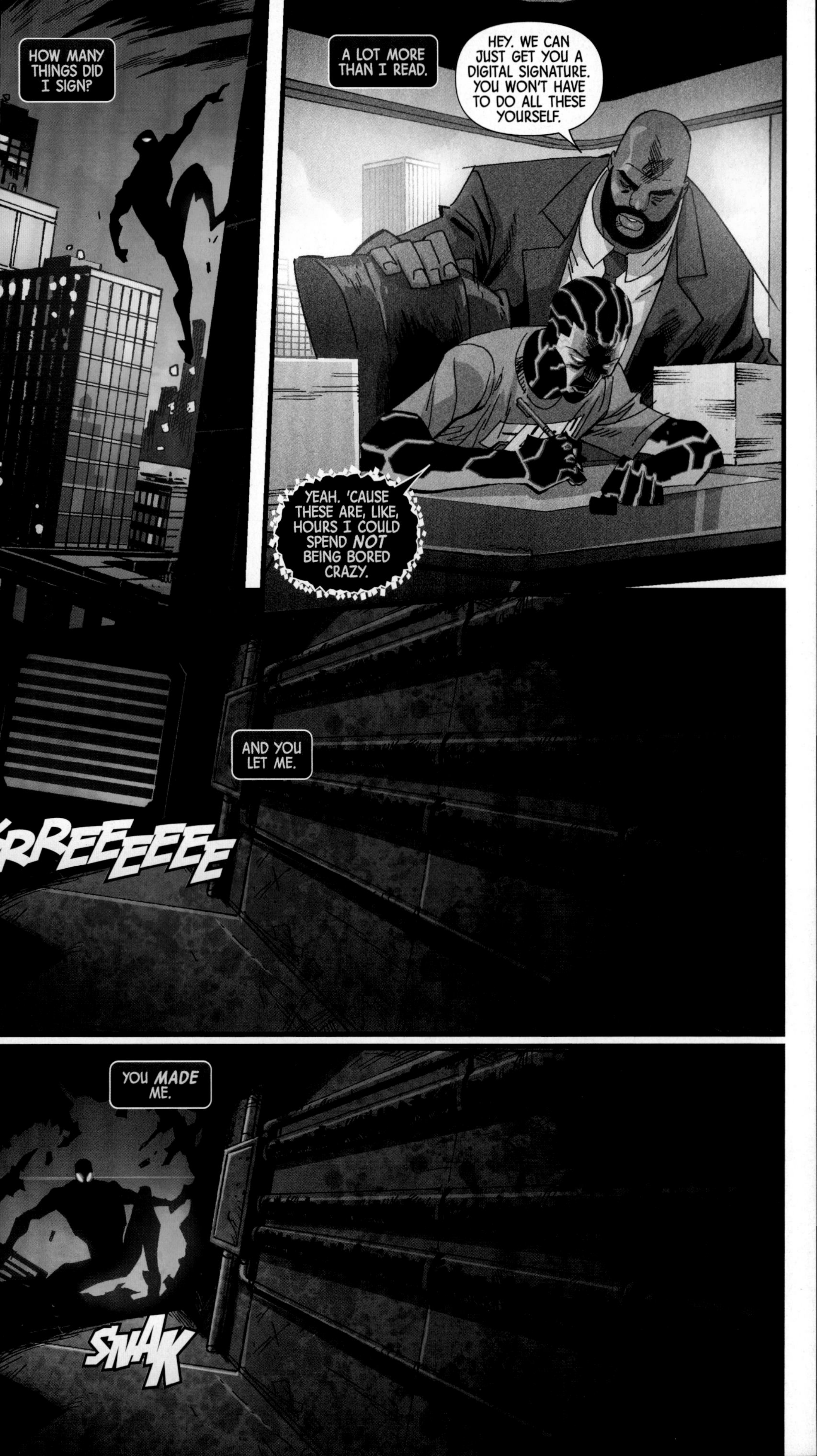
HOW MANY THINGS DID I SIGN?
A LOT MORE THAN I READ.
HEY. WE CAN JUST GET YOU A DIGITAL SIGNATURE. YOU WON'T HAVE TO DO ALL THESE YOURSELF.
YEAH. 'CAUSE THESE ARE, LIKE, HOURS I COULD SPEND NOT BEING BORED CRAZY.
AND YOU LET ME.
RREEEEEEE
YOU MADE ME.
SNAK

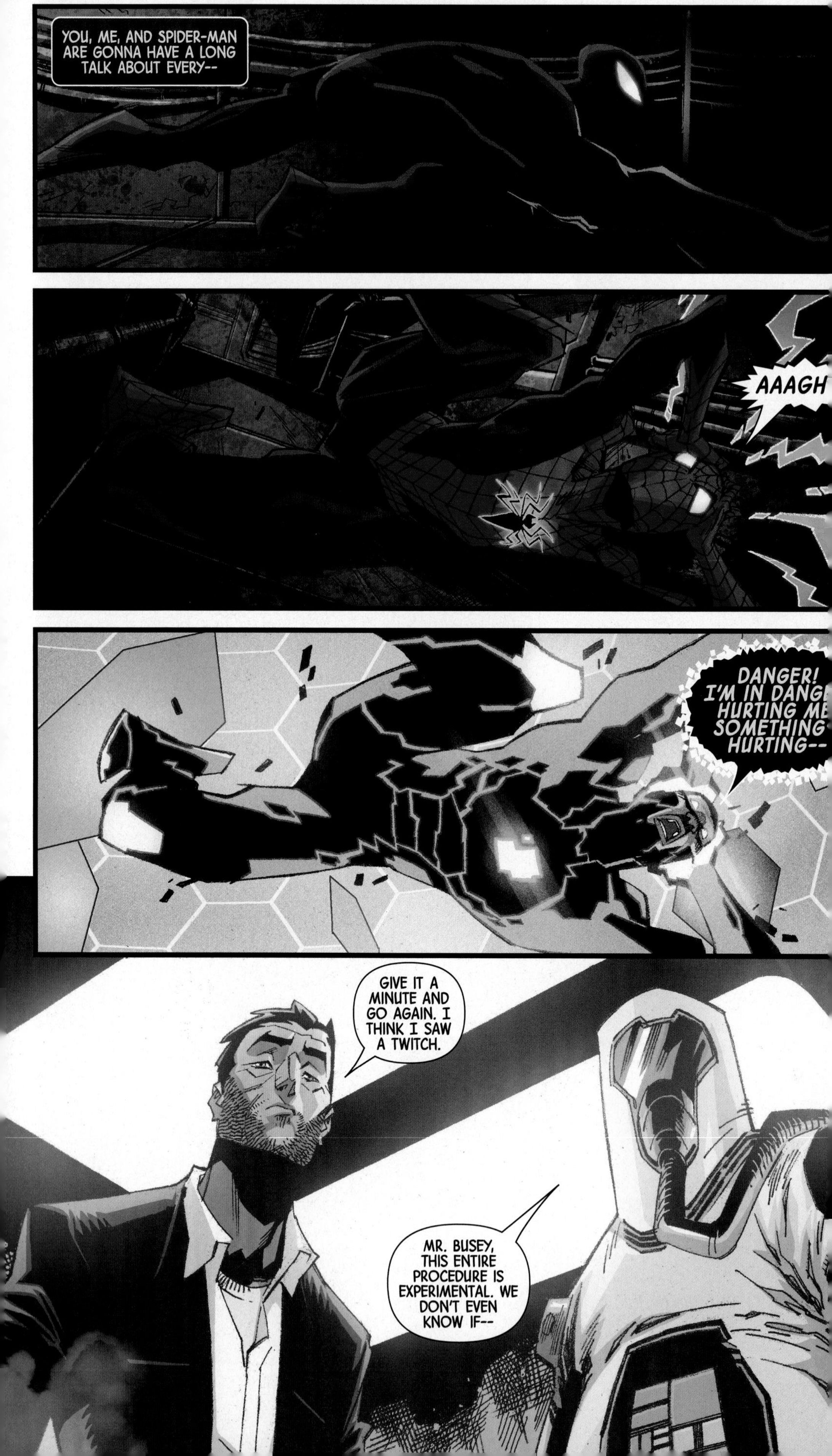
YOU, ME, AND SPIDER-MAN ARE GONNA HAVE A LONG TALK ABOUT EVERY--
AAAGH
DANGER! I'M IN DANG HURTING ME SOMETHING HURTING--
GIVE IT A MINUTE AND GO AGAIN. I THINK I SAW A TWITCH.
MR. BUSEY, THIS ENTIRE PROCEDURE IS EXPERIMENTAL. WE DON'T EVEN KNOW IF--

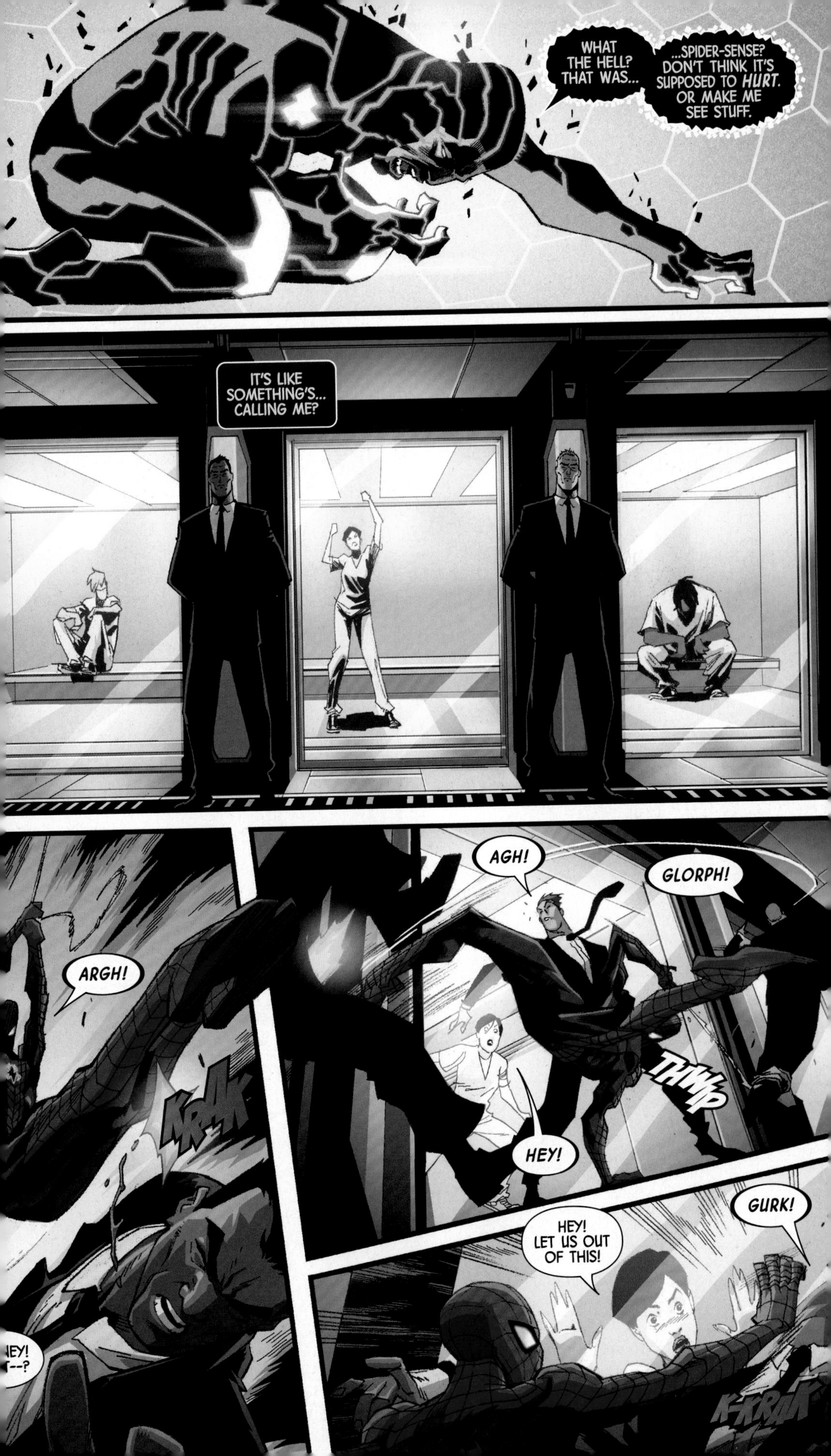
WHAT THE HELL? THAT WAS...
...SPIDER-SENSE? DON'T THINK IT'S SUPPOSED TO HURT. OR MAKE ME SEE STUFF.
IT'S LIKE SOMETHING'S... CALLING ME?
ARGH!
KRAK
AGH!
GLORPH!
THWIP
HEY!
HEY! LET US OUT OF THIS!
GURK!
K-KRAK

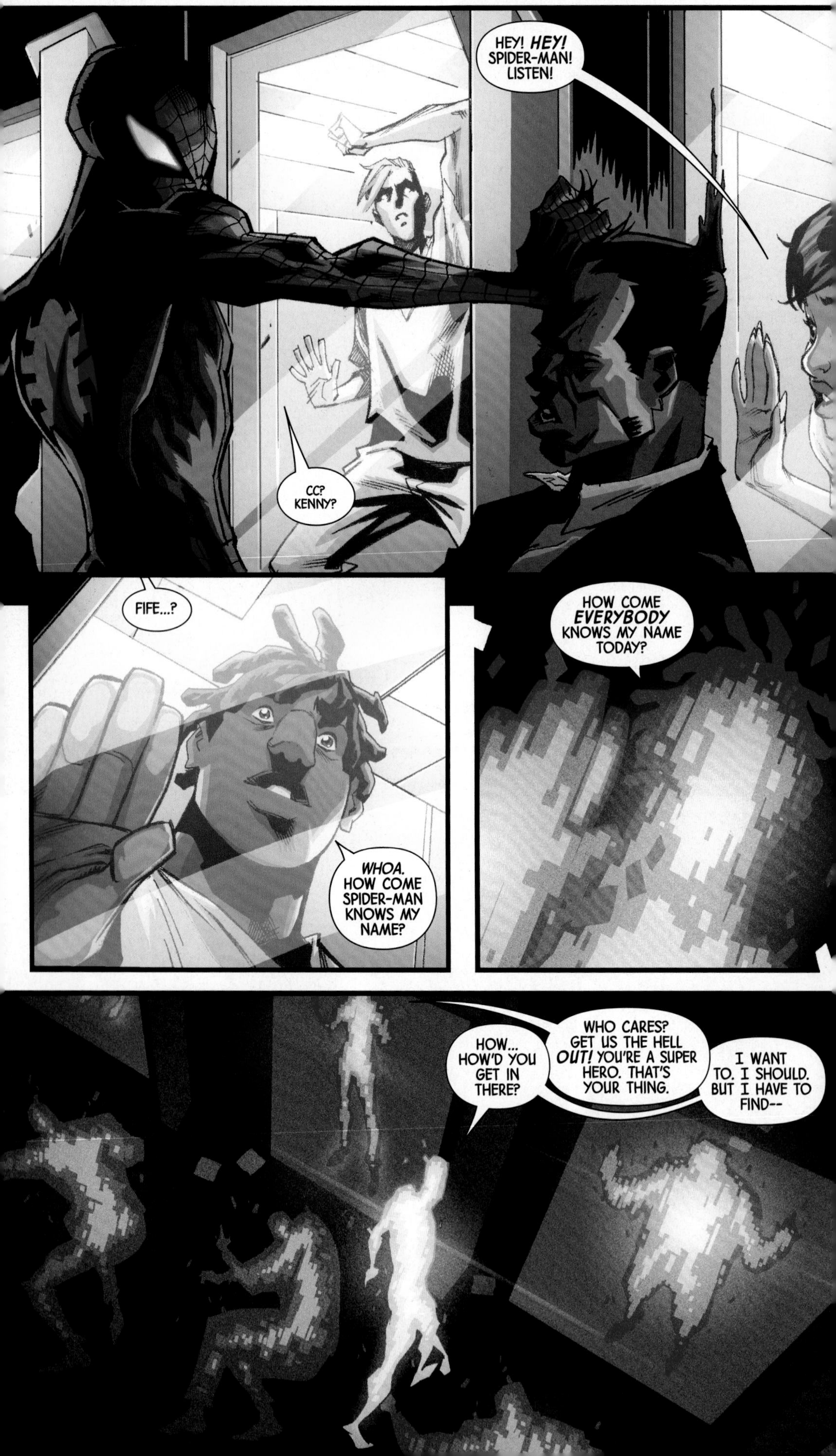
HEY! HEY! SPIDER-MAN! LISTEN!
CC? KENNY?
FIFE...?
WHOA. HOW COME SPIDER-MAN KNOWS MY NAME?
HOW COME EVERYBODY KNOWS MY NAME TODAY?
HOW... HOW'D YOU GET IN THERE?
WHO CARES? GET US THE HELL OUT! YOU'RE A SUPER HERO. THAT'S YOUR THING.
I WANT TO. I SHOULD. BUT I HAVE TO FIND--

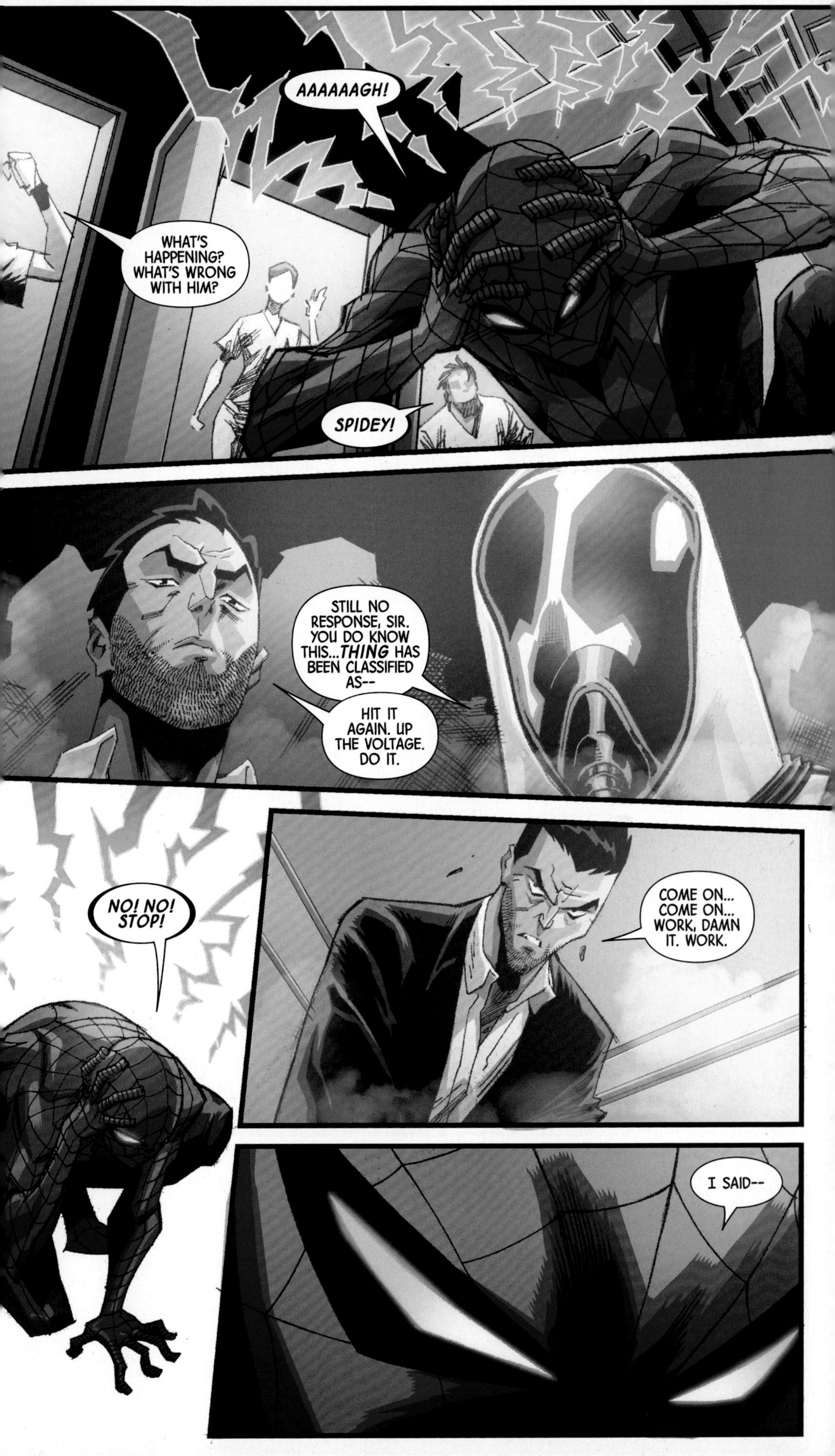
AAAAAAGH!
WHAT'S HAPPENING? WHAT'S WRONG WITH HIM?
SPIDEY!
STILL NO RESPONSE, SIR. YOU DO KNOW THIS...THING HAS BEEN CLASSIFIED AS--
HIT IT AGAIN. UP THE VOLTAGE. DO IT.
NO! NO! STOP!
COME ON... COME ON... WORK, DAMN IT. WORK.
I SAID--

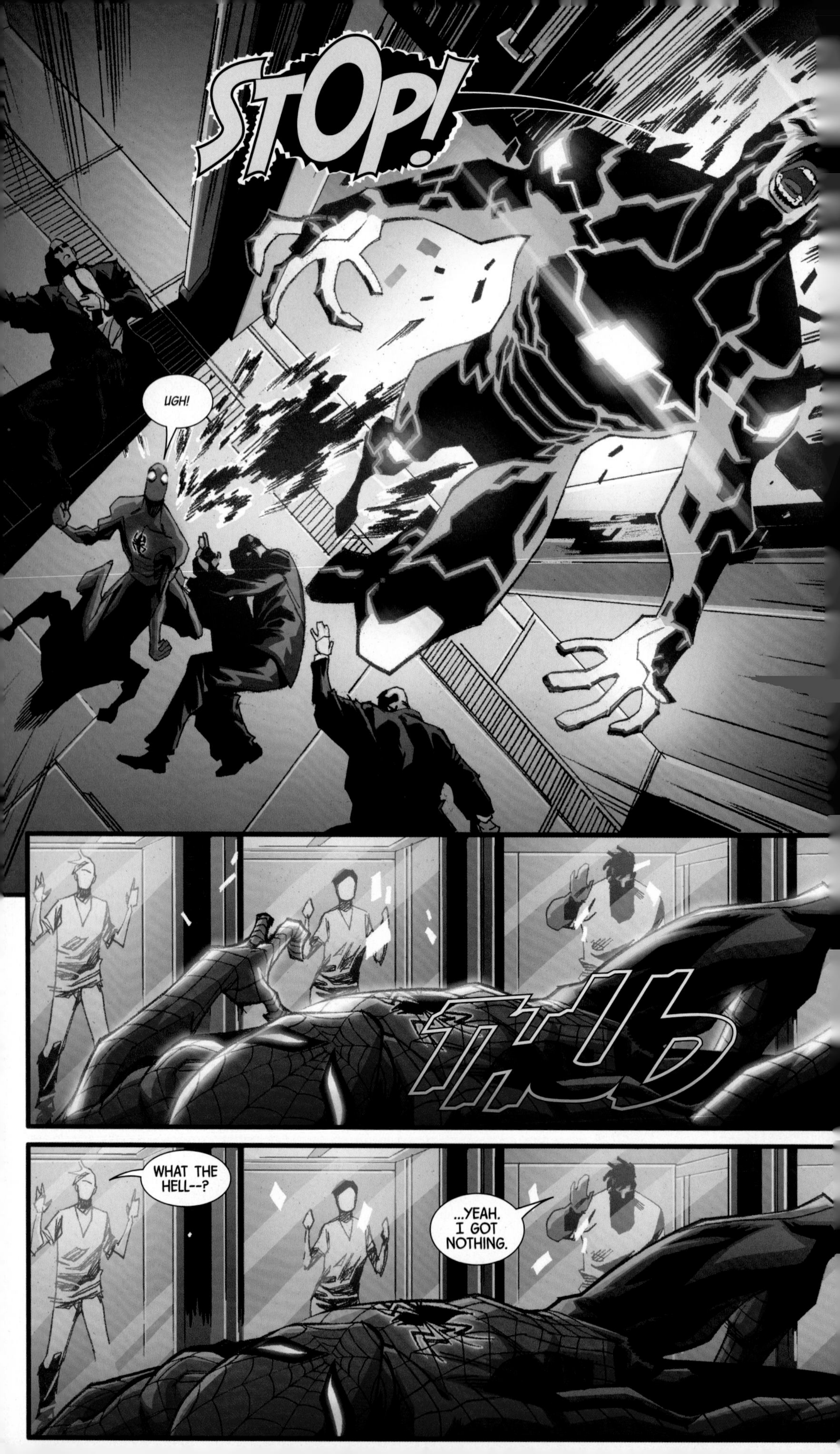
STOP!
UGH!
THUD
WHAT THE HELL--?
...YEAH. I GOT NOTHING.

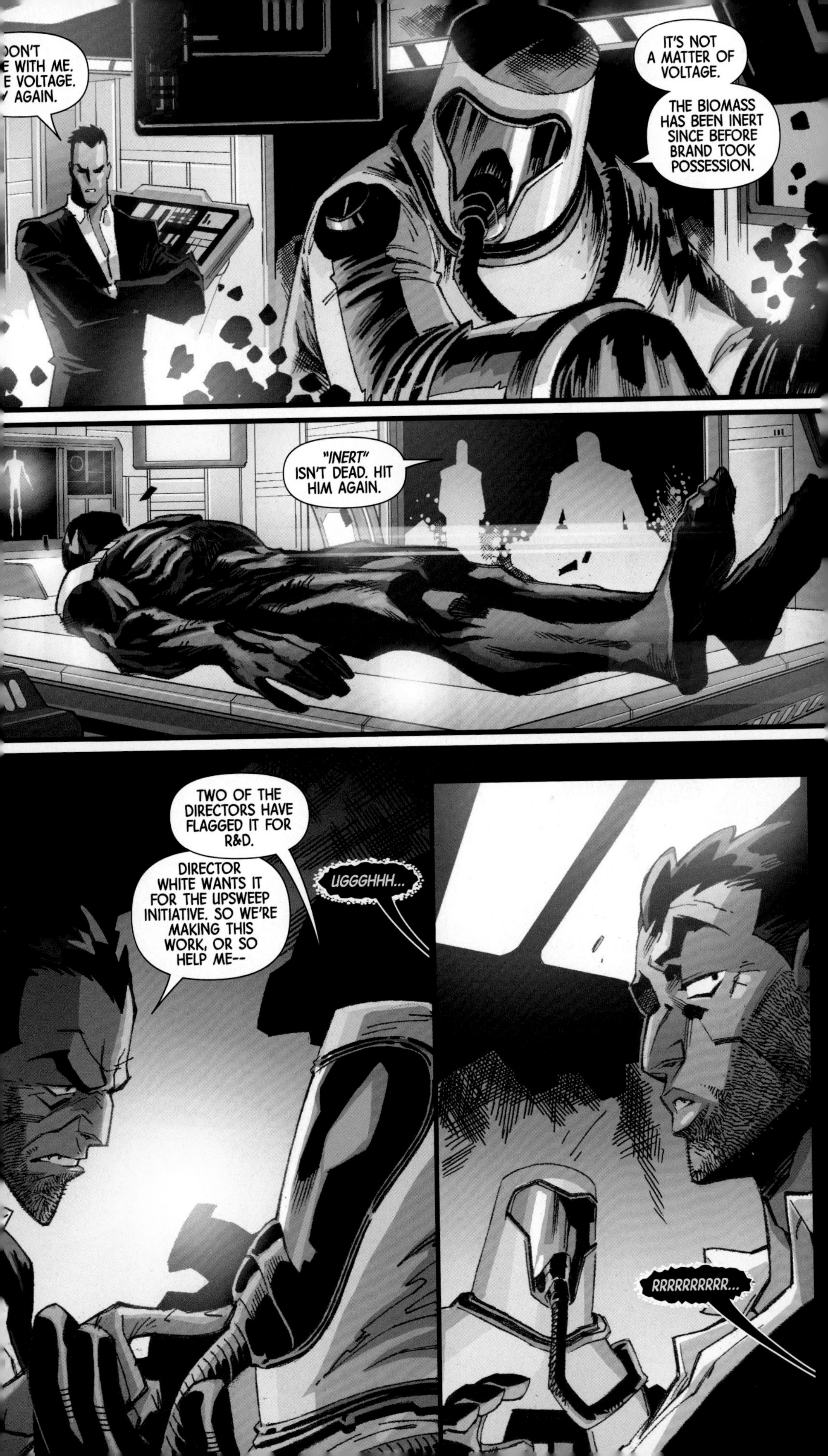

DON'T
E WITH ME.
E VOLTAGE.
AGAIN.
IT'S NOT A MATTER OF VOLTAGE.
THE BIOMASS HAS BEEN INERT SINCE BEFORE BRAND TOOK POSSESSION.
"INERT" ISN'T DEAD. HIT HIM AGAIN.
TWO OF THE DIRECTORS HAVE FLAGGED IT FOR R&D.
DIRECTOR WHITE WANTS IT FOR THE UPSWEEP INITIATIVE. SO WE'RE MAKING THIS WORK, OR SO HELP ME--
UGGGHHH...
RRRRRRRRRR...

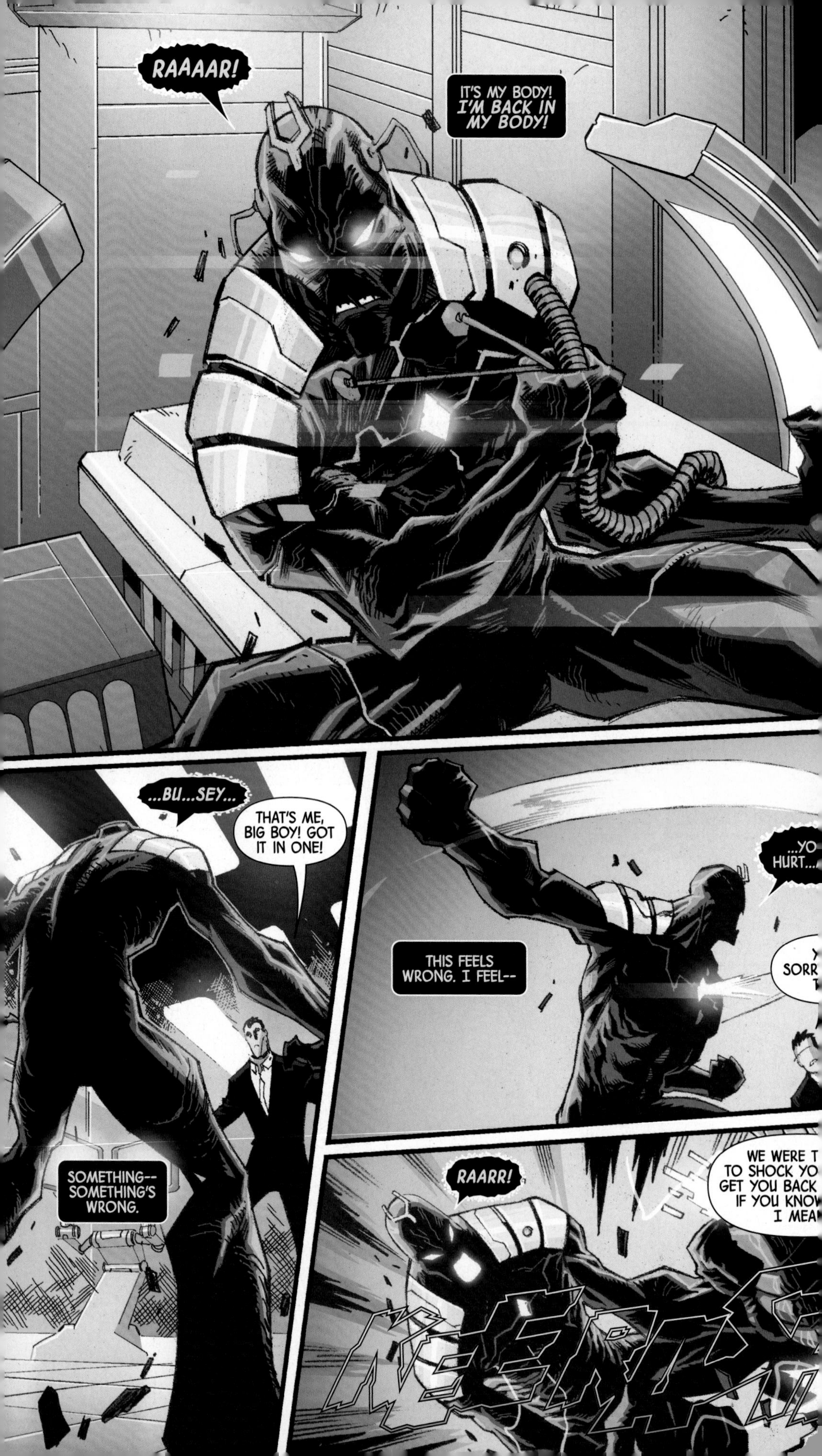
RAAAAR!
IT'S MY BODY! I'M BACK IN MY BODY!
...BU...SEY...
THAT'S ME, BIG BOY! GOT IT IN ONE!
SOMETHING-- SOMETHING'S WRONG.
THIS FEELS WRONG. I FEEL--
...YO HURT...
RAARR!
WE WERE T TO SHOCK YO GET YOU BACK IF YOU KNOW I MEA

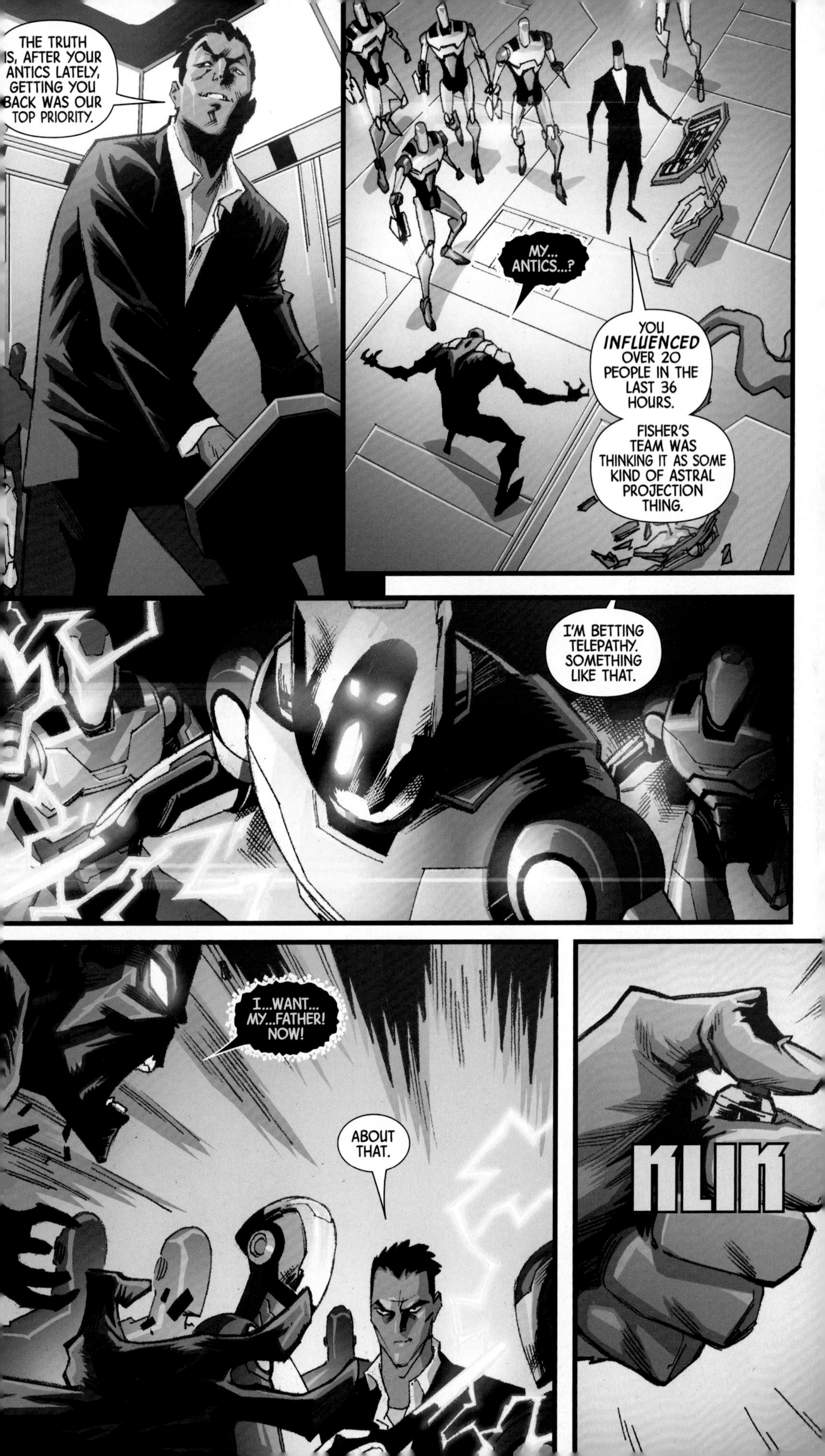
THE TRUTH IS, AFTER YOUR ANTICS LATELY, GETTING YOU BACK WAS OUR TOP PRIORITY.
MY... ANTICS...?
YOU *INFLUENCED* OVER 20 PEOPLE IN THE LAST 36 HOURS.
FISHER'S TEAM WAS THINKING IT AS SOME KIND OF ASTRAL PROJECTION THING.
I'M BETTING TELEPATHY. SOMETHING LIKE THAT.
I...WANT... MY...FATHER! NOW!
ABOUT THAT.
KLIK

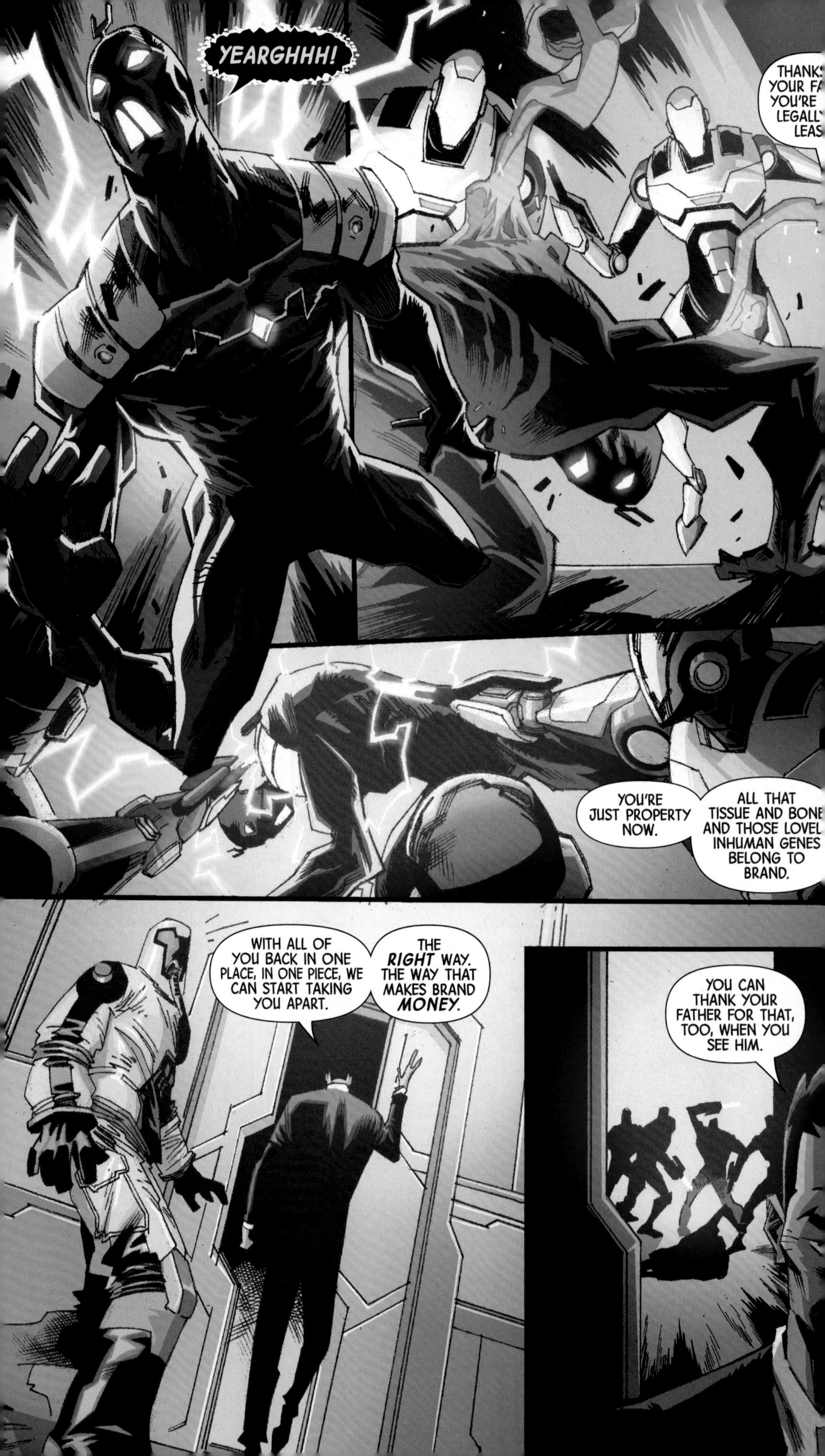
YEARGHHH!
THANKS YOUR FA YOU'RE LEGALLY LEAS
YOU'RE JUST PROPERTY NOW.
ALL THAT TISSUE AND BONE AND THOSE LOVEL INHUMAN GENES BELONG TO BRAND.
WITH ALL OF YOU BACK IN ONE PLACE, IN ONE PIECE, WE CAN START TAKING YOU APART.
THE *RIGHT* WAY. THE WAY THAT MAKES BRAND *MONEY*.
YOU CAN THANK YOUR FATHER FOR THAT, TOO, WHEN YOU SEE HIM.

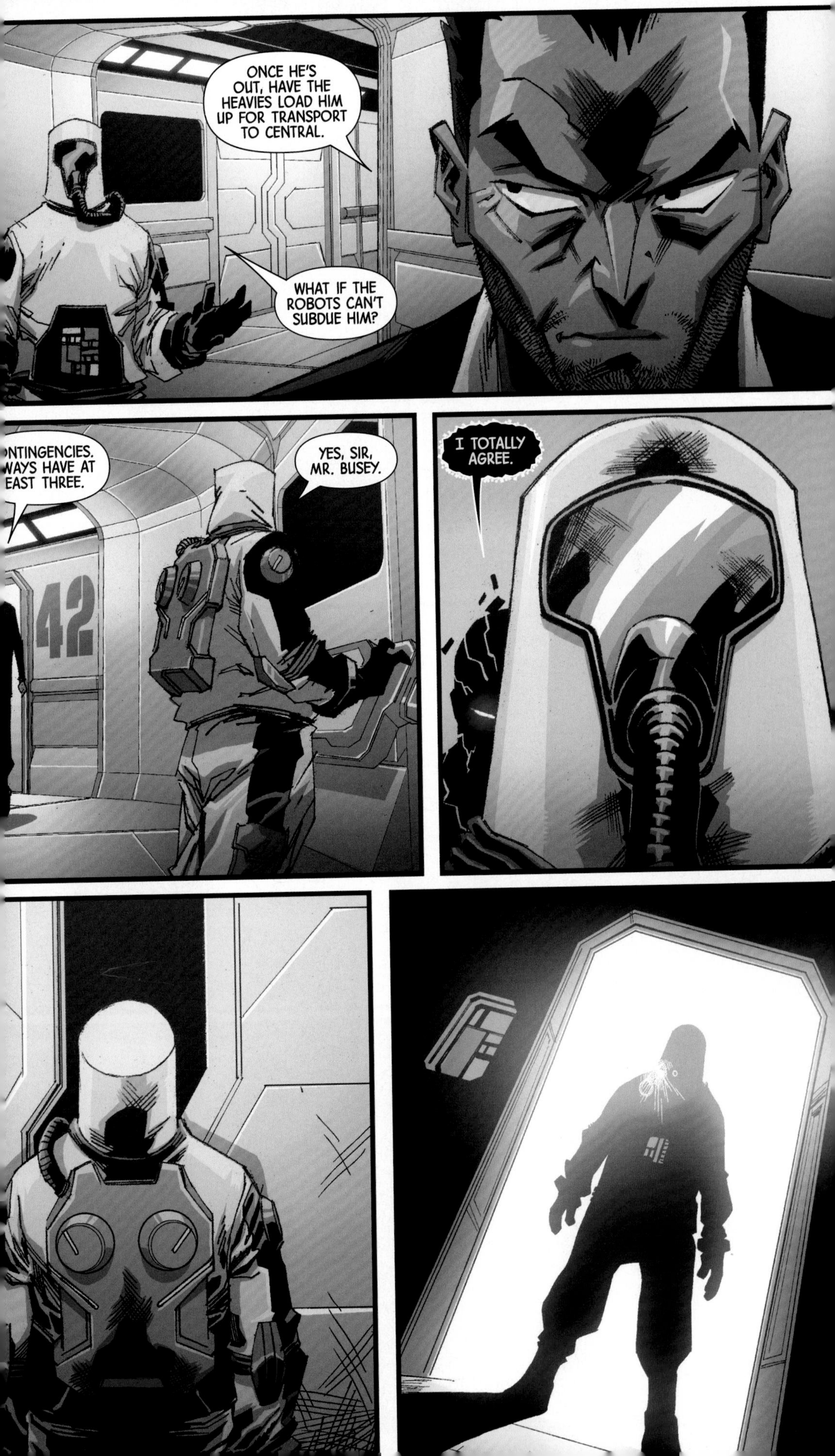

ONCE HE'S OUT, HAVE THE HEAVIES LOAD HIM UP FOR TRANSPORT TO CENTRAL.
WHAT IF THE ROBOTS CAN'T SUBDUE HIM?
NTINGENCIES. WAYS HAVE AT EAST THREE.
YES, SIR, MR. BUSEY.
42
I TOTALLY AGREE.

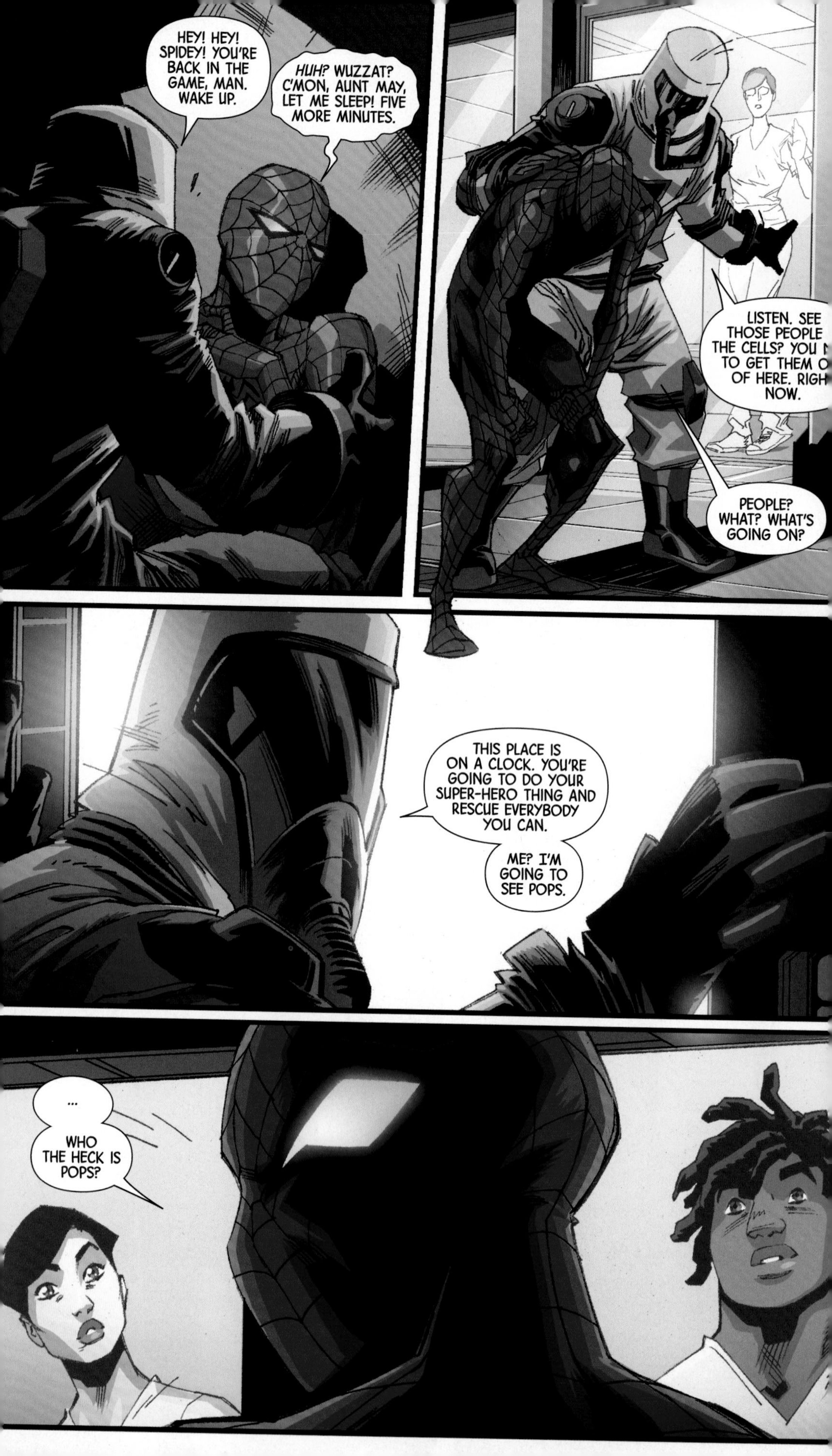
HEY! HEY! SPIDEY! YOU'RE BACK IN THE GAME, MAN. WAKE UP.
HUH? WUZZAT? C'MON, AUNT MAY, LET ME SLEEP! FIVE MORE MINUTES.
LISTEN. SEE THOSE PEOPLE THE CELLS? YOU TO GET THEM OF HERE. RIGH NOW.
PEOPLE? WHAT? WHAT'S GOING ON?
THIS PLACE IS ON A CLOCK. YOU'RE GOING TO DO YOUR SUPER-HERO THING AND RESCUE EVERYBODY YOU CAN.
ME? I'M GOING TO SEE POPS.
...
WHO THE HECK IS POPS?

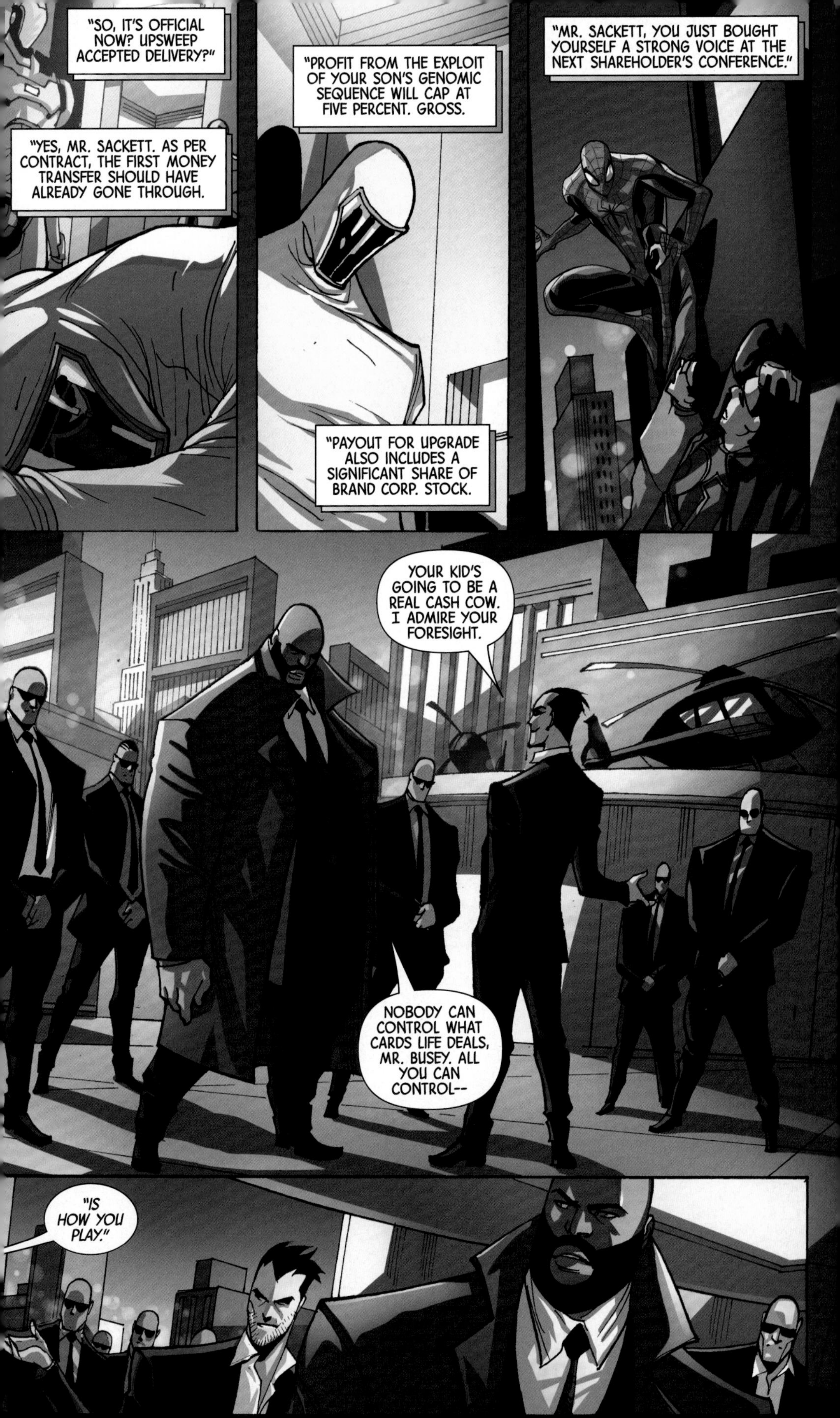
"SO, IT'S OFFICIAL NOW? UPSWEEP ACCEPTED DELIVERY?"
"YES, MR. SACKETT. AS PER CONTRACT, THE FIRST MONEY TRANSFER SHOULD HAVE ALREADY GONE THROUGH.
"PROFIT FROM THE EXPLOIT OF YOUR SON'S GENOMIC SEQUENCE WILL CAP AT FIVE PERCENT. GROSS.
"PAYOUT FOR UPGRADE ALSO INCLUDES A SIGNIFICANT SHARE OF BRAND CORP. STOCK.
"MR. SACKETT, YOU JUST BOUGHT YOURSELF A STRONG VOICE AT THE NEXT SHAREHOLDER'S CONFERENCE."
YOUR KID'S GOING TO BE A REAL CASH COW. I ADMIRE YOUR FORESIGHT.
NOBODY CAN CONTROL WHAT CARDS LIFE DEALS, MR. BUSEY. ALL YOU CAN CONTROL--
"IS HOW YOU PLAY."

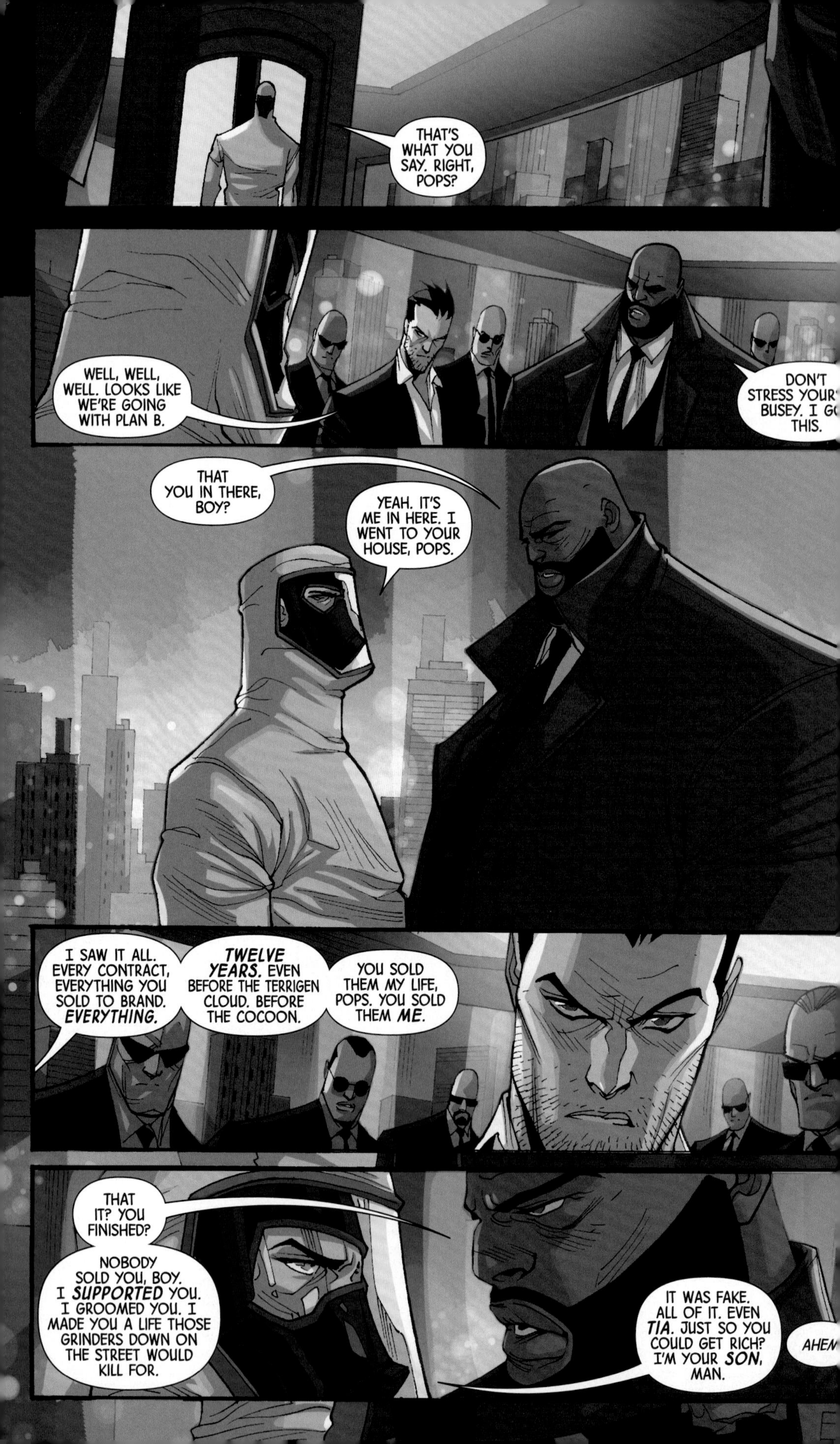
THAT'S WHAT YOU SAY. RIGHT, POPS?
WELL, WELL, WELL. LOOKS LIKE WE'RE GOING WITH PLAN B.
DON'T STRESS YOUR BUSEY. I G THIS.
THAT YOU IN THERE, BOY?
YEAH. IT'S ME IN HERE. I WENT TO YOUR HOUSE, POPS.
I SAW IT ALL. EVERY CONTRACT, EVERYTHING YOU SOLD TO BRAND. EVERYTHING.
TWELVE YEARS. EVEN BEFORE THE TERRIGEN CLOUD. BEFORE THE COCOON.
YOU SOLD THEM MY LIFE, POPS. YOU SOLD THEM ME.
THAT IT? YOU FINISHED?
NOBODY SOLD YOU, BOY. I SUPPORTED YOU. I GROOMED YOU. I MADE YOU A LIFE THOSE GRINDERS DOWN ON THE STREET WOULD KILL FOR.
IT WAS FAKE. ALL OF IT. EVEN TIA. JUST SO YOU COULD GET RICH? I'M YOUR SON, MAN.
AHEM

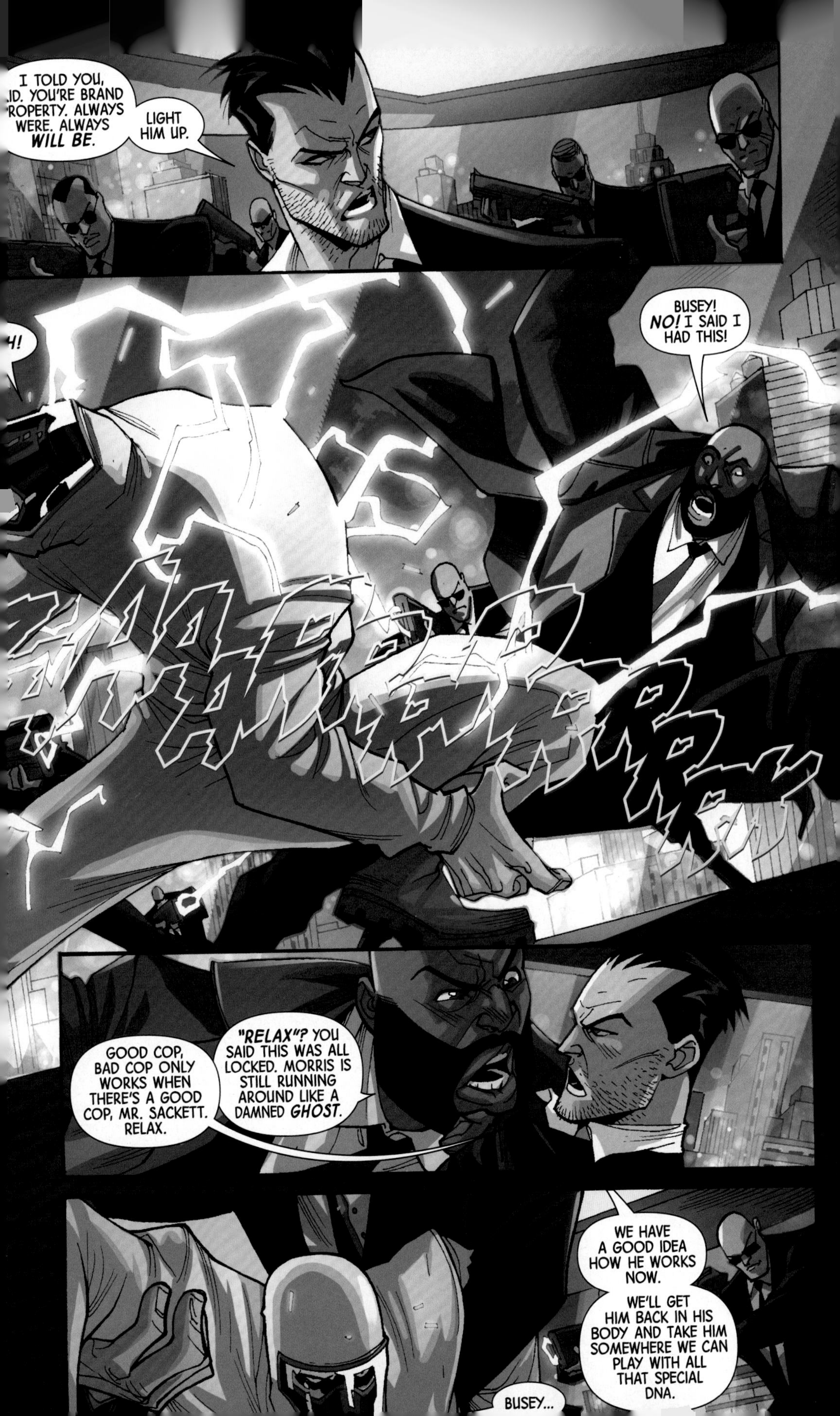
I TOLD YOU, ..ID. YOU'RE BRAND ..ROPERTY. ALWAYS WERE. ALWAYS WILL BE.
LIGHT HIM UP.
BUSEY! NO! I SAID I HAD THIS!
"RELAX"? YOU SAID THIS WAS ALL LOCKED. MORRIS IS STILL RUNNING AROUND LIKE A DAMNED GHOST.
GOOD COP, BAD COP ONLY WORKS WHEN THERE'S A GOOD COP, MR. SACKETT. RELAX.
WE HAVE A GOOD IDEA HOW HE WORKS NOW.
WE'LL GET HIM BACK IN HIS BODY AND TAKE HIM SOMEWHERE WE CAN PLAY WITH ALL THAT SPECIAL DNA.
BUSEY...

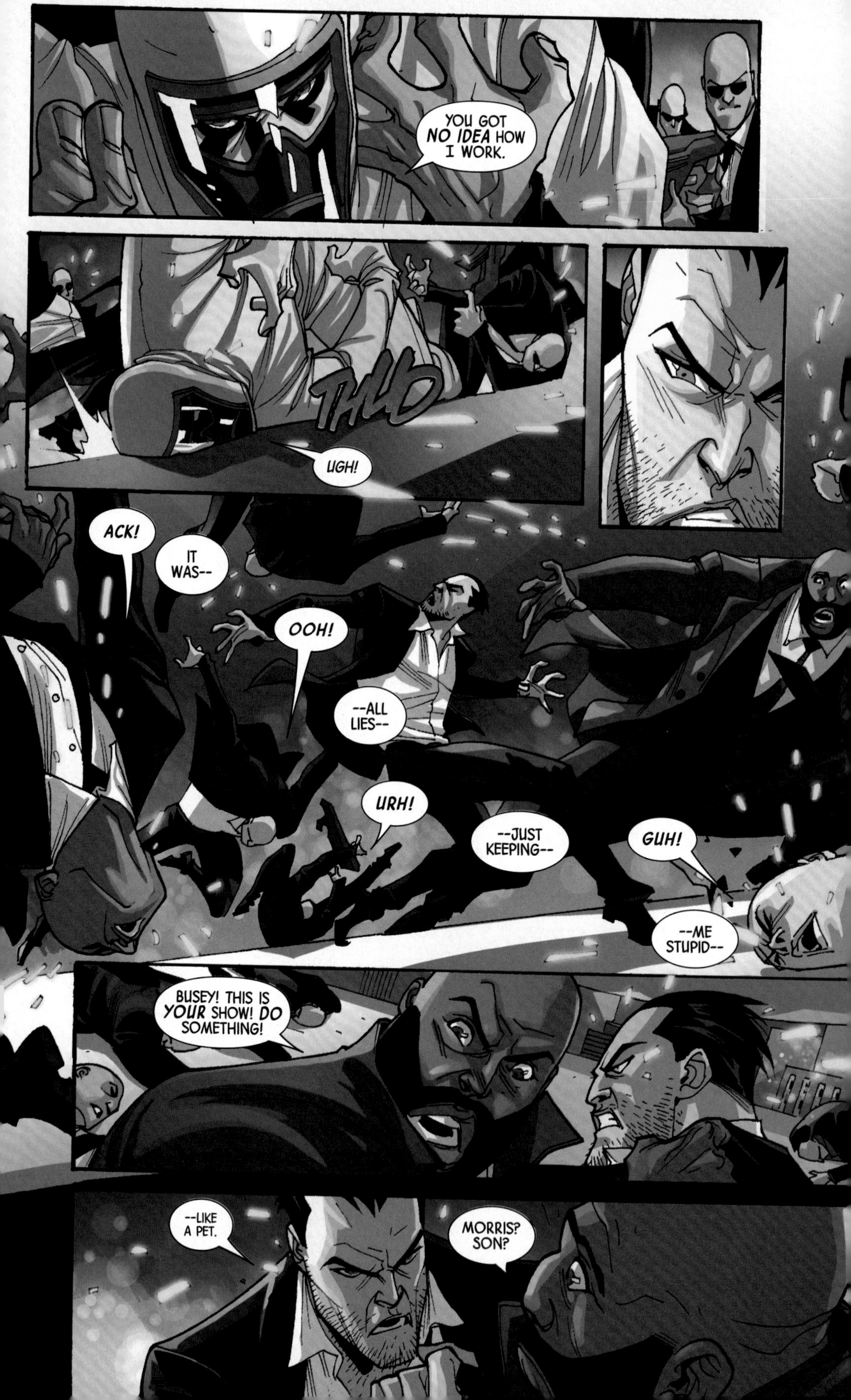
YOU GOT NO IDEA HOW I WORK.
THUD
UGH!
ACK!
IT WAS--
OOH!
--ALL LIES--
URH!
--JUST KEEPING--
GUH!
--ME STUPID--
BUSEY! THIS IS YOUR SHOW! DO SOMETHING!
--LIKE A PET.
MORRIS? SON?

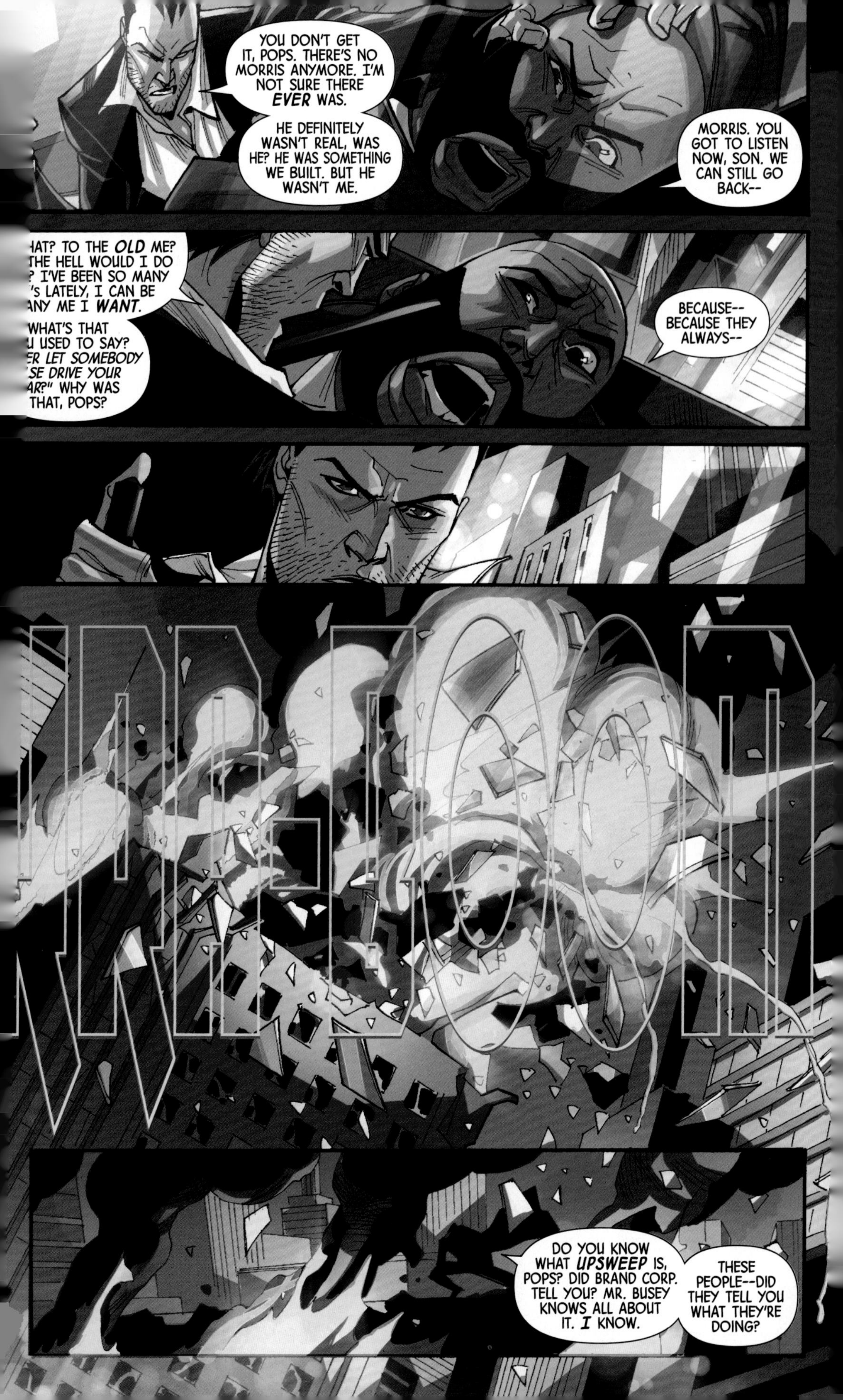
YOU DON'T GET IT, POPS. THERE'S NO MORRIS ANYMORE. I'M NOT SURE THERE EVER WAS.
HE DEFINITELY WASN'T REAL, WAS HE? HE WAS SOMETHING WE BUILT. BUT HE WASN'T ME.
MORRIS. YOU GOT TO LISTEN NOW, SON. WE CAN STILL GO BACK--
HAT? TO THE OLD ME? THE HELL WOULD I DO ? I'VE BEEN SO MANY 'S LATELY, I CAN BE ANY ME I WANT.
WHAT'S THAT U USED TO SAY? ER LET SOMEBODY SE DRIVE YOUR AR?" WHY WAS THAT, POPS?
BECAUSE-- BECAUSE THEY ALWAYS--
DO YOU KNOW WHAT UPSWEEP IS, POPS? DID BRAND CORP. TELL YOU? MR. BUSEY KNOWS ALL ABOUT IT. I KNOW.
THESE PEOPLE--DID THEY TELL YOU WHAT THEY'RE DOING?

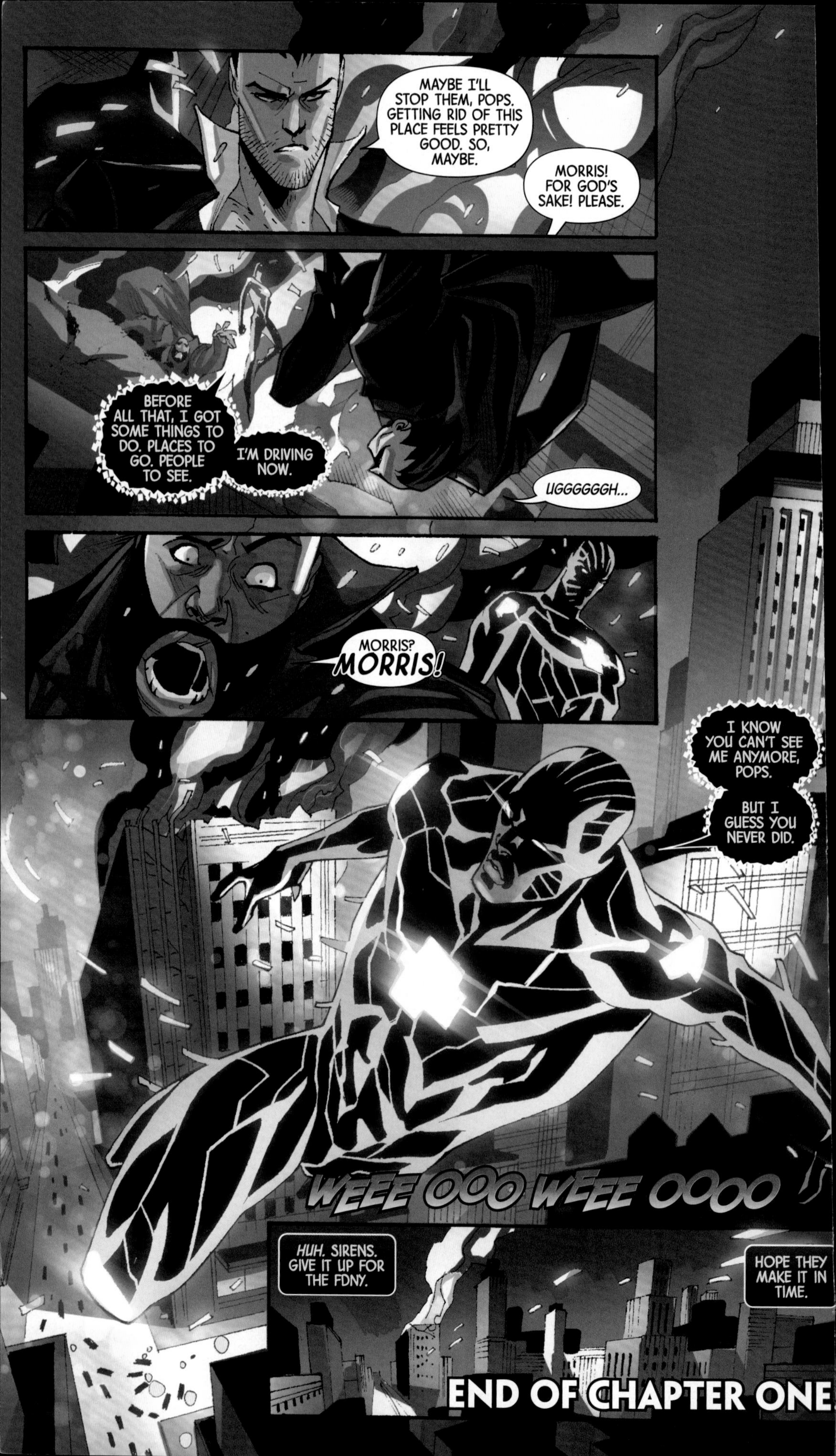
MAYBE I'LL STOP THEM, POPS. GETTING RID OF THIS PLACE FEELS PRETTY GOOD. SO, MAYBE.
MORRIS! FOR GOD'S SAKE! PLEASE.
BEFORE ALL THAT, I GOT SOME THINGS TO DO. PLACES TO GO. PEOPLE TO SEE.
I'M DRIVING NOW.
UGGGGGGH...
MORRIS? MORRIS!
I KNOW YOU CAN'T SEE ME ANYMORE, POPS.
BUT I GUESS YOU NEVER DID.
WEEE OOO WEEE OOOO
HUH. SIRENS. GIVE IT UP FOR THE FDNY.
HOPE THEY MAKE IT IN TIME.
END OF CHAPTER ONE

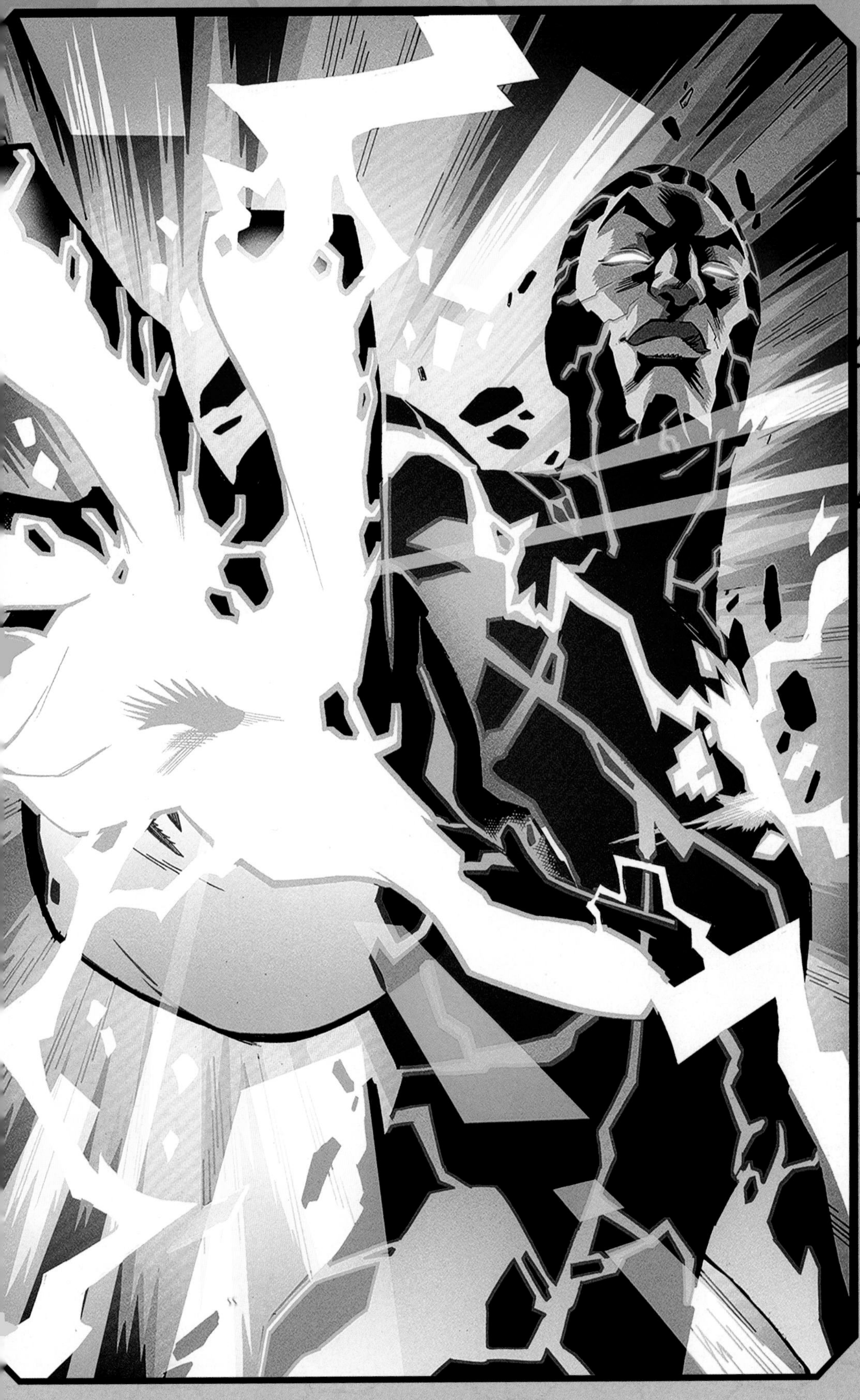

#1 VARIANT COVER BY **KHARY RANDOLPH**

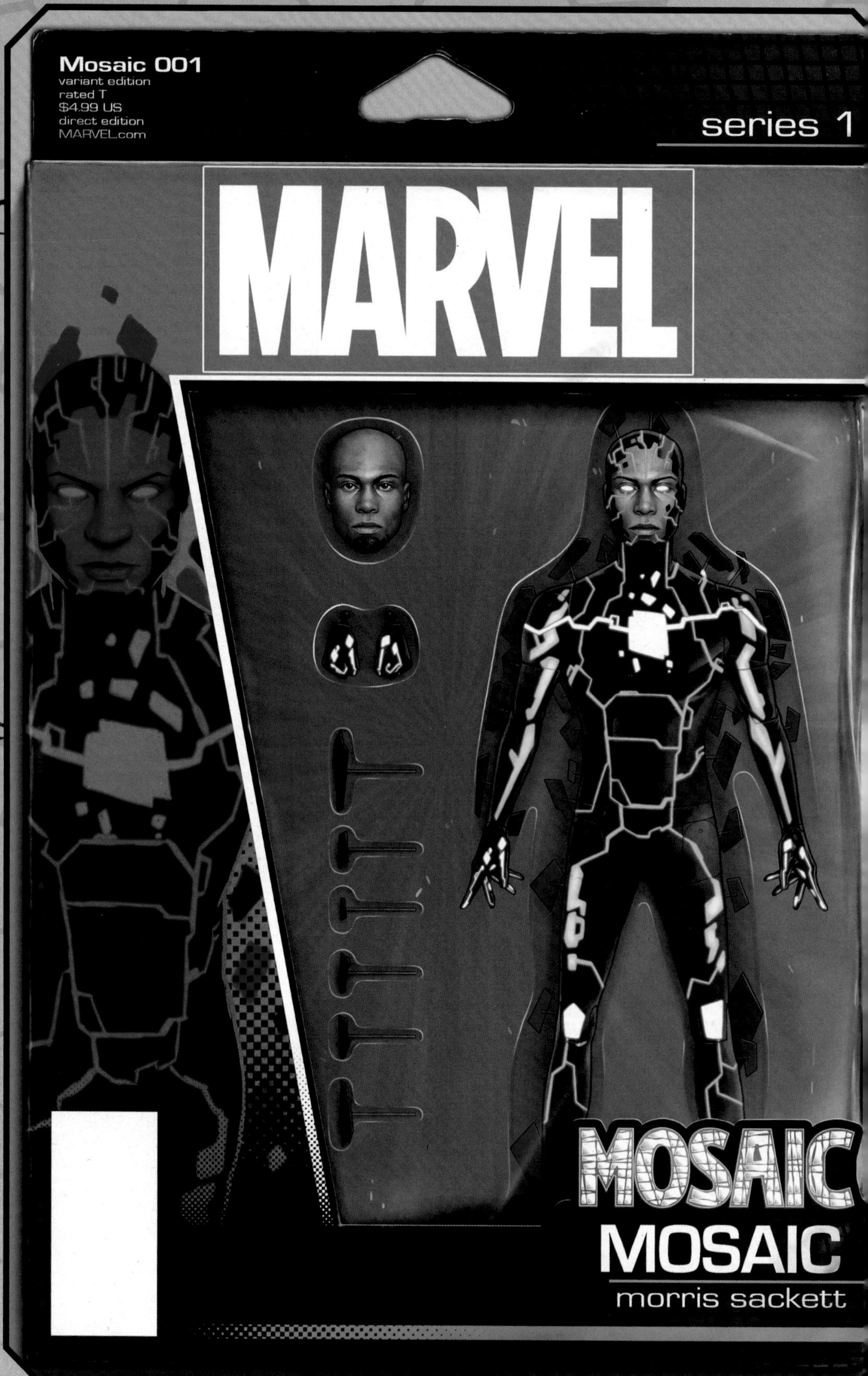
Mosaic 001
variant edition
rated T
$4.99 US
direct edition
MARVEL.com
series 1
MARVEL
MOSAIC
MOSAIC
morris sackett

#1 ACTION FIGURE VARIANT COVER BY **JOHN TYLER CHRISTOPHER**

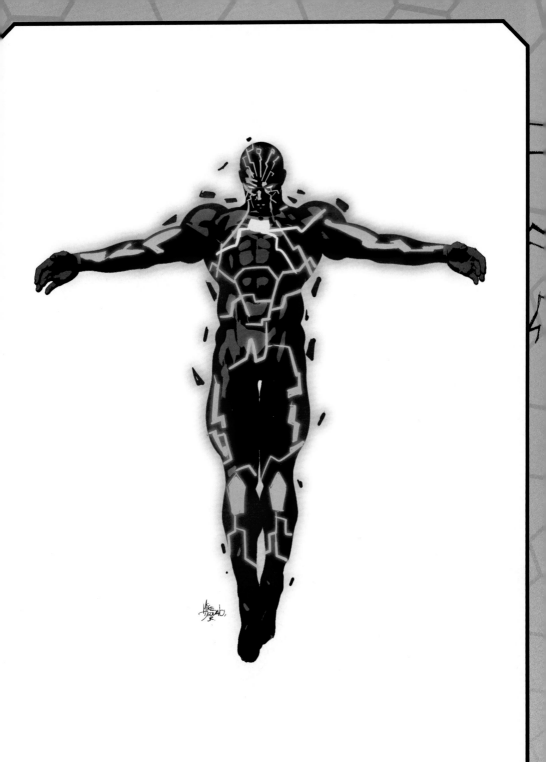

#1 TEASER VARIANT COVER BY **MIKE DEODATO** & **FRANK MARTIN**

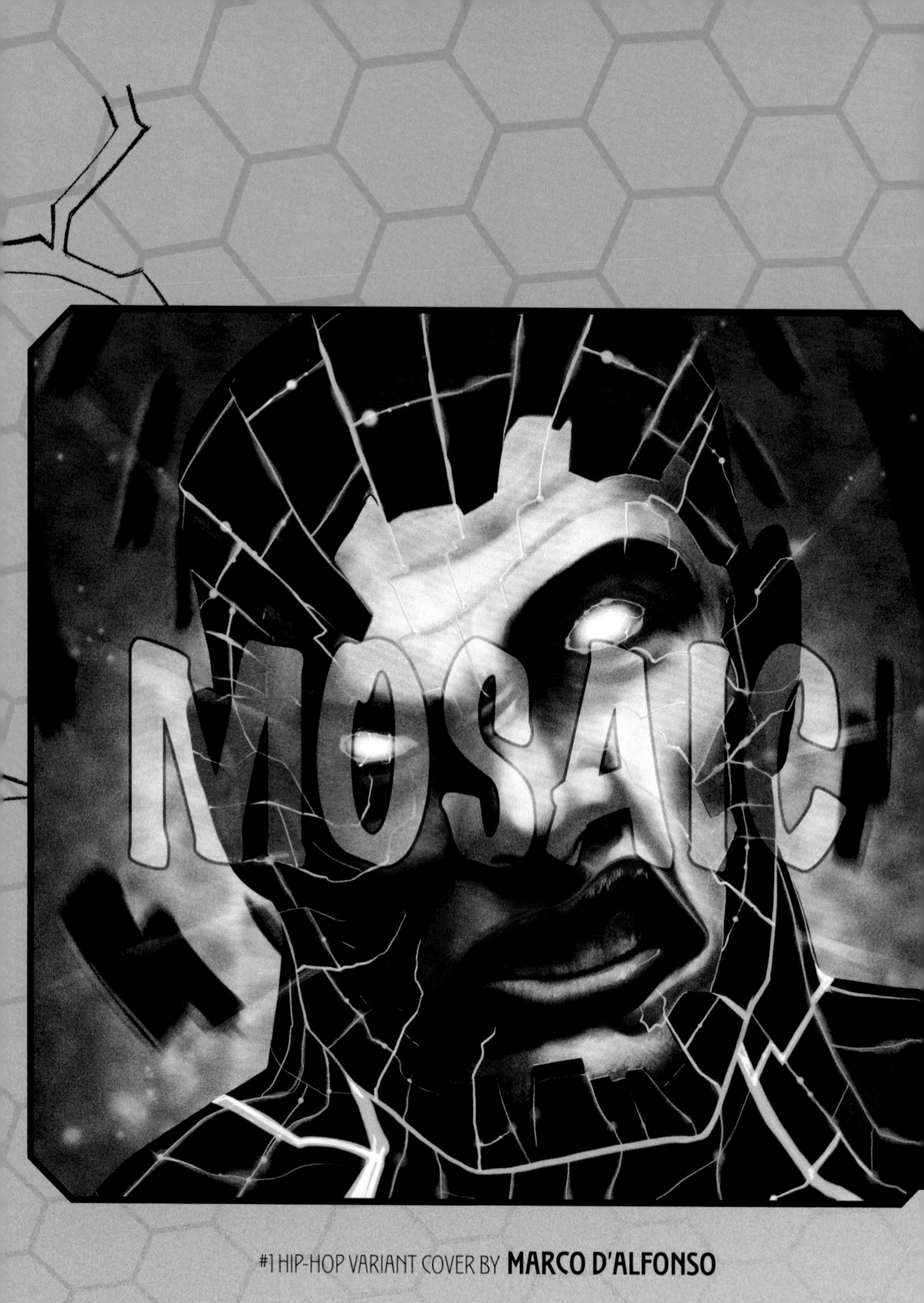
MOSAIC

#1 HIP-HOP VARIANT COVER BY **MARCO D'ALFONSO**

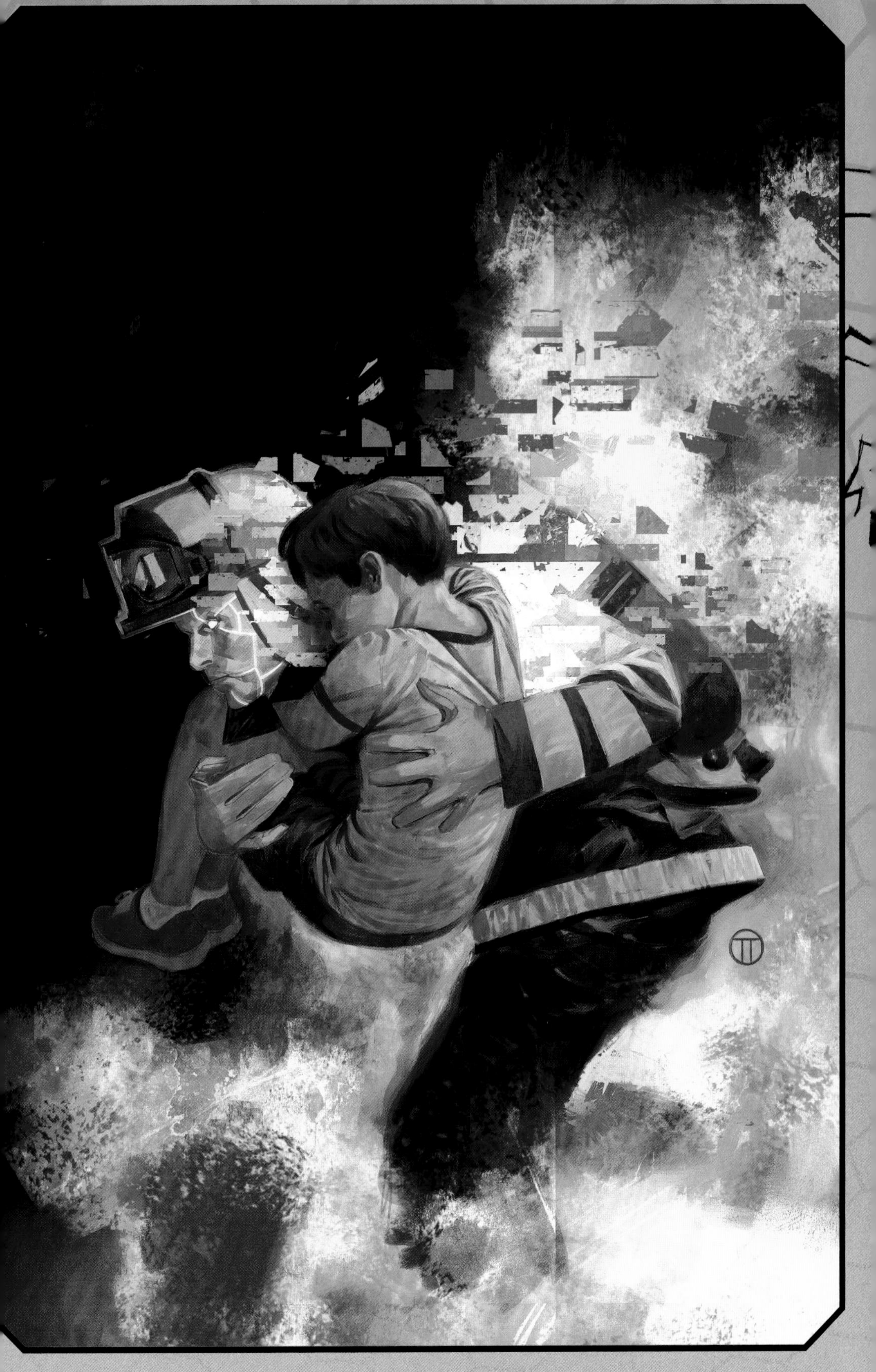

#2 VARIANT COVER BY **JULIAN TEDESCO TOTINO**

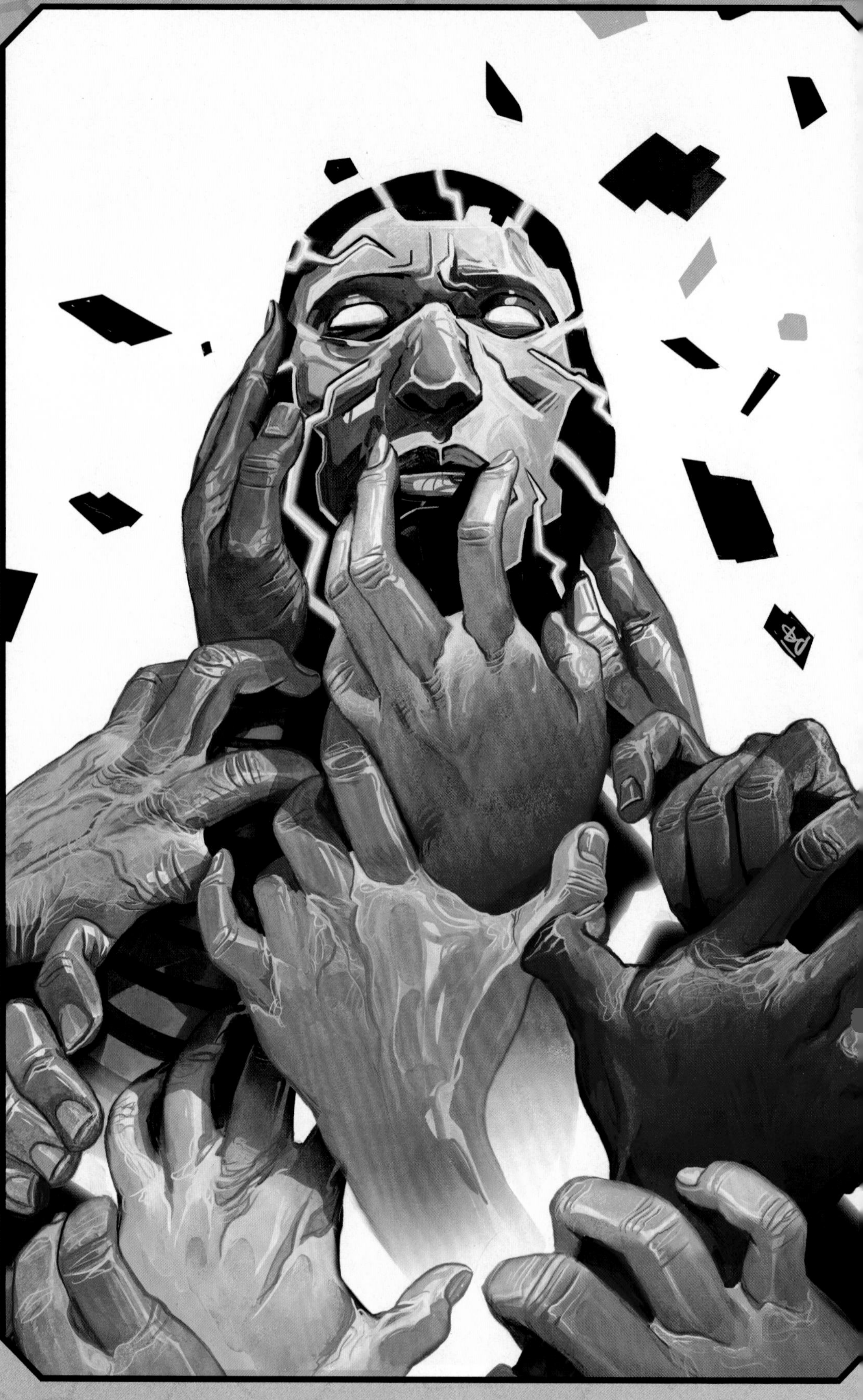

#1 VARIANT COVER BY **MIKE DEL MUNDO**